The Subject in Question

'It is clearly and lucidly written. The theses are clearly formulated, and the arguments clearly laid out. The relations to Kant, Descartes, and some elements of contemporary philosophy make the work still more interesting ... There is nothing in the literature like it.'

J.H. Mohanty, Emory University

The Subject in Question provides a fascinating insight into the difference between two of the twentieth century's most famous philosophers over the key notions of conscious experience and the self. Jean-Paul Sartre's *The Transcendence of the Ego*, published in 1937, is a major text in the phenomenological tradition and sets the course for much of Sartre's later thought. *The Subject in Question* is the first full-length study of this famous work and its influence on twentieth-century philosophy. It also investigates the relationship between Sartre's ideas and the earlier work of Descartes and Kant.

The key theme in *The Transcendence of the Ego* is Sartre's hostility to any essentialist conception of the self. In opposition to Edmund Husserl, the founder of phenomenology, Sartre argues that the ego is not the inner source of one's actions, emotions or character, but rather a construct, a product of one's self-image in the eyes of others. Stephen Priest skilfully shows how Sartre construes consciousness as not essentially Cartesian, but as impersonal, always directed at something other than itself.

The Subject in Question sheds important new light on debates over consciousness and the legacy of Descartes and Kant, the nature of selfhood and personal identity, and the development of the phenomenological tradition.

Stephen Priest is Reader in Philosophy at the University of Edinburgh and a Visiting Scholar of Wolfson College, Oxford. He is the author of *The British Empiricists* (1990), *Theories of the Mind* (1991) and *Merleau-Ponty* (Routledge, 1998), and editor of *Hegel's Critique of Kant* (1987/1992) and *Jean-Paul Sartre: Basic Writings* (Routledge, 2000).

Routledge Studies in Twentieth Century Philosophy

The Subject in Question

Sartre's critique of Husserl in
The Transcendence of the Ego

Stephen Priest

London and New York

To my mother: Peggy Priest

First published 2000
by Routledge
11 New Fetter Lane, London EC4P 4EE

Simultaneously published in the USA and Canada
by Routledge
29 West 35th Street, New York, NY 10001

Routledge is an imprint of the Taylor & Francis Group

© 2000 Stephen Priest

Typeset in Baskerville by Taylor & Francis Books Ltd
Printed and bound in Great Britain by MPG Books Ltd, Bodmin

British Library Cataloguing in Publication Data
A catalogue record for this book is available from the British Library

Library of Congress Cataloging in Publication Data
Priest, Stephen.
  The subject in question: Sartre's critique of Husserl in The
  transcendence of the ego / Stephen Priest.
    p. cm. – (Routledge studies in twentieth century philosophy)
  Includes bibliographical references and index.
  1. Sartre, Jean Paul, 1905–   Transcendance de l'ego. 2. Existentialism.
  3. Phenomenology. 4. Consciousness. I. Title. II. Series.

  B2430.S33 T736 2000
  111–dc21   99–058540

ISBN 0–415–21369–X

Contents

Preface

Consider for a moment some differences between you and everybody else. You look out of your own eyes but you look at or into other people's eyes. You have never seen your own face, nor the back of your own head. In the case of just one human body (the one called your own) you feel yourself to be wholly or largely co-extensive with it. Perhaps you are inside your body or perhaps you are your body, looking out of it. In just *this* body but nobody else's you experience sensations and thoughts. The rest of the world seems physically arranged around you, with your body at its centre. You cannot in the normal course of things encounter your body as one object amongst others in the external world. This, on the other hand, is just how we encounter other people's bodies, as living, speaking, expressive, but as *over there*.

These strange yet intimate phenomenological and physical facts are symptomatic of *being oneself*. We are so used to thinking in a general or abstract way that we fail to notice that *something is me*. Once noticed, this fact is at once obvious and extremely puzzling. For many people, for much of their lives, *being* what they are is an obstacle to *noticing* what they are.

Noticing one's own existence *as one's own* makes possible the understanding of a group of profound and interrelated philosophical questions: What is it for something to be me? Why is something me? What exactly have I claimed about something – a mind, a brain, a body, a whole human being – when I have claimed that it is me?

'What am I?' does not necessarily capture the question. I am no doubt many things (a human being, a man, a biological organism, a thing that thinks, the only person born in *that* place at *that* time, the only person with *that* genetic make-up, etc.). The problem is that none of these facts says what it is for that thing to be me. 'What am I?' does capture the question if it means 'What is it for something to be me?'

The prospects for scientific attempts to answer these questions look grim. This is partly because descriptions of my existence and the theories of science are *antithetical*: I have a capacity to make choices, science is essentially deterministic. I have a past, present and future, science is tenseless. I have a psychological interiority, science only ever explains physical exteriority. Science cannot explain me because *I am the opposite of what science says there is*.

Is there, then, a cogent *phenomenology* of the self; a phenomenology which grounds the physical asymmetries between me and other people? Although Husserl, Heidegger, Sartre and Merleau-Ponty offer phenomenologies of the self which are putatively more fundamental than science, these do not form a homogeneous body of doctrine. The phenomenologists argue against one another. Sartre's first substantial philosophical work, *The Transcendence of the Ego*, is an attempt to refute the answer to 'What am I?' provided by Edmund Husserl in his 'transcendental phenomenology' and replace it with a better one. Here I try to decide whether he succeeds, and see whether either Husserl or Sartre can shed any light on what it is for something to be me.

I have written the book so that it can be read in two ways. On the one hand, it is a critical commentary which tracks Sartre's *Transcendence of the Ego* chapter by chapter. Read this way, it is the first book-length commentary in English on *La Transcendance de L'Ego: Esquisse d'une description phénoménologique* (which first appeared in *Recherches Philosophiques*, VI, 1936–7). On the other hand, the book is written so as to presuppose no knowledge of the philosophies of Husserl and Sartre and may be read as an argumentative analysis of their disagreement over the self.

The first chapter explains Husserl's doctrine of the transcendental ego, so no prior acquaintance with Sartre's target is assumed. The argumentative thread of *The Transcendence of the Ego* is sometimes convoluted and repetitive so I have at two points included summaries of its main sections.

The translation I have used is *The Transcendence of the Ego*, translated and annotated with an introduction by Forrest Williams and Robert Kirkpatrick (Farrar, Straus and Giroux, New York, 1957). Inexplicably, the translation bears the subtitle 'An existentialist theory of consciousness', which has no warrant in the French. Indeed, *prima facie* 'existentialist theory' is an oxymoron.

At the time of writing, philosophy is bedevilled by an alleged distinction between something called 'analytical philosophy' and something else called 'modern continental philosophy'. This preface is not the place to argue the point, but the distinction does not stand up to historical, geographical or philosophical scrutiny. Modern philosophy is in fact several strands of neo-Kantianism (two threads of which cross in Husserl and Sartre).

Nevertheless, there is an important and genuine distinction between using arguments to try to solve philosophical problems and doing anything else. My exegetical method is to interpret the sentences of Sartre, Husserl and others so as to maximise their mutual consistency, because that maximises what they express. My philosophical method is to discover and invent sound arguments for those sentences where they express plausible answers to 'What am I?'.

I am grateful to the governing body of Wolfson College, Oxford, for their generous hospitality during the writing of this book. I thank Tony Bruce, Peggy Priest and Annabel Fraser for their various kindnesses.

Stephen Priest
Department of Philosophy
University of Edinburgh

Abbreviations

CM   Edmund Husserl *Cartesianische Meditationen: Eine Einleitung in die Phänomenologie*, ed. S. Strasser (Martinus Nijhoff, The Hague, 1950)

CMT   Edmund Husserl *Cartesian Meditations: An Introduction to Phenomenology*, trans. Dorion Cairns (Martinus Nijhoff, The Hague, 1982)

CPR   *Immanuel Kant's Critique of Pure Reason*, trans. Norman Kemp Smith (Macmillan, London, 1978)

Ideas I   Edmund Husserl *Ideas Pertaining to a Pure Phenomenology and to a Phenomenological Philosophy, First Book: General Introduction to a Pure Phenomenology*, trans. F. Kersten (Martinus Nijhoff, The Hague, 1983)

Ideas II   Edmund Husserl *Ideas Pertaining to a Pure Phenomenology and to a Phenomenological Philosophy, Second Book: Studies in the Phenomenology of Constitution*, trans. Richard Rojcewicz and Andre Schuwer (Kluwer Academic Publishers, Dordrecht, Boston, London, 1989)

Ideen I   Edmund Husserl *Ideen zu einer reinen Phänomenologie und phänomenologischen Philosophie, II. Buch: Allgemeine Einführung in die reine Phänomenologie*, neu herausgegeben von Karl Schuhmann (Martinus Nijhoff, The Hague, 1976)

Ideen II   Edmund Husserl *Ideen zu einer reinen Phänomenologie und phänomenologischen Philosophie, II. Buch: Phänomenologische Untersuchungen zur Konstitution*, ed. Marly Biemel (Martinus Nijhoff, The Hague, 1952)

KRV   Immanuel Kant *Kritik der reinen Vernunft*, herausgegeben von Ingeborg Heidemann (Philipp Reclamm Jun., Stuttgart, 1980)

TE   Jean-Paul Sartre *La Transcendance de l'Ego: Esquisse d'une description phénoménologique*, Introduction, notes et appendices par Sylvie Le Bon (Librairie Philosophique J. Vrin, Paris, 1985)

References written only as numerals enclosed by brackets are to the English translation of *La Transcendance de l'Ego*: Jean-Paul Sartre *The Transcendence of the Ego*, translated and annotated with an introduction by Forrest Williams and Robert Kirkpatrick (Farrar, Straus and Giroux, New York, 1957).

1 Husserl and the transcendental ego

1 The transcendental ego and the *epoché*

To evaluate Sartre's critique of Husserl in *The Transcendence of the Ego* we need a grasp of some central tenets of Husserl's phenomenology, and the role of the transcendental ego within it.[1]

Husserl's philosophical motivations may be understood as partly Cartesian and partly Kantian. Indeed, this is how he frequently depicts them himself. Husserl shares Descartes' aim of placing all knowledge upon secure foundations; finding some indubitable and incorrigible truths upon which all true beliefs depend for their truth. Like Descartes Husserl is, in a way, an intensely first person singular philosopher but unlike Descartes, Husserl eschews mind–body dualism. Indeed, it is an ambitious but essential part of his phenomenological method to suspend or put in parentheses any metaphysical commitment.

Husserl's motivations are Kantian because, like Kant, he is trying to answer the question: How is knowledge possible? Like the philosophy of the *Critique of Pure Reason*, Husserl's phenomenology is a putative non-empirical grounding or founding of all knowledge, whether scientific, mathematical, commonsensical or philosophical. Like Kant, Husserl grounds knowledge in the 'transcendental' structures of consciousness.

Four phases may be identified in Husserl's philosophical development: a psychologistic and non-phenomenological phase exemplified by *On the Concept of Number* (1887) and *Philosophy of Arithmetic* (1891); a phenomenological and mereological phase exemplified by *Logical Investigations* (1900–1); transcendental phenomenology proper, expressed in the first book of *Ideas* (1913) but in many ways anticipated in the *Lectures on the Phenomenology of Internal Time Consciousness* delivered from 1905; and finally, a concern with the phenomenology of intersubjectivity salient in the 1931 *Cartesian Meditations* based on the *Paris Lectures* (delivered in 1929). As with any attempt to divide a philosopher's intellectual career into 'phases' some elements of one phase may be apparent within another. Husserl's case is made more complex because much of his work has been published posthumously, and an enormous bulk still remains to be published. Of crucial importance in the posthumous publications are *Experience and Judgement* (1973, German 1948), *The Crisis of European Sciences and Transcendental*

Phenomenology (1970, German 1954) and the second volume of *Ideas* (1989, German 1952).

In *The Transcendence of the Ego* Sartre is concerned with what I am calling the third phase of Husserl's philosophy, the transcendental phenomenology of *Ideas*. It reaches its apogee in *Cartesian Meditations* which appeared in French translation in 1931. This phase is distinguished by Husserl's employment of a special device: the phenomenological reduction or *epoché*.

Epoché is the Greek word for 'suspension of belief' and was sometimes used by the ancient sceptics to denote their agnosticism about philosophical or common-sensical assumptions. Husserl uses *epoché* to denote agnosticism about all assumptions about the world outside one's own consciousness. The whole of common sense, or the positing of what Husserl calls 'the world of the natural attitude' (*die Welt der natürlichen Einstellung*) is suspended by the *epoché*, as is the whole of science, philosophy and every other objective ontological commitment. The external world, including other minds and all causal relations, is no longer 'posited'.

Husserl is not endorsing a kind of ontological idealism by his use of the *epoché*. He is not disbelieving in the existence of the external world. He is neither believing nor disbelieving in the external world but using a kind of methodological solipsism to describe just what appears to consciousness with the aim of putting all knowledge on a more secure foundation. 'Methodological solipsism' is not too misleading a term for this, so long as we bear in mind that even one's own existence *qua* living empirical human being is also suspended by the *epoché*.

The use of the *epoché* opens up the field of transcendental subjectivity, transcendental field, or region of pure consciousness (*die Region des reinen Bewußtseins*). Although all ontological commitment to the objective reality of objects in the external world has been suspended, the consciousness of those objects is thereby left untouched, unaffected. The objects themselves are 'reduced' to objects of consciousness, phenomena, or phenomenological appearances. The structures of consciousness itself are thereby opened to phenomenological investigation.

Husserl's phenomenological procedure is both descriptive and essentialist. It is descriptive because no true phenomenologist postulates entities that do not appear, nor provides causal explanations. The phenomenologist is supposed to offer descriptions in a way that is methodologically self-conscious about presuppositions. While many other kinds of philosophy are naively premised on the world as described by science or by common sense, phenomenology asks what the world is like and how any awareness of it is possible.

Phenomenology is essentialist because it seeks the essence of its subject matter: the essence of consciousness, the essence of perception, the essence of a physical object and so on.

If we consider the phenomenological reduction or *epoché*, the concern with description, and the essentialism together, we may obtain a picture of how the Cartesian and Kantian aim of grounding knowledge is to be met.

In phenomenological essentialism it is putatively established that one kind of phenomenon grounds another. For example, phenomenological colour is grounded on extension because through imaginative variation it is established as eidetically impossible that there should be non-extended phenomenological colour. Similarly, Husserl thinks it is of the essence of a physical object that, if it is presented to consciousness, it is presented in a perspectival way, by sides or profiles (*Abschattungen*). It is of the essence of a mental state *not* to be given in this way.

The pure essence (*eidos*) of an object is radically different from that object. It is apprehended though the special faculty of eidetic intuition. It is through the establishing of such hierarchies of dependencies that Husserl hopes ultimately to ground all knowledge.

There are two features of transcendental phenomenology that are particularly important for Sartre's critique in *The Transcendence of the Ego*: the intentionality of consciousness and the ego itself.

As part of his essentialism, Husserl asks what the essence of consciousness is. His answer is that the essence of consciousness is intentionality (*Intentionalität*). Intentionality is the alleged property of consciousness to be *of* or *about* something. For example, there is no seeing without seeing something or other (even if what is seen is illusory). There is no loving without loving someone or something, no thinking without thinking about something, even if what is thought about is wholly imaginary. Influenced by his teacher the Austrian psychologist and philosopher Franz Brentano, Husserl holds that intentionality is mainly necessary and always sufficient for consciousness. He is not as strict as Brentano, who holds that intentionality is always and everywhere necessary and sufficient for consciousness. In *Logical Investigations* Husserl says moods and sensations are mental states but do not exhibit intentionality. What their non-intentional mentality consists in is left unexplained.[2]

Once a distinction is drawn between an act of consciousness and its object or content, we may vary the act type and retain the same type of content or vary the content type but retain the same type of act. Husserl's term for the act of consciousness is *noesis* and he calls the content of the act the *noema*.[3] The eidetic reduction facilitates the description of what is common to a number of acts of the same type. The essence of an act of that type is thereby established. Husserl thinks that knowledge is transcendentally grounded in the structures of consciousness.

Suppose we ask now the further question: How is consciousness possible? Is there anything that grounds consciousness? In particular, are there necessary conditions for the unity of consciousness, or for there being consciousnesses distinct from one another? In the *Lectures on the Phenomenology of Internal Time Consciousness* (delivered from 1905) Husserl unifies the life of consciousness through the *double intentionalities*, transversal and vertical, of the inner temporality of the stream of experiences. Nevertheless, it is in order to answer these and closely related questions that Husserl invokes the transcendental ego.

2 The 'discovery' of the transcendental ego

Sartre uses the term 'transcendental ego' but Husserl uses 'ego' (*Ich*), 'pure ego' (*reine Ich*), 'transcendental ego' (*transzendentale Ich*), 'spiritual ego' (*geistige Ich*), 'ego-pole' (*Ichpol*), 'personal ego' (*persönliche Ich*) and related expressions. It is presumptuous to take it for granted that Husserl's terms have a common referent. In *Ideas* I, Husserl does not use the expression 'transcendental ego' (except in the Preface he wrote especially for the English translation). He uses 'pure ego' to denote the contentless subjective pole of every intentional act. The term 'transcendental ego' is first introduced in the early 1920s in *Erste Philosophie* and *Phänomenologische Psychologie* and appears in *Ideas* II (in §30) which Husserl worked on from 1912 to 1928.[4] 'Transcendental ego' is fully adopted in *Cartesian Meditations* (1931).

In *Ideas* II and *Cartesian Meditations* Husserl does identify the pure ego with the transcendental ego and this allows a holistic picture of Husserl's phenomenology of the self to be extracted. It is this we need to grasp in order to make sense of Sartre's critique.

The transcendental ego is revealed by the *epoché*. When ontological commitment to the world is suspended it is not the case that nothing remains. I remain, not as a certain empirical human being nor as my psychological ego but as a pure ego:

> The *epoché* can [...] be said to be the radical and universal method by which I apprehend myself purely: as ego.
>
> (CMT §8)[5]

Nevertheless, Husserl has the makings of an argument for the transcendental ego. He says

> Let us think of a self-perception as accomplished, but this time in such a way that we abstract from the body.
>
> (*Ideas* II §22)[6]

In that case,

> What we find then is ourselves as the spiritual Ego related to the stream of lived experiences.
>
> (*Ideas* II §22)[7]

If I am conscious of myself, but not conscious of my body, then what I am thereby conscious of is a phenomenological I related to a stream of experiences.

Indeed, so long as the ego exists it is aware of existing: 'The ego is existent for himself in continuous evidence' (CMT §31). The fact that the spiritual ego exists is a *phenomenological discovery*, not the conclusion of a sound argument. Logically, there is no contradiction in the supposition that I am conscious of myself but not my body, but am *not* thereby presented with both a phenomenological ego and a stream of consciousness. There exist three further possibilities: I am presented with an ego but no stream of consciousness. I am presented with a stream of consciousness but no ego. I am presented with neither an ego nor a stream of consciousness but something else: one thought, a Buddhist void, pure presence, the interiority of a soul. There is a logical gap between, on the one hand, the fact of non-physical self-consciousness and, on the other hand, the structure and content of that consciousness.

The transcendental ego is a phenomenological discovery because it is 'what we find in ourselves' (*Ideas* II §22). Who are we? It is essential to distinguish descriptions within and outside the *epoché*. 'Person' is a concept of the natural attitude. It denotes nothing found within the field of transcendental consciousness after the *epoché*. Outside the *epoché* we may use 'we' to denote whoever carries out the transcendental reduction. The chronology of this discovery is as follows: A human being at a time (externally specified) is ignorant of their existence as a transcendental ego. That person at a later time is self-conscious but not thereby conscious of their body nor of themselves *qua* empirical person. Then, at some still later time, that person (externally described) 'finds' (internally described) that they are a transcendental ego 'related' to a stream of consciousness. 'Time' here denotes external time because within the *epoché* the time of the natural attitude is suspended. Husserl allows the use of the first person singular grammatical form throughout the transition from the natural attitude to the phenomenological attitude, from psychological ego to pure ego.

It is not clear what this finding is. It is at least a kind of *disclosure* within transcendental subjectivity, because no other phenomenological route is available for the detection of the transcendental ego. There could in principle be some *nonphenomenological* explanation for the transcendental ego's appearance: for example that the subject is caused to believe in it by a neurological mechanism, at the moment of self-consciousness. Although such an explanation is consistent with phenomenology, it cannot be entailed by it because phenomenology eschews causal explanations. Although belief in the transcendental ego is consistent with its non-existence because its existence does not follow from belief in its existence, 'finding' is not just *coming to believe in* here. The ego appears within transcendental consciousness. It is presented as something rather than nothing so, phenomenologically, or *qua* appearance, it exists. Husserl thinks the transcendental ego is given to consciousness in an indubitable way. This is something that Sartre will call into question.

'Spiritual' (*geistig*) in Husserl's use carries no religious connotation (except *malgré* Husserl) because theological commitments are bracketed by the *epoché*. In Husserl's use of 'spiritual', 'x is spiritual' entails but is not entailed by 'x is non-physical' and the word has the sense of 'pertaining to consciousness'.[8]

It is important to read Husserl's descriptions of the discovery of the transcendental ego phenomenologically, not ontologically, in so far as this distinction can be drawn. Husserl invites us to 'abstract' from the body in thinking of a 'self-perception'. Whatever is thereby phenomenologically presented as non-physical could, arguably, be physical under a non-phenomenological ontological description. Because being physical does not entail appearing physical, and appearing non-physical does not entail being non-physical, Husserl's phenomenology is *prima facie* consistent with competing non-phenomenological ontologies of the mind. Indeed, if this were not the case the abstraction Husserl describes might be impossible or, at best, redundant. Although a critic of the *epoché* might claim it is impossible to be aware of oneself without thereby being aware of the body (a thesis suggested by Merleau-Ponty and some kinds of Buddhism), Husserl's phenomenology cannot possibly entail materialism even though it is consistent with that metaphysical position. Or, if the phenomenology tacitly entailed idealism, then the abstraction might be redundant as the body would already appear as only something that exists for consciousness. Husserl himself some-times calls his philosophy 'transcendental idealism' (*transzendentaler Idealismus*) but that expression is equivocal and cannot plausibly be construed as denoting any strong ontological idealism. What makes ontology of the mind so hard is that in a profound sense Husserl is right: Appearance cannot establish reality. Pheno-menology cannot prove non-phenomenological ontology, even if it grounds it.

Husserl says that the transcendental ego is 'related' to the stream of lived experiences. We need to know what this relation is. A clue is given in other quasi-arguments for there being a transcendental ego:

> The ego grasps himself not only as a flowing life but also as *I*, who live this and that subjective process, who live through this and that cogito, *as the same I*.
>
> (CMT §31)[9]

> I find myself thereby as that which is one and the same in the changing of these lived experiences, as 'subject' of the acts and states.
>
> (*Ideas* II §22)[10]

Three claims need to be separated here: There is something 'one and the same' in the changing experiences. I am that which is 'one and the same'. I am the 'subject' of those experiences. We should add a fourth claim entailed by Husserl's three claims: The 'subject' is identical with that which is 'one and the same' in the changing experiences. If I am identical with what is 'one and the same' and I am identical with the 'subject' then the subject is identical with what is 'one and the same'.

Although Husserl thinks 'I find myself [...] as that which is one and the same in the changing of these lived experiences' is made true by the findings of direct experience, this could be challenged. From a Humean point of view, if I introspect, then there appears no single perennial idea with which I could iden-tify myself or which could explain my idea of myself. Against Hume, and in defence of Husserl, from the fact that no single idea (image, thought, perception) appears in self-consciousness it does not follow that nothing *one and the same* appears. Arguably, there is something constantly present whenever I introspect. For example, that *there is something or other* is constant (except in the rare Buddhist condition of 'no-mind' when ideational and propositional thought ceases but awareness remains).

What we could call the *interiority* of consciousness is always there whatever the changing contents of introspection. The *mentality of content* is similarly perennial in introspection. Finally, and crucially, the property of *being mine* pertains to any content I introspect. The phenomenon of *being me* is disclosed. It is just this phenomenon, I suggest, that Husserl has in mind when he says 'I find myself [...] as that which is one and the same in the changing of these lived experiences' (*Ideas* II §22). It is what Husserl designates 'ownness' (CM §46), *Eigenheitlichkeit* (CM §46). Like Hume, Husserl refuses to identify himself with some idea or mental act. Unlike Hume, Husserl thinks something may be introspected that is not an idea or mental act. The only plausible candidate for this is the phenomenon of 'being me' or the appearance of any or all of my acts as 'being mine'.

I shall argue in this book that although there is such a thing as *being me*, it is peculiarly resistant to description, analysis or explanation. This is the problem of being someone that Nagel insightfully draws our attention to in *The View From Nowhere: What is it for something to be me?* Despite his concern with subjectivity, Sartre does not see that there is a problem about *being me* until *Nausea* (1938), and in *Being and Nothingness* (1943) he states baldly that the problem cannot be solved. Kant is not aware of the problem even though he has discovered transcendental subjectivity. Husserl sees the problem but fails to solve it.[11]

Although Husserl can meet one Humean objection by denying that that which is one and the same is an idea and identifying it with the phenomenon of being me, a new Humean problem arises about this very identification. How can the I that introspects be numerically identical with the I that is introspected (the phenomenon of being me)? Subject and object would have to be identical.

This problem can be overcome. It is not inconsistent to hold that the I that introspects and the phenomenon of being me that is introspected are two aspects of what I am. That the subject *qua* subject is an object, or the object *qua* object is a subject is incoherent, but that subject and object are two parts or aspects of a phenomenological whole is not incoherent.

There is a further problem of how the I that is self-conscious can be justified phenomenologically. If the I is subject then *qua* subject it does not appear to consciousness. Phenomenology only describes what appears to consciousness, so there can be no phenomenology of the subject. The subject *qua* subject is invoked by, but cannot be justified by, phenomenology. True, the *epoché* putatively exposes the transcendental field and the ego-subject for phenomenological scrutiny but this generates the regressive problem of justifying the existence of whatever scrutinises that field, and so on. This is a difficulty in Husserlian phenomenology that Sartre will exploit to the full.

There are two further problems about the identification of the self. How could it be known that 'I am that which is one and the same' in changing experiences? If we concede that there is such a phenomenon as 'being me' and I am directly acquainted with it over time, then that problem is already solved, even if this phenomenon resists adequate phenomenological description and even if 'being me' resists thorough conceptual analysis. However, if what is introspected is not the phenomenon of being me but the constant, or perhaps intermittent, phenomenological property of my experience's being 'mine', then I am being identified with a property of my experiences. This is not Husserl's view but it is close to the one Sartre will adopt. Husserl thinks I depend on my experiences and my experiences depend on me. Sartre thinks I depend upon my experiences but my experiences do not depend on me. It is not clear that Husserl has an argument to forestall this Sartrean construal of the phenomena.

If Husserl could forestall the objection, he would have a ground for his claim that I am the subject of those experiences. It is not clear that the pheno-menology establishes this. As Hume and the Buddhists say, although I may introspect my experiences it is not clear that I introspect myself *qua* subject of them (even if *pace* Hume and the Buddhists, I introspect myself). This is not just because *qua* subject of the act of introspection I am unavailable to that act, but also because it seems intuitively wrong to say that in introspection I am confronted with both my experiences and myself as subject of them.

Husserl does not share this intuition. He thinks that the tripartite structure of consciousness survives the *epoché*. Not only does each act exhibit intentionality, directedness to an intentional content, each act has the same *subjective pole*: a source or origin in the transcendental ego whose act it is. Husserl speaks of 'the Ego as identical pole of the subjective processes' (CMT §31) 'Das Ich als identis-cher Pol der Erlebnisse' (CM §31) and 'the Ego as pole of his acts' (CMT §34) '[…] Ich als Pol seiner Akte' (CM §34).

Is it true, once the objectivity of what is, including the body and the external world, is 'bracketed' by the *epoché*, that this tripartite structure remains?

One of the obstacles to doing transcendental phenomenology, and philosophy of mind, is the contamination of thought by spatial metaphor and spatial images. It is tempting to think of the ego as an object, if not a physical object then a non-physical object, the intentional object as like a physical object, and the mental act relating the two as like a physical relation. Although Husserl is thinking of a mental act as a relation between two relata, ego and intentional object, we have to disregard all physicalist construals of this structure to grasp Husserl's meaning. This is psychologically difficult because we habitually conceive relations and their relata on the model of physical relations (perhaps because we are used to thinking about the external world). Husserl does not free himself from spatial metaphor, indeed he makes use of it.

To decide on the plausibility of his postulation of the transcendental ego we need to inspect its alleged properties and try to unpack his spatial metaphors.

3 The properties of the transcendental ego

i Directedness

Husserl says

> I, the Ego that in each case 'thinks', have directed the ray of the Ego onto what is objective in the act.
>
> (*Ideas* II §22)[12]

and

> In the accomplishment of each act there lies a ray of directedness I cannot
> describe otherwise than by saying it takes its point of departure in the Ego.
>
> (*Ideas* II §22)[13]

Husserl uses the spatial image of a ray to denote the intentionality of an act of
consciousness. It is the ego that directs its 'rays' onto their intentional contents. Now,
it is reasonably clear what it is for a physical ray, a sunbeam or the beam of a searchlight, to be directed towards a physical object. In these cases the sun and the
searchlight respectively have a causal role in illuminating what they are directed
towards. Physical rays have a physical direction. It is less clear what it means for the
transcendental ego to direct its acts to its contents, once the physical connotations of
'ray' are subtracted. Husserl himself feels a difficulty at this point when he uses
'I cannot describe otherwise than [...]'. This is partly the seeming ineffability of
the self but it is also the seeming ineffability of intentionality.

There are two kinds of way of characterising intentionality: phenomenological and theoretical. Phenomenologically, we find a form of words, or a detail of
description, that will capture the 'aboutness' of the mental. Theoretically, we
eschew phenomenology and try to find some explanation sufficient for intentionality in terms of mental representations or neural processing systems. *Pace*
Husserl, what intentionality is cannot be 'read off' the phenomena and *pace*
several philosophies of mind, the neurological is not sufficient for the intentionality of the mental. *Pace* Cartesianism, there is no *a priori* obstacle to intentionality
being wholly physical, or there being wholly physical intentional systems or relations. A photograph is a photograph of some subject. A footprint is a footprint of
some boot sole etc. The intentionality is there and is wholly physical. It obtains
in virtue of a causal relation and a qualitative similarity between object and
representation. What is hard to see is how any physical mechanism, however
complex, could be sufficient for the intentionality of the mental. It is the
phenomenology of intentionality that is difficult to construe physically, not intentionality *per se*.

The directedness of the transcendental ego consists in its being a director; the
director of its mental acts towards (in some non-spatial sense of 'towards') their
contents.

Rather as Husserl makes the scholastic assumption that all consciousness (with
the exception of moods and sensations) is consciousness of some object, so he
makes the Cartesian assumption that all consciousness of the world is by some
subject. Any consciousness is someone's consciousness:

> Anything belonging to the world, any spatio-temporal being, exists for me –
> that is to say, is accepted by me – in that I experience it, perceive it,
> remember it, think of it somehow, judge about it, value it, desire it, or the
> like. Descartes, as we know, indicated all that by the name *cogito*.
>
> (CMT §8)[14]

After the *epoché* this owner is no longer the empirical human being, nor the psychological ego of scientific psychology and everyday life, but the transcendental ego.

Is Husserl right? There are other ways of describing the inside of consciousness, Buddhist or Humean for example, which do not carry this entailment. The Buddhist freeing of attachment (*upadana*) from thoughts and their objects and the resultant cessation of desire (*raga, tanha*) is in many ways strikingly analogous to Husserl's *epoché*. Yet the Buddhist conclusion is that there is no ego but selflessness, or soullessness (*nairatmya*), which implies that acts of awareness have no persistent inner owner. It is not self-evident that the Buddhists and the Humeans are wrong and it is a philosophy of the self consistent with theirs that Sartre will endorse.

ii Indubitability

Husserl speaks of 'the Ego given in absolute indubitability as the "*sum cogitans*" ' (*Ideas* II §22). Something is indubitable if it cannot be doubted, so the existence of the transcendental ego is indubitable if it is not possible to doubt it. There are different kinds of impossibility, so what kind does Husserl have in mind here?

He says the ego is given in *absolute indubitability*. This at least means that once I am reduced to it, I cannot be more certain of anything than I am of my own existence *qua* transcendental ego. It might also mean that certitude about the existence of the ego does not admit of degrees. It is certainly never the case that the ego is dubitable once disclosed.

The impossibility could still be psychological, logical or metaphysical. Construed psychologically, Husserl means it is not a psychological option for me to (sincerely) doubt my own existence *qua* transcendental ego. This in turn divides into the claims that I cannot doubt that I exist, and I cannot doubt that I am a transcendental ego. I can perhaps form the words 'I do not exist' or 'I am not a thinking being' but I can never believe them if I understand them. On this reading we are not constituted in a way that allows us to doubt that we exist. The thought makes sense to us. We can even think the thought 'It is true that I do not exist'. What we cannot do is think it sincerely. Similarly, once we have enacted the *epoché* and the transcendental field is exposed it is not a psychological option not to identify oneself with the transcendental ego.

If this is what Husserl means, it is doubtful that it is true. It is an entailment of the Buddhist doctrine of no-mind that a person can be in a state of consciousness where their psychology is so to speak 'dissolved'. They feel themselves to be Humeans (although not, of course, under that description). The existence of such states is sufficient to refute the indubitability of the self as transcendental ego or as *sum cogitans*. The Buddhist or Humean states do not have to be veridical for the Husserlian view to be refuted.

Could the impossibility be logical? It is not clear that sentences like 'I do not exist' and 'I am not thinking' are self-contradictory, though they could be made to entail contradictions on some interpretations. Rather, such claims are self-stultifying. They may be uttered or thought just on condition they are false. Their falsity is a necessary condition for their production. Even the plausibility of this may be doubted on a 'no-self' view. If there is no self that thinks, but only thinking, then 'I' denotes nothing, except perhaps the thinking itself. Even then, if there can be thinking without a thinker it seems redundant to claim that thought has to think itself, or thinking does its own thinking. What could that consist in except the thinking itself going on? Similarly, 'I exist' is false if 'I' refers to nothing. If 'I exist' is thought or uttered then something certainly exists but it is not clear that it has to be what the 'I' denotes. It is still less clear that if 'I' denotes it has to denote the transcendental ego.

Could the impossibility be metaphysical? Is it metaphysically impossible for me to doubt that I am a transcendental ego? Something is metaphysically impossible if and only if in every possible world it is not the case. Is there a possible world in which I doubt that I am a transcendental ego? Of course there are many, including all the possible worlds in which one is sceptical of Husserlian phenomenology. Is there a possible world in which Husserl's *epoché* is executed but no transcendental ego revealed? There are many: Buddhist worlds, Humean worlds, Sartrean worlds. Sartre's phenomenology of the self in *The Transcendence of the Ego* may be construed as one such possible world.

iii By no means whatsoever something mysterious or mystical

In his desire to establish phenomenology as a strict science (*strenge Wissenschaft*) Husserl shares with other post-Kantian philosophers a horror of the mystical and the metaphysical and an urge to transparency. He says about the ego:

> As what is absolutely given, or what can be brought to givenness in the a priori possible view of fixating reflection, it is by no means whatsoever something mysterious or mystical.
>
> (*Ideas* II §22)[15]

Something is absolutely given if nothing else has to be given in order for it to be given, and it is given as it is. The findings of reflection are *a priori* because they are known independently of sense experience. However, it is not clear that Husserl is right to suppose that the ego's being absolutely given entails that there is nothing mysterious or metaphysical about it. He thinks that because it is given immediately and as it is, nothing further is true of it. This inference is invalid and the conclusion almost certainly false. Even if something is given as it is, not all of it might thereby be given. It is probably false that all of the ego is given because, as Husserl concedes, there is something seemingly ineffable about the self. There is the Nagelian problem of what it consists in for something to be me. Ineffability, or even apparent ineffability, entails mystery.

Indeed, the self is arguably mystical because it seems to admit of no naturalistic explanation. My own existence cannot be logically derived from any set of purely naturalistic premises no matter how long and complicated. From premises of the form '*x* exists' we cannot validly infer 'I am *x*'. Even from 'This particular unique *x* exists' we cannot validly infer 'I am *x*'. Although the logical independence of descriptions is not enough to establish the ontological independence of entities we have very little idea of what is said about something when it is said that I am it. I am, it seems, out of this world. Nevertheless, and paradoxically, the phenomenon of being me may be intuited.

iv Numerical identity over time

Husserl maintains that the transcendental ego, *qua* that which has my thoughts and experiences, remains numerically identical over the time it takes for those thoughts and experiences to occur. Consider some set of experiences occurring over some length of time. If those experiences are experiences of just one person then one and only one transcendental ego is the subject of all of them and exists over all of that time. If that transcendental ego exists at any of that time then that transcendental ego exists at all of that time.

What are Husserl's grounds for this? Two sorts of ground are implicit in his text. He thinks the transcendental ego is revealed whenever an act of consciousness is revealed within the transcendental field after the *epoché*. Second, he thinks the transcendental ego accounts for the unity of consciousness.

It is right that whenever I introspect, any mental phenomenon of mine appears to have the phenomenological property of being mine. This, however, is only sufficient to establish a qualitative similarity between those acts. It does not establish the numerical identity over time of a psychic subject or owner of them. It is extremely tempting to make the slide from the qualitative similarity of a property to the numerical identity of an entity. The slide, however, is not a logically valid one. The phenomenological property of the acts feeling like mine might not be what their being mine really consists in.

Even if the transcendental ego may be introspected as a perennial accompaniment of my acts, it does not follow that it is their owner, that which 'has' them. Even if it is that which has them, the necessary and sufficient conditions for the unity of consciousness might lie elsewhere. They might account for my 'having' my experiences.

Sartre's strategy in *The Transcendence of the Ego* will be to accept the 'personal' nature of one's mental states but argue that the existence of the transcendental ego is actually inconsistent with the unity of consciousness. He then tries to account for that unity in a different way.

Husserl thinks the transcendental ego does not exist independently of its mental acts. He speaks of 'the transcendental ego [as] inseparable from the processes making up his life' (CMT §30). This inseparability is entailed by his view that ego and act are mutually dependent:

The Ego cannot be thought of as something separated from these lived experiences, from its 'life', just as, conversely, the lived experiences are not thinkable except as the medium of the life of the Ego.

(*Ideas* II §22)[16]

However, from the fact that the ego never appears phenomenologically unaccompanied by one of its acts, it does not follow that it could not exist without its acts. Again, phenomenology does not establish ontology. Also, it is not clear that ego and act are unthinkable independently of one another. Plausibility would be lent to the ego as unifier of consciousness if it predated and postdated an act as well as lasted through it. If the ego depends on its acts, support is given to the view that it is a property of them.

v Necessity

Husserl claims that a kind of contingency pertains to mental states but a kind of necessity pertains to the ego:

At least, considered eidetically, any *cogito* can come and go, even though one may doubt that every *cogito* is necessarily something transitory and not simply, as we find it, something in fact transitory. In contradistinction, the pure Ego would, however, seem to be something essentially necessary.

(*Ideas* I §57)[17]

Any token mental state exists contingently, not only because it might not have existed but also because it is temporary. Although a type mental state may exist intermittently, if tokens of that type exist at different times and do not exist at some intervening times, it does not necessarily exist intermittently. It is a contingent fact about any token mental state that it exists temporarily and a contingent fact about any type mental state that it exists intermittently because in principle any mental state might have been perpetual.

On the other hand, the transcendental ego 'seem(s) to be something essentially necessary' (*Ideas* I §57). Husserl does not say what kind of necessity pertains to the transcendental ego. There are three possibilities: necessary existence, necessary properties, and a necessary relation to experience. I shall consider each in turn.

It seems doubtful that the transcendental ego necessarily exists. If we make the background metaphysical assumption that it is a contingent fact that there is something rather than nothing at all, argument would be required to show that the existence of the transcendental ego is an exception. It does not seem contradictory to say that there might have been no transcendental ego.

If it could be established that the transcendental ego exists in all possible worlds then it would follow, in just that sense, that the transcendental ego necessarily exists. However, it is not clear that Husserl is committed to such a large claim. He thinks the transcendental ego is a condition for the possibility of this world, the actual world, being given to us. Even if we said that the imagining of any possible world tacitly presupposes a point of view, and more controversially, thereby presupposes a transcendental ego, we have still only made a claim indexed to the actual world (our world).

However, the existence of the transcendental ego could be argued to be necessary in a weaker, quasi-Kantian sense. For Husserl the transcendental ego is a necessary condition for the world. In *Ideas* the world is the totality of things. In the later Husserl it is construed as the ultimate horizon and so inseparable from transcendental subjectivity. On both construals of 'world' the transcendental ego grounds the 'perspectival' world as we know it. The ego is then transcendental in this neo-Kantian sense of 'necessary for the world of our experience'. If the transcendental ego is necessary for the world as we know it, then the existence of the world as we know it is a sufficient condition for the transcendental ego. This is not the same thing as saying that the transcendental ego necessarily exists. However, it is equivalent to saying that the transcendental ego is necessary in a weakened sense of 'necessary', viz.: 'p is necessary if and only if nothing in the world (as we know it) can refute p'. So, on this interpretation the existence of the transcendental ego is not logically necessary ('There is no transcendental ego' is not contradictory) but it is still necessary in a strong sense. Nothing we can ever come across can refute the claim 'There is a transcendental ego'.

Another possibility is that Husserl thinks the transcendental ego possesses its properties essentially or necessarily. For some property of the transcendental ego, F, not only is the transcendental ego F but the transcendental ego could not not be F. Different reasons could be adduced for this claim: it would be contradictory to say the transcendental ego is not F. The transcendental ego could not exist unless it were F. The transcendental ego could not be what it is (the transcendental ego) unless it were F. Through Husserl's process of eidetic intuition it appears that the transcendental ego could not lack some of the properties it has.

Finally, Husserl could mean that the transcendental ego is essentially or necessarily related to its experiences. We have already seen that the transcendental ego depends upon its experiences. If, as Husserl thinks, the ego is the subject of experiences and accounts for the unity of consciousness then it is a necessary condition for them (at least *qua* someone's). It follows that experience is sufficient for the transcendental ego. However, to say that the transcendental ego is necessarily related to its experiences is not to say that it necessarily exists. It is to say that the inference from experience to transcendental ego is a logically valid one. The validity of that inference is not a modal property of the ego itself.

Husserl does not just say the ego seems to be 'necessary'. He says it seems to be 'essentially necessary'. If something is necessary, what additional information is supplied by saying it is essentially necessary? If 'essentially' just means 'necessarily' then Husserl's concept is that of an iterated modality and the difference is just between: 'Necessarily p iff $\square\ p$' and 'Essentially necessarily p iff $\square\ \square\ p$'. But the ego possesses its modality *de re* and 'essentially' does not just mean 'necessarily'. Suppose x is essentially F if and only if either x could not exist unless x was F or x could not be x unless x were F. If we conjoin this definition with the idea of an object possessing a property necessarily: *x* is *F* and *x* could not not be *F*, then we have the following interpretation of Husserl's 'essentially necessarily': '*x* is essentially necessarily *F* if and only if *x* is necessarily *F* and either *x* could not exist unless *x* were *F* or *x* could not be *x* unless *x* were *F*.

Clearly, in order for this schema to be informative the grounds for holding that *x* is necessarily *F* have to be different from the grounds for holding that *x* is essentially *F*.

Husserl's claim that mental states 'come and go' and are therefore contingent (exist contingently) seems unproblematic, so long as we understand it as a claim about types. It does not make much sense to talk about token mental states 'coming and going' if we individuate them through their unbroken temporal locations. If we give up that assumption then obviously we may say 'This is the same headache as the one I had yesterday' where this does not mean another token of the same type.

If something exists intermittently there is a sense in which it does follow that it exists contingently, so long as we assume that each thing exists either neces- sarily or contingently and nothing exists neither necessarily nor contingently. It follows because if something exists intermittently it sometimes does not exist, *a fortiori* it is possible that it does not exist, and that is just what it is for something to exist contingently. If something exists necessarily, it not only exists, it is not possible for it not to exist so it cannot exist intermittently.

The only serious objection to the soundness of this argument is the logical possibility that something necessarily exists intermittently, not in the sense of something that exists contingently (or non-necessarily), having the property of periodically ceasing to exist necessarily, but in the sense of something that neces- sarily exists when it exists but does not always exist. This must in fact be the modal status of the transcendental ego in Husserl (if it exists necessarily) because he thinks the transcendental ego only exists when its experiences exist. Its experi- ences do not always exist so it does not always exist. The only way of reading this claim consistent with the necessary existence of the transcendental ego is to say it necessarily exists when it exists.

vi *Transcendency within immanency*

What exactly is the appearance of the transcendental ego within consciousness after the *epoché*? Husserl says:

> there is presented in the case of that Ego a transcendency of a peculiar kind – one which is not constituted – a transcendency within immanency.
>
> > (*Ideas* I §57)[18]

Something is immanent if and only if it is directly present to consciousness. Something is transcendent if and only if it is presented to consciousness as not directly present to consciousness. For example, the back and one side of a visible physical object are presented to consciousness as not directly presented to consciousness if the front is being directly (visually) presented. A physical object is constituted. Consciousness constitutes it as a whole physical object for us. In the case of the transcendental ego the transcendence in immanence is not constituted from outside itself. In the developed philosophy of *Cartesian Meditations* the transcendental ego constitutes itself. It has a genesis, a history and an 'auto-constitution'. It has a genesis because it begins to be when a mental act begins to be. It has a history because it accumulates properties; the property of having been subject of act 1 at *t1*, of act 2 at *t2*, and so on. It has an auto-constitution because 'The ego is himself *existent for himself* in continuous evidence; thus in himself, he is *continuously constituting himself as existing*' (CMT §31) 'Das ego selbst ist für sich selbst seiendes in kontinuierlicher Evidenz, also sich in *sich selbst als seiend kontinuierlich konstituierendes*' (CM §31).

The transcendental ego makes itself be and makes itself what it is (it has no prior 'essence'). Husserl says that in its *full concretion* the ego is correctly designated by the Leibnizian term 'monad'. Ego, act and content are given *as if* that is all there is. This is why Husserl says, 'Consequently the phenomenology of this self-constitution coincides with phenomenology as a whole' (CMT §33) 'In weiterer Folge ergibt sich die Deckung der Phänomenologie dieser Selbstkonstitution mit der Phänomenologie überhaupt' (CM §33) and this is why Sartre's attack is potentially so subversive of the Husserlian project.

The transcendence of the transcendental ego is its existence as the subject of absent mental states when it is presented immanently as subject of present mental states. The fact of its transcendence can be intuited directly in its immanence. Why this should be so, Husserl does not say. In particular, the transcendental ego is not constituted as transcendent in the manner of a physical object, so that explanation is unavailable, even though Husserl calls the ego's self-constitution 'transcendental self-consititution' (CMT §31 footnote). However, Husserl thinks 'transcendency within immanency' captures the phenomenology.

Interestingly, Husserl does not choose to write 'immanency within transcendency'. *Prima facie* this is an accurate phenomenological description. Experiences occur over times, such that any experience later than a given time and before a later time is 'within' those two times. From the point of view of that experience, the transcendental ego is transcendent at those earlier and later times.

Husserl uses 'transcendency within immanency'. The act of phenomenological reflection to which the ego is immanently presented is the same act that detects earlier and later experiences as having the same transcendental ego as subject. It is this numerical identity over time possessed by the ego that makes it transcendental in respect of any one experience at any one time (when, available to direct reflection, it is immanent.) In reflection it is grasped as both immanent and transcendent but in immanence, so it is grasped as transcendence in immanence.

In summary, then, we may say that Husserl thinks the transcendental ego is an ineliminable subject of experience revealed by his *epoché* or phenomenological reduction. It is that which has all one's experiences. It unifies states of consciousness as one's own, exists always and only when they do and has an *auto-constitution*. Its existence is indubitable within the framework of transcendental subjectivity and its existence is in some sense necessary. With this picture of Husserl's doctrine of the transcendental ego in mind we may turn to Sartre's critique.

2 The theory of the formal presence of the I

Summary

Sartre seeks to refute Husserl's claim that the unity of consciousness is a product of the I and argues that the I is a product of the unity of consciousness. Sartre is partly able to escape the fundamentally Kantian framework of the debate. Sartre accounts for the unity of consciousness by a holism about the mental: acts of consciousness unify themselves as parts of one and the same consciousness through their intentional objects. In addressing the problem of individuating consciousnesses, Sartre rejects the view that consciousness is a substance. He draws a distinction between reflective and pre-reflective consciousness which will be crucial to his developed existential phenomenology in *Being and Nothingness*. The question of whether consciousness entails self-consciousness is discussed. In distinguishing states of consciousness with and without the I, Sartre concludes that the I only appears to reflecting consciousness. Sartre draws a distinction between the I and the me; that psycho-physical whole human being who I am. Sartre argues that the existence of the transcendental ego is inconsistent with the freedom of consciousness. In his break with Husserl's Cartesianism Sartre nevertheless accepts the certainty of the *cogito*. Distinguishing a third 'level' of consciousness, reflection on reflection, Sartre tries to avoid the danger of an infinite regress. Sartre offers a phenomenology of pre-reflexive consciousness based on memory and argues that pre-reflexive consciousness contains no I. Sartre denies that the I is the 'source' of consciousness but concludes that the I is an existent. The I is intuited. The I appears to reflective consciousness but the I falls before the *epoché*.

1 Sartre on Kant's 'I think' doctrine

Here I establish both that Sartre has an unusually accurate understanding of Kant's thesis of the transcendental unity of apperception and that the dispute between Sartre and Husserl mainly takes place within a Kantian framework. Sartre's reading of Kant on self-consciousness is incorporated into his own critique of Husserl so we need to be clear on what it is.[19]

By an 'accurate' or 'correct' understanding of some thesis I mean one which allocates propositions to indicative sentences in such a way as to maximise their mutual consistency, or internal consistency *qua* set. The rationale for this interpretation of 'accurate' or 'correct' is that to the extent to which a set of sentences is internally inconsistent it expresses no propositions. It does not say anything.

On this definition, an interpretation may be accurate even if it is not the interpretation the author intended. In practice, however, common conventions about the allocation of meanings in ordinary language, and the author's own concern for consistency, make it unlikely that any interpretation will diverge radically from the author's own. To borrow a distinction drawn by Bernard Williams, on my view there is not a vast divergence between the answer to What does it mean? and the answer to What did it mean?[20]

Although accuracy admits of degrees because the set of mutually consistent propositions could be larger or smaller on some interpretations, 'correct' is an absolute notion because if an interpretation is correct then there is no other interpretation on which the set of mutually consistent propositions could be larger. This is nevertheless logically consistent with there obtaining more than one correct interpretation because that is just for there to obtain more than one set of allocations of propositions to indicative sentences on which the maximal number of mutually consistent claims is expressed.

Kant's thesis of the transcendental unity of apperception is a claim about the fundamental possibility of experience. One of Kant's projects in the *Critique of Pure Reason* is the establishment of the conditions singularly necessary and jointly sufficient for experience as we know it. The most primordial of such necessary conditions, the condition for all conditions that has itself no condition, is the transcendental unity of apperception (*transzendentale Einheit der Apperzeption*). This doctrine has been much misunderstood and much misrepresented but one thing is clear about it. It is a thesis about self-consciousness.[21]

Sartre reports Kant's thesis accurately when he says 'the I Think must be able to accompany all our representations'.[22] The crucial point, which has been missed by many Kant commentators, from Hegel to Strawson, is that Kant is talking about a possibility, a potential or a disposition and not necessarily about an actuality.[23] Sartre sees the possibility of misunderstanding when he asks whether we need to conclude that an I in fact does accompany each of our representations from the fact that it could. Sartre rightly sees that any such putative inference would be a *non sequitur*.

Kant's thesis of the transcendental unity of apperception is this: It must in principle be possible for any of a person's thoughts or experiences to be a self-conscious thought or experience as a necessary condition for its being theirs. Kant's formulation is as follows:

> It must be possible for the 'I think' to accompany all my representations; for otherwise something would be represented in me which could not be thought at all, and that is equivalent to saying that the representation would be impossible, or at least would be nothing to me.
>
> (CPR B131–2)[24]

If it were in principle impossible for some thought or experience to be had self-consciously, to be self-ascribed in the having of it, then it would not make sense to say that such a putative mental episode had an owner, was someone's.

Clearly, from this thesis it only follows that there obtains a disposition to self-consciousness, not a realisation of that disposition and *a fortiori* not a realisation of the disposition all the time that the disposition obtains. Not only is Sartre right to note that this inference does not go through but he also sees that Kant rejects the thesis that every thought or experience is occurrently self-conscious. He says that this would be a distortion of Kant's view.

That Sartre is unusual in interpreting Kant correctly on this point follows from the fact that many Kant commentators have misascribed to Kant the 'occurrent' view of self-consciousness. They think that Kant thinks that every thought is a self-conscious thought.

Although Sartre has it right that the transcendental unity of apperception is a dispositional thesis, in common with nearly every other commentator on the *Critique of Pure Reason* he wrongly ascribes to Kant a representational theory of thought and perception. This misunderstanding derives from a pervasive mistranslation of the German word 'Vorstellung' by the French 'représentation' and the English 'representation'. In many ordinary contexts 'representation' would be an appropriate translation of 'Vorstellung' but not in translating Kant, unless we take 'representation' just to be a term of art to cover the field of intentionality that need not literally carry the sense that objects are mentally re-presented. Kant is at pains to repudiate the quasi-Lockean thesis that perceiving something consists in mentally representing it. Rather, objects are transcendentally constituted by the possibility of the perception of them according to Kant. C.D. Broad has made the ingenious if somewhat tenuous suggestion that 'Vorstellung' in the *Kritik der reinen Vernunft* be translated as 'presentation' rather than 'representation'.[25] This is philosophically satisfactory because it is consistent with the direct realism ('empirical realism') which Kant wishes to espouse as consistent with his transcendental idealism.

Although Sartre wrongly ascribes to Kant the view that there are perceptual representations, he rightly points out that the transcendental unity of apperception is putatively a formal rather than an ontological thesis. This is what Sartre means when he says that Kant has nothing to say about the existence of the 'I think'. This is right because it is Kant's view that any thought could in principle be formulated using the prefix 'I think that … '. It amounts to the putatively purely formal requirement (or requirement of 'transcendental logic') that any experience in a self-same mind that endures over time is possibly a self-conscious experience.

2 Is Kant's 'I think' doctrine true?

Whether Kant's doctrine of the transcendental unity of apperception is true may be doubted. Clearly, Kant has provided a sufficient condition for the unity of consciousness and the unity of consciousness is a necessary condition for experience if by 'experience' we denote a set of experiences in one mind. The transcendental unity of apperception is sufficient for the unity of consciousness because if a set of thoughts could be the self-conscious thoughts of a subject then it follows that those thoughts are had or 'owned' by that subject. It would be inconsistent to maintain that they could belong to someone else. The unity of consciousness is a necessary condition for experience because the numerical identity of a subject over the time it takes for an experience to happen is a necessary condition for that experience being one rather than more than one experience. This is because we individuate experiences partly through their owners. Although uncontroversially a subject has and so *a fortiori* may have more than one experience one experience cannot be and so *a fortiori* is not had by more than one subject. (Here I am thinking of experience tokens or particulars and not experience types.)

However, it is doubtful that Kant has provided a necessary condition for the unity of consciousness. This is because there is no incoherence in the supposition that the unity of consciousness may be accounted for in other ways than by the truth of the thesis of the transcendental unity of apperception. Not only may some ontological realism about the subject be true, some kind of spiritualism or Cartesianism for example, but a series of experiences could be experiences of a single subject without it being the case that that subject could even in principle be conscious of having those experiences. It is false that the only reason why a subject could not even in principle be aware of having an experience is that that experience was not had by that subject. There are other possibilities. For example, a subject of experience may simply lack the cognitive capacity for self-consciousness. However such a capacity may be realised it might not be realised for some subject. In that case it might not even make sense to hold that such a subject is capable of self-conscious experience. We would not wish to make that a conclusive ground for saying that such a subject was not a subject of experience. There is no contradiction in the supposition that a series of experiences occur in one and the same mind over a period of time but that mind is not a self-conscious mind and so could not be conscious of those experiences.

If this argument is sound then Kant has at most shown that the unity of consciousness is a necessary condition for experience and the transcendental unity of apperception is a sufficient condition for experience. He has not shown that the transcendental unity of apperception is necessary for the unity of consciousness so he has not shown that the transcendental unity of consciousness is necessary for experience.

3 Is Kant's 'I think' doctrine purely formal?

Although Sartre is right to claim that Kant intends the transcendental unity of apperception to be a purely formal thesis it is less clear that it can be. I mean, it is not clear that the thesis can be true without being given some ontological interpretation or other. To draw an analogy, it is uncontroversial that the proofs of pure mathematics and logic are formal in the sense that they obtain in virtue of their mathematical or logical 'form' and not in virtue of any one interpretation of them. They are valid irrespective of what their component sentences are true of. However, it is not clear that there could be soundness in logic without material truth and there could not be material truth without material truth conditions and that implies an ontology; some ontology or other. Similarly, although formal proof in mathematics holds irrespective of interpretations it is not clear that there could be mathematics without, in some sense, mathematical reality; if not Platonic numbers then at least computation or numbers of things.

The transcendental unity of apperception, however intended by Kant and understood by Sartre, cannot be utterly formal because it is true of something: it is true of any set of experiences which belong to a single subject. What we need to know is in virtue of what exactly it is true rather than false that any presentation to a subject may be truly prefaced by 'I think that … '. Of course, just as a mathematical or logical statement may be given an interpretation and be true under that interpretation so the transcendental unity of apperception may be given an ontology of the person and be true of experience in virtue of that ontology.

As Sartre rightly points out, Kant is not committed to the existence of a transcendental ego. Indeed, he is arguably committed to the view that there is no such thing. There is no irreducibly subjective source of consciousness in Kant's philosophy and it is the important negative thesis of the Paralogisms chapter of the *Critique of Pure Reason* that the subject is not a substance. However, suppose we ask what the truth conditions are which make the transcendental unity of apperception obtain. A number of internally coherent yet mutually competing answers might be given.

A disposition may obtain without being exercised so it is not a necessary condition for the existence of a disposition that it be realised. However, the exercise of a disposition is a sufficient condition for the existence of that disposition. Suppose then 'I think' prefaces one of someone's thoughts, it logically follows that that thought is a self-conscious thought and something like the transcendental unity of apperception is true. That exact doctrine does not have to be true because from the fact that 'I think that … ' prefaces one particular thought or experience it does not follow that it does or has to preface any arbitrary other of them or could preface all of them. We still do not know what a thought's being someone's as opposed to some else's consists in. Still less do we know what it consists in for a thought to be mine. Some ontological content has to be given to the thesis for it to be true.

It is this problem which provides Husserl with the philosophical motivation for the postulation of the transcendental ego. Kant's purely formal condition for the possibility of experience cannot ground real material experience.

Kant, Husserl, and even Sartre in these opening pages of *The Transcendence of the Ego*, operate within the framework of transcendental philosophy in a broad sense of 'transcendental philosophy'. As Sartre puts it:

The problem, indeed, is to determine the conditions for the possibility of experience. (32)[26]

Sartre's repudiation of Husserl's doctrine of the transcendental ego is an essential part of his transition to the existential phenomenology of *Being and Nothingness*. Does he thereby remain a transcendental philosopher? We understand 'transcendental philosophy' too liberally if we say it is the attempt to specify all the non-empirical necessary conditions for experience. On this view, Plato and Aquinas emerge as transcendental philosophers because they think, respectively, that the Forms and God are non-empirical conditions for the possibility of experience. 'Transcendental philosophy' is anti-metaphysical philosophy. Paradigmatically, in Kant, the non-empirical conditions for experience are formal, not metaphysical (that is the point of transcendental logic). Naturally, there is room for a transcendental philosopher to nevertheless be a metaphysician *malgré lui*. If we allow that there is anti-metaphysicial transcendental philosophy, then Kant, Husserl and Sartre endorse such philosophy.

For the later Sartre the necessary conditions for experience are existential. The Heideggerian existential category 'being-in-the world' (*être-au-monde, in-der-Welt-sein*) replaces the transcendental ego. It is not so much I who grounds the world as my being in it. To the extent that Sartre is describing non-metaphysical conditions for the possibility of experience that are at least not straightforwardly empirical he remains a transcendental philosopher despite his endorsement of existential phenomenology.

Sartre agrees with Kant that one of the conditions for the possibility of experience is that I can always regard one of my thoughts or experiences as mine (32). It follows that in a very broad sense Sartre endorses something like the transcendental unity of apperception. Unlike Kant but like Husserl he will wish to give it a content – an ontological realisation, but unlike Husserl but like Kant he will wish to deny that this content is the transcendental ego.

The profound metaphysical problem of what it is to be me escapes Kant, Husserl and Sartre at this point. Despite their rather Cartesian obsession with the ontology presupposed by the use of first person singular grammatical constructions Kant in his transcendental idealism, Husserl in his transcendental phenomenology and Sartre in his critique of Husserl do not come close to feeling the metaphysical mystery of one's own existence. This is missed despite Husserl's attempts to ground the world in the irreducibly subjective source of consciousness which I am, and Kant's rewriting of Descartes' *cogito* as 'Ich denke'. What transcendental philosophy and even first person singular Cartesianism miss is what causes Roquentin's horrified disgust in *Nausea* and what Nagel sees in *The View From Nowhere*: There is a mystery about what it is for a portion of what is to be myself. How can something be me?[27]

Now, it need not be a sign of inadequacy that a profound metaphysical problem does not arise for a theory. It might be a sign of the theory's correctness. But this is not the case with transcendental philosophy's failure to solve the Nagelian problem of the self. Even if we accept Christopher Peacocke's suggestion that subjective and objective descriptions might differ in sense but not reference, the problem of what it is for something to be me remains.[28] We still do not know what I have said about something when I have said that I am it. Nor is the problem solved if first and third person descriptions of the person are mutually dependent, say because I can only think of myself as myself if I can pick myself out in an objective picture of the world, or if others can in principle identify me. None of these observations shows why something is me. None of them explains what it is for a portion of the universe to be me.

I shall return to this problem towards the end of this book in examining the limits of the Kantian framework within which both Husserl and Sartre operate. Now I conjecture a reason why this problem passes these thinkers by. Husserlian transcendental phenomenology and Sartrean existential phenomenology are both deeply conservative philosophies from a metaphysical point of view. They are as committed as linguistic analysis and post-structuralism to the conservative neo-Kantian orthodoxy that transcendental metaphysics is impossible. They think it in a way inevitable that people will engage in metaphysics but this putative enquiry can yield no knowledge.

This neo-Kantianism is intellectually debilitating for many reasons but two are these: unless we see the problems we are going to be unable to solve them. We will be subject to them nonetheless. Second, a necessary condition for the advance of knowledge is bold conjecture outside established frameworks of thinking. Neo-Kantianism is anathema to such conjecture. Kant says we cannot solve the problems. Indeed, his thesis is even more thoroughly conservative and pessimistic because he thinks we are so constituted as to be unable to solve the problems.[29]

Husserl and Sartre are incapable of doing metaphysics because they never escape the Kantian cognitive prison. This prevents them feeling the mystery and appreciating the intractability of the problem of what it is for something to be me. Indeed, Sartre, like Kant and Husserl, can only understand the problem of the self as a formal problem or an ontological problem. In a way the problem is ontological, but it is not a problem about whether to postulate an extra entity. It is a problem about what it is to be someone, viz. oneself.

4 Hypostatisation

Sartre says that in Kant commentators there is a 'dangerous tendency' to construe the Kantian conditions for the possibility of experience ontologically, of 'making into a reality the conditions'. It is of precisely this that he considers Husserl guilty. Husserl reifies the transcendental unity of apperception into the transcendental ego. Husserl misconstrues a formal condition for the possibility of experience as an ontological claim, not of course an ordinary ontological claim about the content of the world of the natural attitude but about an item of transcendental ontology: something that exists in the transcendental field.

The engagement between Sartre and Husserl is over form and content, over whether the unity of consciousness (and so the possibility of experience) may be accounted for in terms of Kant's transcendental logic or whether recourse has to be made to the ontology of Husserl's field of transcendental subjectivity. Although Sartre is right to say

> To make into a reality the transcendental I, to make of it the inseparable companion of each of our 'consiousnesses', is to pass on fact, not on validity, and to take a point of view radically different from that of Kant. (33)[30]

It does not follow that such a misconstrual of Kant is not the solution to the problem of the unity of consciousness and the possibility of experience. After all, if experience exists and if the unity of consciousness exists it is hard to see how their existence could be accounted for in wholly non-ontological terms. Arguably, only something that exists can account for something that exists.

It will be Sartre's considered view that both a phenomenology and an ontology of the ego are possible but a phenomenology and an ontology radically distinct from those of Husserl. It follows that Sartre himself breaks with the Kantian view that the philosophy of the self belongs to purely formal or transcendental logic. Kant thinks the unity of consciousness and the possibility of experience can be grounded without recourse to ontology and without a phenomenology of the self. In the end Sartre will agree with Husserl that this is impossible but his own conclusions will be fundamentally inconsistent with Husserl's.

One merit of Sartre's reading of Kant is that it is anti-psychologistic. It is a poor philosophical reading of Kant to construe transcendental logic as a kind of non-empirical psychology, however useful such an appropriation may have proved for developmental psychology or cognitive science. As Sartre points out, if Kant is read this way he can only be construed as constructing an unconscious mind: a framework for the possibility of experience that is not available to introspection. Sartre rightly says that Kant's concern is not with the way in which empirical consciousness is in fact constituted. Rather, Kant is trying to itemise the necessary conditions for any self-conscious experience whatsoever. He is trying to decide on the *a priori* conditions for the possibility of any consciousness; what has to be the case in order for there to be consciousness. Indeed, Sartre thinks that any putative reification of the Kantian conditions for the possibility of experience will be subject to precisely the kind of 'critique' Kant advances in the *Critique of Pure Reason*. He says:

> To cite as justification Kantian considerations on the unity necessary to experience would be to commit the very error of those who make transcendental consciousness into a pre-empirical consciousness. (33)[31]

It is a central tenet of the *Kritik der reinen Vernunft* that any object of knowledge is, at least in principle, a possible object of experience. We cannot think that which we cannot experience. Clearly, this principle is violated by knowledge of the existence of a consciousness that is pre-empirical because '*x* is pre-empirical' entails '*x* is non-empirical' and '*x* is non-empirical' entails '*x* is not a possible object of experience'. But if it could be known that there is a non-empirical consciousness something could be known which is not a possible object of experience. We could think something we could not experience.

Sartre is right to construe Kant as writing in a way that is ontologically neutral with regard to any positive but non-metaphysical view of the self. As Sartre puts it:

> If we associate with Kant, therefore, the question of validity, the question of fact is still not broached. (34)[32]

By 'validity' here Sartre is indicating the Kantian notion of *Gultigkeit* which means 'validity' not in the logical or deductive sense but in the sense of 'justifica-tion' or 'legitimation'. This idea of validity is an idea of possibility; the idea of that which makes experience possible in the transcendental sense.

Sartre is correct to construe Kant as ontologically neutral here. For example, it is clear that Kant thinks that there can be no experience without the unity of consciousness whatever the unity of consciousness consists in. Kant thinks there can be no unity of consciousness without 'owned' experiences whatever the self consists in. Kant is trying to write generally: about what the self must be like whatever it is. In fact a good construal of 'formal' in 'Kant's transcendental logic is formal' is 'ontologically neutral'.

Kant's account is not neutral in a negative sense. He wishes to explicitly rule out some metaphysical ontological options. Conspicuously he attempts to refute the thesis that the self is a substance and, *a fortiori*, the quasi-Cartesian thesis that the self is a mental substance. When Sartre insists that the question of fact has not been broached he means that Kant's transcendental account is consistent with several ontologies of the self.

Kant tries to account for the unity of consciousness by the transcendental unity of apperception and tries to account for experience by the unity of consciousness. Sartre however regards it as an open question whether the self is explained by the unity of consciousness or whether the unity of consciousness is explained by the self. There are other options which Sartre does not consider. For example, there might be a relation of mutual dependence between the self and the unity of consciousness such that one is necessary and sufficient for the other. There might be no self or there might be no unity of consciousness or there might be neither. The self might be reducible (in various senses of 'reducible') to the unity of consciousness but the unity of consciousness might not be reducible to the self, or the unity of conscious might be reducible to the self but the self might not be reducible to the unity of consciousness.

We should turn now to Sartre's critique of Husserl's attempt to ground the unity of consciousness in the transcendental ego.

5 Subjectivity and synthesis

The dispute between Husserl and Sartre is over the answer to this question:

Is the I that we encounter in our consciousness made possible by the synthetic unity of our representation, or is it the I which in fact unites the representations to each other? (34)[33]

The question is posed in a Kantian vocabulary: Synthesis is the mental act of combination whereby it is made possible for several perceptions to be perceptions of one and the same object, or several thoughts to be thoughts of one and the same object. The question is whether the I is constituted and so made actual by the unity of acts of consciousness in synthesis, or whether even the unity of acts in consciousness of objects is made possible by the I. Husserl takes the second of these views. Sartre takes the first. In doing so he makes a radical break with the Kantian framework. It is profoundly anti-Kantian to maintain that the I is a product of synthesis.

Husserl thinks the I is transcendental in the sense that it is a condition for both consciousness and the world as presented to consciousness. Sartre will wish to argue, on the contrary, that such a position is phenomenologically illegitimate and the I is one object of consciousness amongst others. A clue to this approach is already given when Sartre talks about the I 'that we encounter in our consciousness' (34). This suggests that the I is something we are conscious of rather than something which is conscious.

Sartre's thesis that the I is encountered in consciousness produces a regressive problem that he only addresses later on in *The Transcendence of the Ego*: Who or what encounters the I? His sustained answer will be: that psycho-physical whole human being who I am. Sartre is only able to argue for this existential solution much later in the book because it depends upon a prior critique of the *epoché*: a demonstration that the subject of experience is in the world and is not a structure of 'reduced' consciousness.

Husserl's view that the I makes the synthetic unity of consciousness possible is vulnerable to an objection levelled at Kant by Susan Hurley.[34] If all unity is the product of acts of synthesis, and the I cannot make the unity of consciousness possible unless it is itself one, then the I must itself be a product of acts of synthesis and cannot be the ground or source of synthesis. Thus Husserl must undermine his account of the basic-ness of the transcendental ego by postulating some mysterious primary synthesiser 'behind' the I, and he is anyway launched into an infinite and vicious regress. Sartre's alternative of grounding the I in synthesis avoids this entire problem.

Sartre draws the distinction between Kantian and Husserlian approaches to consciousness as follows: Kantianism is critical but phenomenology is descriptive. Although criticism and description are mutually distinct in that criticism is a kind of demystification or drawing of conceptual limits while description is supposedly passive and reportive, the difference between Kant and Husserl is not so clear-cut as Sartre believes.

It is clear that Husserl's use of the *epoché* may be construed as a kind of critique of consciousness, and Husserl himself allows that Kant was the first philosopher to truly engage in phenomenology, in the *Transcendental Deduction*.[35]

It follows that Husserl is partly a critical philosopher and Kant partly a descriptive philosopher or phenomenologist. Nevertheless, Sartre is correct to claim that phenomenology putatively proceeds essentially by intuition, by acts of immediate awareness of phenomena, uncontaminated by linguistic or other forms of preconception.

Also, Husserl thinks that intuition puts us in the presence of the thing. The Kantian distinction between objects of intuition or phenomena and things as they are in themselves is thought not to arise in the Husserlian framework. In fact however there is at least a close analogue of this distinction in the difference between the objects of the natural attitude and the purely intentional objects of the phenomenological reduction. If Kant's things as they are in themselves are not construed as metaphysical items but as not numerically distinct from ordinary commonsensical objects (those objects as they are, rather than as they appear) then they are numerically identical with the objects of Husserl's natural attitude, even if by definition they never appear *qua* things in themselves, only *qua* appearances.

Whether this is right or not, Sartre's view of Husserl's phenomenology as 'a science of fact' is correct or, at least, this is how Husserl conceived his own projects. Husserl thinks he is founding a rigorous essentialism that will justify and explain the possibility of empirical science. He refers to phenomenology as rigorous science (*strenge Wissenschaft*).[36]

Sartre infers from the claim that phenomenology is a science of fact that problems of the relation of consciousness to the I are existential problems. This inference needs extra premises to go through. Existential problems are problems about existence or about the nature of what exists, so if the problem of the relation of consciousness to the I is an existential problem then it is a problem about the existence of that relation or the nature of that relation.

This inference is valid if (but not only if) all facts are existential facts. However, although if something is a fact then it is the case, it is not clear that this is exactly the same thing as saying that something exists. Sartre has himself claimed that it makes no sense to ask within a narrowly Kantian framework what transcendental consciousness can be. The thought is that transcendental consciousness exists as a condition for experience whatever it is.

If we construe 'existential' narrowly, so that existential problems are the problems of human existence, then the inference certainly does not go through because not all facts, not even all phenomenological facts, are facts about the nature of human existence. The 'human' component of this description is suspended by the *epoché*. But suppose we construe 'existential' widely, and allow a distinction which Sartre accepts between the formal conditions for experience as claimed by Kant, and the material or phenomenological conditions as claimed by Husserl. Then in a sense Kant's facts are not existential facts; they are just the fact that certain synthetic *a priori* propositions are true and that if this were not the case rational self-conscious experience would not be possible. This leaves room for Sartre to say that Husserl's phenomenological facts, if they are facts, are existential facts. Husserl would have to be an existentialist *malgré lui* but if the two classes of fact, formal and existential, are not only mutually exclusive but collectively exaustive then Sartre has to be right.

Sartre says, I think correctly, that there is something in common between Kant's transcendental consciousness and the transcendental consciousness revealed by Husserl's transcendental reduction. Indeed this claim makes it look as though the relation is identity:

> Husserl [...] discovers the transcendental consciousness of Kant, and grasps it by the *epoché*. (35)[37]

It is certainly an essential part of Husserl's phenomenology that transcendental subjectivity is revealed in the *epoché*. This can be seen in the *Paris Lectures*, *Cartesian Meditations* and *Ideas*. Also, Husserl's transcendental subjectivity and Kant's transcendental unity of apperception share a similar fundamental function: they make experience possible. But Sartre draws the crucial difference as follows: [transcendental] consciousness is not 'a set of logical conditions' (35) 'un ensemble de conditions logiques' (TE 18) 'It is a fact which is absolute' (35) 'c'est un fait absolu' (TE 18). It is arguable that the difference between Kant and Husserl which Sartre draws sharply is in fact one of degree. For example, suppose as Kant thinks there can only be experience on condition a set of *a priori* sentences is true, then we may still ask what makes those sentences true, and enquiry into the true conditions of synthetic claims will require mention of material facts, not merely formal facts even if (as Kant supposes) the synthetic *a priori* sentences express necessary truths. Further, suppose Husserl is correct in thinking that transcendental subjectivity is revealed by the *epoché* and is a condition for consciousness in the world. Then we may ask what transcendental subjectivity is in a material or ontological sense as Sartre suggests, but we may also give Husserl's claim a quasi-Kantian formal construal. If what Husserl says is true then, for example, if there is experience of the world then a certain claim is true: the claim that transcendental subjectivity in some sense exists. Conversely, unless there was in some sense transcendental subjectivity then there could not be consciousness of a world. To this degree Husserl's claims are as formal as Kant's and Kant's as material as Husserl's. Both are saying, if not A then not B, but if A then B and each is committed to giving A and B some minimal content. Sartre, I think, construes Kant too formally and Husserl too materially.

The reason why the formal and the material are not as readily separable as Sartre supposes is that Kant is not just engaged in logic and Husserl is not just describing empirical contingencies. In fact both Kant and Husserl say the status of their claim is synthetic *a priori* – a status with formal (i.e. necessary and *a priori*) and material (i.e. synthetic) components.[38]

Sartre says about Husserl's transcendental consciousness:

this consciousness is no longer a set of logical conditions. It is a fact which is absolute. (35)[39]

I would wish to rewrite the first part of this so that it reads: this consciousness is no longer just a set of logical conditions, or better, not just a set of formal conditions. Husserl fills out (to put it metaphorically) the formal dimension of the Kantian framework. He is answering a question which according to Sartre is unanswerable within the Kantian framework: What are the conditions for experience materially? (Sartre cannot say 'ontologically' here because ontological commitments are bracketed by the *epoché* although Sartre will allow this sort of talk in his phenomenological ontology in *Being and Nothingness.*) I think Husserl is entitled to ask this question within the Kantian framework and, again, Sartre's prohibition of this is a consequence of his construing Kant formally but Husserl materially.

What does Sartre mean when he says Husserl makes transcendental consciousness into an absolute fact? Fact is clear enough: If something is a fact then it obtains or is the case, or put it another way, a certain sentence is made true. Husserl's transcendental subjectivity is an absolute fact in Sartre's sense as follows: It is a condition for the experience of the world that is not itself grounded. As we have seen, if A grounds B then A makes B possible, or B would not be possible but for A. But if A is an absolute condition then A grounds B but there is no ground for A. This is at least true of A if A is an absolute condition, but there is more: A is the ground of A, or A makes itself possible, or A is the reason for A. Now, a rather vacuous modal point needs to be cleared up here. If we ask what makes something possible, then it is going to be trivially or tautologically true that everything features amongst the conditions for its own existence: A if and only if A. This is not what Sartre means, because it is a condition of anything at all. We want a construal which captures absolute conditions in particular. If A is an absolute then A is cause of itself; it makes itself be what it is. This is the formula Sartre will use in his own account of consciousness but here he is ascribing it to Husserl's transcendental subjectivity. I think Sartre is half right about this. If we look at *Cartesian Meditations* and *Ideas* then it is clear that transcendental subjectivity is the ground of the world but is not grounded. That is the part Sartre has right. Husserl does not claim that transcendental subjectivity is the cause of itself or the reason from itself or that it makes itself be or that it makes itself be what it is. However, it may well be that Husserl is committed to that view implicitly even though he does not state it. It would seem to be open to Sartre or anyone else to develop logical implications of a philosopher's view.[40]

There is one other way of construing 'absolute' here. Suppose something is an absolute fact, then this might mean not only is it the case but it could not not be the case, or not only is the sentence reporting it true but it could not not be true. In other words, all and only absolute facts are reported by necessary truths, or absolute facts are facts which make necessary truths true. Now, there is a reason for and against reading 'absolute' this way, in the context Sartre is considering. Suppose the fact of transcendental subjectivity is an absolute. In a sense we do not wish to make it a necessary truth that anything exists, even transcendental subjectivity, because arguably it is a contingent fact that that there is something rather than nothing, but the existence of transcendental subjectivity is logically consistent with the view that there might not have been anything. Suppose, on the other hand, given that there is something rather than nothing there is transcendental subjectivity. This view can be extracted from Husserl if we mean 'what is' by his 'world'. Transcendental subjectivity, after all, not only constitutes the world but is its ground: it makes what it is be and be what it is. Then transcendental subjectivity would be an absolute in the sense that the existence of the world is sufficient for transcendental subjectivity.

But everything is in the last resort contingent upon the existence of the world for Sartre; and for Sartre it is a contingent fact that there is something rather than nothing. The being of what is is a brute and even unacceptable fact in the developed philosophy in *Being and Nothingness*. This is a reason for thinking Sartre does not mean by 'absolute fact' 'fact which makes a necessary truth true'.

A reason for adopting this reason is that Husserl (following Kant) thinks the sentences asserting the ground of the world are synthetic *a priori* necessary truths.[41] This means that in some sense they could not be false. If we read 'world' to mean 'what is' then 'necessary' means 'necessary *tout court*' – or 'not subject to qualifications'. But if we give 'world' a weaker reading to mean something like 'set of possible objects for consciousness' then 'necessary' means something like 'necessary given there is experience', or 'guaranteed to be the case if a world is given to consciousness'. This would make transcendental subjectivity into an absolute if it is the case that there is consciousness of a world.

Sartre denies that transcendental subjectivity is an absolute in any of these senses. Even in the minimal sense that transcendental subjectivity is an absolute if and only if it is the ground for the world but itself is not grounded it will turn out for Sartre to be false that it is absolute. His view will be that transcendental subjectivity does not ground the world and consciousness of it, but rather is itself an object in the world for consciousness. This would turn the tables on Husserl because it makes what was transcendental subjectivity contingent on consciousness of the world, not consciousness of the world contingent on it. Before we can appraise this reversal a great deal of further argument and description needs to be evaluated.

There are several points on which Sartre is in substantial agreement with Husserl. For example, Sartre accepts that consciousness constitutes the world. Intentional objects are made what they are by intentional acts. So Sartre accepts the *noema/noesis* distinction, and is willing to call consciousness 'transcendental' in so far as it has this constituting function:

> it is indeed this transcendental consciousness which constitutes our empirical consciousness, our consciousness 'in the world', our consciousness with its

psychic and psycho-physical me. For our part, we readily acknowledge the existence of constituting consciousness. (35–6)[42]

Sartre also accepts from Husserl the phenomenological reduction of the pre-philosophical ego. As he says, the psycho-physical me is a transcendental object which falls before the *epoché*. His disagreements are as follows. Once the ego has fallen before the *epoché* there is no further irreducibly subjective ego remaining. This is the most profound disagreement between Husserl and Sartre.[43] It will further follow from this that the only ego there is is transcendent but not transcendental. Far from being a condition for consciousness, consciousness is a condition for it. As Sartre puts it:

> Is not this psychic and psycho-physical me enough? Need one double it with a transcendental I, a structure of absolute consciousness? (36)[44]

Suppose (as Sartre wishes) we reply 'No, there is no need' or 'No, to do so would be phenomenological extravagance'. Then, Sartre thinks, four consequences follow:

1   Consciousness becomes impersonal.
2   The I only appears at a level of humanity as an aspect of the me.
3   The unity of consciousness makes the 'I think' possible.
4   It is possible that there should be absolute impersonal consciousness.

The first and fourth of these are closely related so may be treated together.

Sartre says about (1):

> The transcendental field becomes impersonal; or, if you like 'pre-personal', without an I. (36)[45]

The transcendental field is what is revealed by the *epoché*. For example, for Husserl it is consciousness as constituted and grounded by transcendental subjectivity. What Sartre is claiming is that from a phenomenological point of view we are in a position to speak of consciousness without a subject after the *epoché*. Consciousness itself is revealed by the transcendental reduction but no owner of consciousness, or put in Kantian terms, no subject of experience. This implies that it makes sense, on one level at least, to speak of consciousness without thereby being committed to the view that there is something or someone that is conscious, or to speak of experience without something or someone that experiences. This is a contentious philosophical issue. For example, it could be that there is something incoherent about the idea of an unowned or, more strangely, unhad experience. An experience is necessarily undergone, enjoyed, or 'had' and if so, then it is had, undergone or enjoyed by someone or something or other. But conversely it is possible that the appearance of incoherence is generated by the subject–verb–object form of our grammar. It does not make sense perhaps to speak of experience but no experiencer in our language. But perhaps Sartre can force our language to be about what is directly phenomenologically given (even if this means doing violence to our grammar).

Under (4) Sartre contemplates the possibility that there might be consciousnesses which are not or do not have personalities, or are not anybody's. This would seem to be possible if an impersonal consciousness is possible. If it is a necessary condition of being a personality to be a person and if there are no persons without subjects of experience then if there is no subject of experience then there are no persons and so no personalities. It follows then that Sartre's possibility is an actuality if it is true that there is no irreducibly psychic subject but there are consciousnesses. It would remain true of course that there are persons and personalities pre-phenomenologically, or at the level of the natural attitude, but 'subject', 'person' and 'personality' would fall before the *epoché*.

Sartre's (2) appears ambiguous. 'At the level of humanity' would imply 'only at the level of the natural attitude' because it is only within the natural attitude that we may talk about humans and humanity. Yet the I as part of the me, the active part, would seem to be open to phenomenological description, i.e. to description in the world of the phenomenological reduction. Although there is an ambiguity here there is no contradiction because the views are in fact mutually consistent. We simply need to add the thesis that the I may appear as part of the me both in the natural attitude and after the phenomenological reduction. Suppose that is true. The question now is what makes the I the active component of the me. The me is an object, perhaps commonsensically contrasted with the I as subject, so the me appears to the I. It is the latter claim that Sartre wishes to reject. There is no I that the me appears to. Rather there is the me as object with two components, one active and one passive. Within the Kantian framework one way in which the subject–object distinction is drawn is that the subject is active (a *spontaneity* as Kant puts it) but the object (at least as an object of sensibility) is passive (a *receptivity* he says). This is more clearly a distinction between intellect and sense in Kant but it carries over in Sartre and Husserl as part of the subject–object distinction. Now, Sartre is saying the me is an object but nonetheless contains a subjective–active component. The I is the me as thought or experienced as an active subject. Oneself as active subject is one object of thought amongst others and so cannot possibly, *qua* that, really have the status of subject of experience. The subject is part of the object.

Sartre's point (3) is an inversion of a traditional picture of Kant's doctrine of the transcendental unity of apperception in the 'Transcendental Deduction'. Suppose it is the Kantian view that that the 'I think' be capable of accompanying any of my experiences is a necessary condition of their being mine. In a sense the I think is then prior to or is a ground of experience. Indeed Kant sometimes calls it an original condition. Sartre is reversing the picture because he thinks the unity of consciousness is a condition for the possibility of the 'I think'. It follows that the I think cannot 'help to create' consciousness. Rather consciousness is its 'foundation' (36).

For this reason Sartre finds greater value in Husserl's treatment of consciousness in *Logical Investigations* than in *Ideas*. In *Logical Investigations* the Husserl of 1900–1 does not attempt to ground the world and consciousness of it in the constituting activities of the transcendental ego. However, in *Ideas* the Husserl of 1913 transformed phenomenology into an egology, a study of the ego, as that which fundamentally grounds the world and consciousness of it. Indeed, as Sartre points out, the Husserl of *Logical Investigations* already possesses the idea of the self (the me) as constituted by synthetic acts of consciousness. Sartre agrees with that. Sartre's position is that the picture is redundant:

> This I would be, so to speak, behind each consciousness, a necessary structure of consciousness whose rays would light upon each phenomenon presenting itself on the field of attention. (37)[46]

Indeed, Sartre could have pointed out here that if the metaphor of 'behind' is apposite then such an ego cannot appear to consciousness and if phenomenology is the description of what appears to consciousness as it appears there can be no phenomenology of the transcendental ego.

6 The unity of consciousness

The idea that one's consciousness is necessarily a unity, is in principle indivisible, is a psychologically compelling one. It is not the claim that it is impossible to think two thoughts simultaneously (although on some criteria for individuating thoughts that might be the case), it is the claim that a consciousness *qua* someone's is necessarily single. Otherwise, we could not make sense of putatively numerically distinct thoughts being episodes within a self-same consciousness, and the grounds for saying that this consciousness is mine and this someone else's would seem undermined.[47]

Sartre accepts the necessary unity of consciousness but rejects the thesis that its unity is bestowed by a Husserlian transcendental ego. He has two grounds for this rejection. First, the transcendental ego is redundant because the unity of consciousness may be accounted for without its postulation. Second, the existence of a transcendental ego is actually incompatible with the fact of the unity of consciousness. We could put these points in this way: The existence of the transcendental ego is not a necessary condition for the unity of consciousness and the existence of the transcendental ego is a sufficient condition for the impossibility of the unity of consciousness.

Is either of these claims true? I shall pursue the question of whether the transcendental ego would make the unity of consciousness impossible in the section below. Sartre thinks the transcendental ego is redundant because he thinks it is the objects of consciousness which make its unity possible. It is the synthesising activity of several mental acts in constituting one and the same intentional object which enables us to say that it is one and the same consciousness which is directed towards that object. It is not that which is conscious which bestows unity on consciousness but that which consciousness is of.

An objection might be brought against this thesis. *Prima facie* it is neither necessary nor sufficient for one act of consciousness to be part of the same consciousness as some numerically distinct act of consciousness that they have the same intentional object.

It is not necessary because the intentional objects of a putative unified consciousness may change. Besides, it could in principle turn out on other grounds that two acts of consciousness are episodes within one and the same consciousness without its being the case that they are directed towards the same intentional object. Indeed, if this were not the case one person could not experience different things.

It is not sufficient because from the fact that two mental acts take the same intentional object it does not follow that they are parts of one and the same consciousness. This is because two mental acts could exist in two numerically distinct consciousnesses yet still take the same intentional object. If this were not the case then different people could not experience the same thing.[48]

Even if these objections may be met, Sartre faces a further difficulty. The view that the intentional object constitutes the unity of consciousness sounds more plausible when we are dealing with short-term sequences of experiences (e.g. counting) than when the objects and experiences are widely separated in time and nature. The objects counted have a causal role in making my sequence of thoughts a case of that mental unity called 'counting' (even if I miscount). However, it is hard to see how this account could be extended to explain how my present experience of drinking red wine in London could be part of the same consciousness as my perception twenty years ago of a tree in Spain.

For Sartre it is the world which constitutes consciousness rather than the reverse. Even though series of intentional conscious acts make the world what it is for consciousness, without the world there could be no consciousness. In his rather compact idiom, consciousness constitutes itself as awareness of itself in the face of an object.

Is Sartre entitled to the view that the transcendental ego is redundant for the unity of consciousness? Suppose we leave on one side for the moment the claim that it might even be incompatible. Then, I think, Husserl could reply that the existence of the transcendental ego as a structure of consciousness is a sufficient condition for the unity of that consciousness. To see this, consider what is involved in the notion of a subject of experience.

Consider some series of experiences where we wish to know the grounds for claiming those experiences are episodes within one and the same consciousness. Now, it is going to be a sufficient condition for that that those experiences have a single owner or subject. Bracketing questions about the subjective nature of time, suppose the series is constituted by numerically distinct experiences occurring over a time interval, then if some subject of an experience at an earlier time is numerically identical with some subject of an experience at a later time then the earlier experience and the later experience are experiences in one and the same consciousness.

It could be objected that this analysis simply begs the question. By saying that there is one and only one consciousness for each subject of experience it seems to be excluded stipulatively and *a priori* that one and the same subject should have or constitute more than one consciousness. I do not think this charge is terribly damaging. It has after all been allowed that a single subject may think numerically distinct thoughts simultaneously, and not much more sense than that may be attached to a single subject being or having more than one consciousness. At least, if we attach much more sense to it, for example in multiple personality or split brain cases, then we have to give up talking about a single or self-same subject of experience over time from a subjective point of view. If we accept that then we have to accept that the existence of the Husserlian transcendental ego is a sufficient condition for the unity of consciousness, so long as we understand (as Husserl and Sartre do) a Husserlian transcendental ego as a structure of consciousness: its subjective pole or that which is conscious but not to be found as some item within consciousness.

To show that the transcendental ego is not redundant to the unity of consciousness it would have to be shown that there is no way other than postulating a transcendental ego in which the unity of consciousness could be accounted for. Even if the previous argument is sound it has only been shown that the transcendental ego is sufficient for the unity of consciousness, not that it is necessary, and showing that it is necessary is much more difficult because that requires showing that any *prima facie* competitor for bestowing the unity of consciousness could not in fact fulfil that role.

Prima facie there exist several such competitors. For example the unity of consciousness might depend on the indivisibility of the soul, or the unity of consciousness might depend (contingently or causally) on the identity of the brain (even though this is not a claim a phenomenologist can easily make *qua* phenomenologist). Or consciousness might be the sort of entity which is in principle indivisible *qua* consciousness. If so, it does not make sense to deny the unity of consciousness much as it does not make sense to say that phenomenological red is unextended.

Husserl thinks it is phenomenologically self-evident that the unity of consciousness is constituted by the transcendental ego. The trouble is, what is here phenomenologically self-evident to Husserl is not phenomenologically self-evident to Sartre.

7 Sartre's holism

Following Brentano entirely, and Husserl largely, Sartre says 'consciousness is defined by intentionality' (38), 'la conscience se définit par l'intentionalité' (TE 21). He thinks all and only mental phenomena exhibit that directedness towards some object or content which we call 'intentionality'. In other words, the intentional is necessary and sufficient for the mental.

Suppose that intentionality is the essence of the mental, or intentionality makes the mental what it is. With this assumption we may examine Sartre's alternative account of consciousness's unity.

To say that Sartre's account is an alternative to Husserl's is perhaps rather misleading. Sartre thinks that Husserl is in possession of a broadly accurate account of the unity of consciousness but then unnecessarily postulates a transcendental ego to account for that very same unity. Sartre says that consciousness 'unifies itself by escaping from itself' (38), 'elle s'unifie en s'échappant' (TE 21).

Let us take first the claim that consciousness escapes from itself. Sartre never abandons the view that consciousness is 'transparent'; that consciousness is consciousness of itself. Despite this he wishes to make room for the claim that consciousness is 'absorbed' in its intentional object. It is possible to make intuitive or pre-phenomenological sense of this by remembering that there are times when one is no doubt conscious of something or other but not conscious of being conscious. There seem to be periods when persons are conscious without thereby being occurrently self-conscious. If we were asked later what we were conscious of we could perhaps answer correctly and there might be various reasons for this. We might remember the object, or infer that we were conscious of the object on the basis of remembering the object in a particular way. Or it could be that consciousness is implicitly a kind of self-consciousness even when there is not any direct act of attention focused on the consciousness of the object. These possibilities would seem to be open. But clearly, there is a kind of 'escape' from self-consciousness or consciousness's reflection upon itself involved when one's attention is absorbed by the object of consciousness. It could be that these distinctions admit of degrees that are not readily captured by the distinctions available to us at present.

But Sartre says more than that consciousness escapes from itself. He says that by doing this it unifies itself. The thinking here is that unless there existed an intentional object there could exist no unity of consciousness. (I mean by 'exist' here 'exist *qua* intentional object'. I do not mean that the intentional object need have some non-phenomenological existence.) Putatively, phenomenological existence *qua* intentional object, or *qua* object of consciousness, is a sufficient condition for the unity of the consciousness of that object. Sartre thinks intentionality is constitutive of the unity of consciousness. Why is this?

Sartre proffers a kind of holism of the mental. It does not make much sense to talk about a single act of consciousness taking a single intentional object wholly in abstraction from numerically distinct actual and possible acts of consciousness which jointly contribute to the synthesis of that object as the object that it is. Sartre provides us with the following example:

> The unity of a thousand active consciousnesses by which I have added, do add, and shall add two and two to make four, is the transcendent object 'two and two make four'. (38)[49]

It is only against the background of a multiplicity of acts of consciousness that we can speak of, for example, a particular thought that two plus two make four. The fact that is thereby thought counts as the one that it is in virtue of its transcendental constitution.

Sartre is not saying that empirical agreement or anything like that makes it the case that two plus two equal four. Clearly, from the fact that n people agree that p it does not follow that p, and Sartre knows that. Indeed, he calls 'two plus two equal four' 'this eternal truth' (38) so I take it he thinks that it is necessary.[50] He is concerned with its constitution as an object for consciousness: what the fact as a fact thought by us consists in. The fact that two plus two equals four is a transcendent object of consciousness according to Sartre. He means it is not something which exists *qua* fact only amongst the contents of consciousness. Its being the fact that it is transcends or is not exhausted by any consciousness of it. The possibility of its being an object for a particular act of consciousness, its being possible for example that I think it now, has transcendental conditions. Unless a multitude of other mental acts were possible, concerning addition, subtraction, the meaning of '+' and '=', etc. then this putatively isolated fact would not be thinkable. If that is right, then there cannot exist acts of consciousness in isolation from other acts of consciousness, and if that is right then it only makes sense to talk of numerically distinct acts of consciousness if such acts are in principle parts of some consciousness as a whole. For this reason Sartre says:

Whoever says 'a consciousness' says 'the whole of consciousness'. (39)[51]

This is an interesting line of argument which, if sound, does succeed in grounding the unity of consciousness in the intentional object and therefore makes the transcendental ego redundant.

There are however a number of problems for it. Perhaps the most fundamental is this. Suppose we maintain that the intelligibility of an object of experience *qua* this or that sort of object presupposes the possibility of a variety of acts of consciousness. Suppose we allow further that the set of acts of consciousness thus presupposed must turn out to be parts of one and the same consciousness; otherwise their content could not be presupposed in the intelligibility of the object to a single act of consciousness. On the face of it this looks like a respectable and familiar quasi-Kantian line of argument. The trouble is that it arguably proves too much.

Suppose the transcendental conditions for the possibility of the unity of consciousness are in fact social or public. For example, suppose it is a condition for two plus two equals four being not a fact *tout court* but a fact for some consciousness that other consciousnesses agree that this is indeed a fact. We would not wish to claim that that constituted good grounds for saying that putatively numerically distinct consciousnesses must actually turn out to be parts or aspects of one and the same consciousness. This is an option that Hegel takes up.[52]

In *The Phenomenology of Spirit* Hegel wishes to maintain the individuality of the various consciousnesses whilst maintaining at the same time that they are aspects or perspectives of one and the same consciousness. Suppose however we just wish to retain the individuality of consciousness: retain good grounds for saying that your mind is not mine and mine is not yours. These grounds would seem not to be forthcoming from any view which makes the constitution of the objects of consciousness *qua* the sorts they are transcendentally and intersubjectively constituted. Indeed, *prima facie*, the notion of intersubjectivity is undermined. The options would seem to be these: atomistic intelligibility of experience or Hegel.

8 Consciousness makes itself

Sartre accepts, indeed emphasises, that synthesis is temporal:

> A principle of unity within duration is nonetheless needed if the continual flux of consciousness is to be capable of positing transcendent objects outside the flux. Consciousness must be perpetual synthesis of past consciousnesses and present consciousnesses. This is correct. (38–9)[53]

This statement expresses a fundamental area of agreement with two characteristically Husserlian views: the view that consciousness constitutes its objects, and the view that any single act of consciousness is made possible by protention and retention.[54]

Sartre has already argued that it is the intentional object of consciousness which makes consciousness a unity. Now he is suggesting that it is certain facts about consciousness which make the object of consciousness what it is for consciousness. So the process is two-sided: The intentional object provides the unity of consciousness, but consciousness 'posits' its intentional object and makes it be what it is for consciousness. We should think of these as reciprocal processes, or as synthesised (*aufgehoben*) in Hegel's dialectical sense.[55]

Sartre's claim about time is that past acts of consciousness have to be in some sense present in any given act of consciousness in order for the objects of consciousness to be posited, or experienced as objects existing independently of consciousness. Any act of consciousness directed towards some object presupposes other acts in the same consciousness, but those other acts that are past acts must be 'read into' the present one to make it consciousness of an object of a mind-independent sort.[56]

If *per impossibile* there were solitary acts of consciousness then there could be no grounds for claiming that the objects of such acts are transcendent. As Sartre puts it, unity within duration is required for the positing of objects 'outside the flux' (39). The distinction between what is 'in' consciousness and what is 'outside' it is only possible if certain sorts of objects, paradigmatically physical objects, are posited. Nevertheless, within the minimal Husserlian framework which Sartre accepts, the existence for example of a physical object for consciousness is an achievement of consciousness, an achievement of synthesis.

Sartre's thesis that consciousness must be a synthesis of past and present acts of consciousness is not only consistent with but semantically similar to Husserl's protention–retention distinction. That is the view that in any act of consciousness of some object an anticipation of the nature of the object is read into it and a quasi-memory of the nature of the object retained in the perception of it. In the *Lectures on the Phenomenology of Internal Time Consciousness* Husserl considers the example of the consciousness of a tune. Clearly, Sartre is reporting half of this picture when he claims a synthesis of past and present consciousness obtains. Sartre's thesis of past and present synthesis is entailed by but does not entail Husserl's doctrine of protention and retention.

It might be objected that the description Sartre has given of the 'principle of unity within duration' (38) is incoherent. He has said that consciousness is a synthesis of past and present consciousnesses, but he does not just mean that consciousness in general is such a synthesis. He means present consciousness is a synthesis of past and present consciousness. The difficulty is that something present is putatively both present and past but arguably it is logically impossible for anything to be both present and past because 'present' and 'past' are mutually exclusive predicates. (There is a clear sense in which they are not mutually exclusive; what was past may now be present; in other words something may last from then to now. But this is not Sartre's meaning here.) Sartre seems to be committed to the view that what was past is present *qua* past and that would seem contradictory.

To make sense of this we need to view it in the context of Sartre's account of the present moment. In *Being and Nothingness* he commits himself to a view of the present as the is been. This violence to the tense categories of ordinary language is necessary according to Sartre to break down our rather static compartmentalised view of time as divided cleanly between past, present and future. In fact the putative present is perpetually ceasing to be future and perpetually becoming past and this change constitutes the essentially dynamic quality of the present. The synthetic unity of past, present and future is prior to their analytical separation. In *originary synthesis* room would seem to be left for the past, in this case past acts of consciousness, to be, or at least to be becoming, present. The distinction between past, present and future is blurred in reality if not in language. The ekstasies of time are separable in abstract thought but not in what is phenomenologically given.

So, we have a new way of thinking of the unity of consciousness. Although it remains true that consciousness is unified through its intentional objects, it is true in addition that 'It is consciousness which unifies itself' (39). This is intended by Sartre as a complementary claim, not one which competes with the thesis that unity is provided by the object. After all, consciousness was not without any role in the constitution of the unity of its object. The several acts of consciousness have to be directed towards their intentional object not just so that we can speak of one and the same consciousness but so that we can speak of one and the same object. It would be fair to say that consciousness unifies itself before the object or in the face of the object, or the several acts of consciousness fuse into one single consciousness by being directed towards one and the same object, even though an equally legitimate way of thinking of this process is: the object counts as one and the same transcendent object for consciousness because the several acts of consciousness are directed towards it.

It might be objected to this description that it is circular: A unifies B and B unifies A but either the prior unity of A is a condition for the unity of B or the prior unity of B a condition for the unity of A but not both. I think Sartre's reply would be that it is one process that is being described in two ways here and not two separable processes. Although consciousness is not identical with its objects, the two are inseparable.

We are now in a position to interpret Sartre's claim that 'consciousness refers perpetually to itself' (39). This may be unpacked in two complementary ways. First, any given act of consciousness presupposes certain past acts of consciousness for the constitution of its intentional object. Second, in mentioning an act of consciousness one is implicitly making reference to the whole consciousness of which that act is a part. This is because its being the act that it is, its being the act directed towards a particular intentional object and an intentional object of that type, depends upon its location holistically as one act of consciousness amongst others. So when Sartre says 'whoever says "a consciousness" says "the whole of consciousness"' this is not the Hegelian point that talk of an individual consciousness presupposes the existence and nature of consciousness in general (a social and ultimately spiritual consciousness). Rather it is the claim that in a sense in referring to a part of consciousness one has referred to the whole of which it is a part.

This is a rather contentious claim philosophically. Suppose someone claims that if I refer to a part of x then I refer to x, then there is a sense in which this is true and a sense in which it is false. It is false in the sense that if I refer to a part of x I have not thereby referred to the whole of x *qua* that whole and 'the whole of x' is one plausible meaning of 'x'. However, it remains true that if I refer to a part of x it is x that I have referred to; that very object rather than another. In referring to a part of x it was a part of x that I was referring to. Sartre really needs the second of these two thoughts rather than the first in order for his point about consciousness to go through. If I refer to a particular act of consciousness I am implicitly referring to a consciousness as a whole because any act of consciousness is a part of a whole consciousness. Despite this, it remains true that 'act of consciousness' does not mean the same as 'consciousness as a whole'. The second of these is used to refer to a consciousness as a whole individual consciousness.

The force of Sartre's holistic conception of consciousness is to make the transcendental ego redundant. Indeed, to the extent that Husserl shares this holistic contention he does not need to postulate an I as the unifying subject of consciousness either, as Sartre emphasises. Sartre thinks the self-unification of consciousness in the face of its object may take place without any recourse to the postulation of a transcendental ego, and so the unity of consciousness may be fully accounted for without any subjective source of unity.[57]

Sartre is correct in this thought to the extent that his descriptions of how the unity of consciousness is possible are logically independent of any claims about the existence of the I as subject. Unless we make it analytic that if there is consciousness then there is a subject of consciousness then Sartre's claim goes though. The only ontological resources he has used are consciousness and the intentional object, and the only plausible line of objection to this strategy would be to insist that 'consciousness' and 'object' have no legitimate use unless some use is given to 'subject'. If we accept there may be 'impersonal' or 'pre-personal' consciousnesses in Sartre's sense that leaves just the objection that 'object' needs 'subject' for semantic contrast. There are two possibilities: either it does or it does not, and a Sartrean reply may be constructed for each.

If there are no objects without subjects then it is open to Sartre to maintain that the subject is not a Husserlian transcendental ego. It might for example be consciousness itself, and there might not be any irreducibly subjective source of consciousness. Or, the subject might be the whole person, that psycho-physical whole which each of us essentially is. In either case 'object' is given a semantic contrast without the postulation of the transcendental ego.

In any case, it is open to Sartre to maintain that there are objects in his sense without this claim depending on a possible use for 'subject'. This is because 'object' here means 'intentional object' or 'object of consciousness' and in order for it to be true that there is something which consciousness is consciousness of, it does not have to be true that there is something which is conscious, or at least, this is only required if it is independently true that there is no consciousness without something which is conscious and to say that without argument is to beg the question against Sartre.

The effect of these arguments, if they are sound, is to abolish the transcendental subject, the left-hand side of the traditional phenomenological triad subject–consciousness–object. Sartre's developed strategy will be to incorporate what was designated 'subject' as part of what is designated 'object'. Briefly, the subject is an object.

9 Individuality

A defender of the transcendental ego might mount the following defence. Consciousnesses are individual consciousnesses. In other words, choose any consciousness you like, it is just that consciousness which it is and not any of those consciousnesses that it is not. This is on the face of it a rather vacuous modal point because it is a logical property of anything that it is just what it is and not anything that it is not. In *Being and Nothingness* Sartre will maintain, rather provocatively, that consciousness is what it is not and is not what it is, but this claim requires separate treatment to unpack it as saying something coherent.[58] But, so the objection goes, not only is it true that this consciousness is not that but my consciousness is not yours and your consciousness is not his and so on. Indeed, the individuality of consciousness consists in precisely that fact that each consciousness is logically 'owned' by the subject of that consciousness. This means that if two putatively numerically distinct consciousnesses are to turn out to be in fact one and the same consciousness this is only because that which owns the one consciousness is numerically identical with that which owns the putative other. It is a logically necessary condition of two putatively distinct consciousnesses being numerically identical that they have a single subject, and it is logically sufficient for their being one and not two that they have a single subject. So if we ask the questions: What makes my consciousness mine and yours yours? and What stops my consciousness being yours and yours mine? the answer can only come in the quasi-Kantian analytic and formal mode: mine is mine and yours is yours. In other words yours is owned by you or you are the subject of yours and mine is mine or I am the subject of mine. If we ask the question of what I am, the Husserlian reply comes: I am a transcendental ego or irreducibly subjective source of consciousness.

Sartre's aim is the demolition of this entire picture of the individuality of consciousness as bestowed by the transcendental ego. Instead he says:

> The individuality of consciousness evidently stems from the nature of consciousness. Consciousness (like Spinoza's substance) can be limited only by itself. (39)[59]

Spinoza thinks there is only one substance, the totality of what is, which may be named either *deus* 'God' or *natura* 'Nature' in virtue of its two essential properties: thought and extension.[60] A substance is that which stands in no need of anything else in order to exist, and Spinoza clearly thinks that the only thing of which this could be true is the whole of what exists. Now, Sartre is saying that consciousness is in at least one respect like a substance in Spinoza's sense. Spinoza's substance is 'limited only by itself' in that there is nothing other than it which may constrain its being what it is. Any constraint on its nature arises from its nature and is not imposed by anything other than it.

This picture may be usefully contrasted with that of physical objects. If we ask what makes a certain physical object the thing that it is then this may be given either a causal or a logical construal. Construed causally it means something like: What causes this physical object to be how it is? and the answer could come in this form: It interacts causally with other physical objects. Construed logically the question means: What makes this physical object just the thing it is and not any of the things it is not? and the answer again, arguably, could come in terms of other physical objects. For example, it is arguably a necessary condition for one physical object not being identical with a putative other that they occupy numerically distinct portions of space-time. On this view, if two putatively distinct physical objects turned out to occupy numerically the same portion of space-time then they would turn out to be one and the same physical object. (This view of physical objects is not beyond doubt. Suppose two spatially distinct physical objects fused by occupying the same space, and then bifurcated by once again occupying numerically distinct spaces. It seems true to say that during the period of fusion two physical objects occupy the same space at the same time, even though talk of 'two physical objects' here is parasitic on talk of spatially distinct objects. On this view there is no *a priori* objection to an infinite number of physical objects occupying a place at a time.) Paradigmatically, something is not a physical object unless it can interact with other physical objects and paradigmatically, something is not a physical object unless it occupies a place distinct from other physical objects at a given time.

Now, I think Sartre is saying that nothing like these two sorts of criteria for determining the nature of physical objects is applicable in the case of consciousness. Consciousness makes itself be what it is. It is not caused to be what it is by anything other than the consciousness that it is. Also, it does not make much sense to talk about consciousnesses occupying spatio-temporal locations, so in stating the logical conditions for the numerical distinctness of consciousnesses, recourse cannot be had to things outside consciousness, in the 'external world'. The same two sorts of criteria would seem to be equally redundant in determining the nature of Spinoza's substance.

There is an important disanalogy between Spinoza's substance and consciousness of which Sartre must be aware. For Spinoza there exists only one substance, but for Sartre there exists more than one consciousness. So the problem arises for Sartre of how one consciousness is to be distinguished from another. Clearly for Spinoza there is no analogous problem of how one substance is to be distinguished from another. Sartre does not spell out clearly this disanalogy nor his solution to the problem it raises, but I think a Sartrean answer may be constructed. Any consciousness is presented to itself as if it could be the only thing that exists. In other words, solipsism is thinkable and this captures a possible phenomenology of consciousness. Arguably only consciousness is directly presented to consciousness and, even if that is false, other consciousnesses are not presented to any one consciousness. So, one consciousness not being another and this being a knowable fact depends upon the restricted type of epistemological access each consciousness has to consciousness. It is directly aware of itself but not of another. Sartre does not state this explicitly and parts of it are inconsistent with what he says elsewhere, but he does say, for example, that 'consciousness refers perpetually to itself' (39) and 'consciousness is consciousness of itself' (40). It is also perhaps implied by this:

> Thus it [consciousness] constitutes a synthetic and individual totality entirely isolated from other totalities of the same type. (39)[61]

One consciousness is entirely isolated from another. This is something phenomenologically given about consciousness; it is intrinsic to its nature that its only direct access is to itself and not to another consciousness. This, so to speak, prevents one consciousness merging with another, or one consciousness being another. This is what Sartre means when he says that the individuality of consciousness stems from its own nature and not from anything outside itself.

If Sartre has succeeded in saying something meaningful and true here then he has thereby succeeded in making the transcendental ego redundant as that which bestows individuality on consciousness. He has not yet accounted for the seeming personality of consciousness – its seeming to be mine, yours, and so on, but he has perhaps shown that personality is not necessary for individuality.

Consciousnesses may be distinguished from one another without recourse to mentioning their subject, and this leaves logical room for there being in a sense no subject. Indeed, he will go on to argue that personality is produced by consciousness, not *vice versa*:

> The phenomenological conception of consciousness renders the unifying and individualising role of the I totally useless. It is consciousness on the contrary, which makes possible the unity and the personality of the I. (40)[62]

We see here starkly put the reversal of the Husserlian order of priorities. The I does not constitute consciousness. Consciousness constitutes the I.

10 Pre-reflective consciousness

Sartre maintains famously and perhaps paradoxically that 'consciousness is conscious of itself' (40), 'la conscience est consciente d'elle-même' (TE 23). What does this mean? A clue, if not an explanation, is given by his claim that 'The type of existence of consciousness is to be consciousness of itself' (40), 'le type d'existence de la conscience c'est d'être conscience de soi' (TE 23–4). So consciousness's consciousness of itself is the way or manner in which consciousness exists. It could not be nor be what it is unless it had a certain internal reflexive relation. Although 'being conscious of' sounds like a relationship and 'being conscious of itself' sounds like a reflexive relationship, these would be rather misleading interpretations of the nature of consciousness in Sartre's view. This is because consciousness's being consciousness of consciousness is something which characterises *pre-reflexive* consciousness for Sartre. This is a kind of consciousness quite distinct from self-consciousness, or the mental act of being aware of some mental state of mine which he calls reflective or reflexive consciousness. Pre-reflexive consciousness is the sort of conscious state we are in when we are not consciously reflecting on our own mental states yet still conscious. But if pre-reflective consciousness is consciousness of consciousness then it is not clear what prevents pre-reflective consciousness collapsing into reflective consciousness. It seems *prima facie* that Sartre is committed to the incoherent view that pre-reflective consciousness both is and is not a kind of consciousness. There is however a way of dispelling this appearance of paradox.

The solution is to distinguish between two kinds of self-consciousness which are assimilated in the ordinary language term 'self-consciousness'. Self-consciousness may be consciousness of self or consciousness of consciousness. Reflexive consciousness is consciousness of self, or a kind of consciousness of consciousness in which the self or 'the me' appears. Pre-reflexive consciousness is a kind of consciousness of consciousness in which no self appears. Pre-reflexive consciousness is an implicit consciousness of consciousness or a subliminal awareness of the awareness itself in being aware. Clearly pre-reflexive consciousness is not just consciousness of consciousness even if, as Sartre maintains, its being this is essential to its being what it is. Pre-reflective consciousness is our ordinary typical awareness of the objects and the people which surround us and it is this awareness which is implicitly or subliminally an awareness that it is an awareness.

If this dispels the appearance of paradox we may now ask whether it is true. It would seem not to logically follow from 'x is aware of y' that 'x is aware of being aware of y'. x's awareness of being aware of y (if we assume the awareness is veridical) is logically sufficient for the truth of 'x is aware' but it would seem not to be necessary. Indeed, it seems commonsensically plausible to assume that there are things we are or have been aware of without being aware that we are or were aware that we are or were aware of them.

Even if it does not logically follow from the fact that a being is conscious that that being is implicitly or explicitly conscious of being conscious, it might still be true that at least some beings are conscious of being conscious when they are conscious.

An argument could be deployed to demonstrate this. Suppose it is true that some person 'x' perceives some object 'y'. Suppose further that x is interviewed about the perception of y and x is able to assert truly that it was indeed y that he perceived. It might be maintained that this supplies a kind of evidence for the conclusion that x was not only aware of y when aware of y but was further aware of being aware when being aware of y, and even aware of being x in being aware of y.

If this is evidence then it is evidence of only a weak or inductive kind. The reason for this is: from the fact that x is able to truly assert that he perceived y it does not logically follow that he was aware of being aware in perceiving y. It might be for example that x is presently able to remember y and presently assumes that the reason he can remember y is that it was in fact the case that he was perceiving y, and clearly this is quite consistent with the possibility that he was not aware of being aware when being aware of y and was not aware of being aware of y in being aware of y. The view that in being aware of y x was aware of being aware or aware of being aware of y is only one possible explanation of x's present ability to claim correctly that it was y that x was aware of.

Are there then any good grounds for Sartre's claim that pre-reflexive consciousness is consciousness of itself? It is clearly of no use to say that it feels as though this is true, or that it appears to consciousness that when there is consciousness there is consciousness of this consciousness, or that consciousness is consciousness of this consciousness, or that consciousness is consciousness of being conscious of consciousness. Even if we could be sure that such meta-acts of consciousness were veridical they would at best show that there is consciousness of consciousness when there is consciousness of consciousness, and this rather tautological fact could be established *a priori* irrespectively of whether it is true in fact that if someone is conscious they are thereby conscious of being conscious.

There is then a problem about the verification of Sartre's claim. If we say that it is apparent to consciousness that it is consciousness of itself then the claim

becomes vacuous and uninformative, or true *a priori* irrespective of the phenomenological facts about consciousness. But if we say it is not by some act of
consciousness that we know that consciousness is consciousness of itself then we
are faced with the problem, which may be insuperable, of how we could even in
principle come to know that Sartre's claim is true.

Despite these severe philosophical difficulties for Sartre's claim it is not necessarily a false one, still less a meaningless one. Meaning is not so closely tied to
verifiability to make it nonsensical, and from the fact that we cannot know the
truth value of a claim it does not follow that that claim is not true. I leave it open
then as a logical possibility that Sartre is right: Ordinary pre-reflexive consciousness is implicitly an awareness of itself.

It is worth mentioning the relation between Sartre's notion of pre-reflexive
consciousness and two competing tendencies in the philosophy of mind: one
Cartesian and one Freudian.[63]

Any Freudian conception of an unconscious would seem to logically imply
the view that a person may be in a mental state yet be ignorant of both the existence and the nature of that mental state. This is in fact what is essentially meant
by calling a mental state 'unconscious'. Conversely, any Cartesian conception of
the mental must preclude this possibility because an incorrigibility thesis is part
of Cartesianism. This is the view that if a person is in a mental state then they
know they are in that mental state.

I do not mean to suggest that Freudianism and Cartesianism are collectively
exhaustive epistemologies of the self. There are other options, notably those
which claim that one's first-person perspective on one's own mental states is
neither infallible, incorrigible, nor absolutely transparent, but in general offers
full, correct and immediate access. Moreover, knowing is factive. So a person
may, *ex hypothesi*, believe they are in a certain mental state and not know they are
– either because they are wrong, or because they are not justified in believing it
(i.e. if, *ex hypothesi*, the contents of certain mental states are determined by factors
beyond the first person singular perspective, the subject may not know what he
thinks until he has carried out an investigation of his socio-physical environment).

Now, it is clear that, barring certain interesting facts about self-deception,
Freudianism and Cartesianism are to this degree mutually inconsistent theories
about the mental. This is because if a person is in a mental state, on pain of
contradiction, either they know they are in that mental state or they do not know
they are in that mental state. Of course we may say in exception to this that a
person knows they are in some mental state under a certain description, *qua*, for
example, a mood, but does not know they are in that mental state under another
description, *qua*, for example, brain process. Nevertheless, the claim that there is
an unconscious appears self-contradictory within a Cartesian framework, and
Cartesianism appears false, at least for a large class of mental states, within a
Freudian framework.

Sartre is located within this scheme of things as follows: He is Cartesian about
incorrigibility and repudiates any idea of an unconscious. The only ambivalence

is how Cartesian he is about incorrigibility and how anti-Freudian he is about the unconscious.

With regard to the unconscious, in chapter 2 of *Being and Nothingness* Sartre develops the idea of self-deception he calls 'bad faith' (*mauvaise foi*). Bad faith is an endemic kind of self-deception in which human beings hide from themselves the reality of their own freedom. Suppose being free entails being in a mental state (for example, of deliberation). The issue then arises of the logical relations between bad faith and Cartesian incorrigibility.

Bad faith is open to several interpretations. On any of them bad faith is distinct from mere ignorance. On one reading, a person in bad faith does know what mental state they are in but refuses to acknowledge it. It is not that such a person is ignorant of their own mental state. On another construal, a person has the propositional self-knowledge that they are in some mental state but adopts a behavioural disposition which suggests (to themselves and others) that they are not in that state. To the extent that the disposition constitutes a belief, it is a belief which is inconsistent with their propositional belief that they are in that mental state. On another construal a person possesses both the propositional belief and the propositional disbelief that they are in some mental state but does not notice the inconsistency. If the existence of bad faith logically implies that a person has numerous false beliefs about themselves and amongst these beliefs are beliefs about the person's own mental states then the existence of bad faith is inconsistent with Cartesian incorrigibility: A person is in a mental state, and holds a false belief about the existence or nature of that mental state. Construed in that way, the doctrine of bad faith is incompatible with full-blooded Cartesianism about the incorrigibility of first person singular present tense psychological ascriptions. Damagingly, the doctrine of pre-reflexive consciousness implies that same Cartesianism. This tension, it seems to me, is unresolved in Sartre's philosophy as it stands.

One way of resolving it would be to drastically weaken Sartre's Cartesianism from 'If a person is in a mental state they know this', to: 'If a person is in a mental state they believe this'. Then the pre-reflexive idea of a person being aware of the mental state that he is in would be captured, but room would be left for the first person singular present tense psychological ascriptions to be corrigible.

There is a parallel problem about bad faith and Freudianism. If a person is in bad faith they hold at least one false belief about at least one of their mental states. It follows that under at least one description there exists a mental state that they misidentify or misascribe a property to. But this is arguably part of what it means for a mental state to be unconscious, and the doctrine of pre-reflexive consciousness implies that there are no unconscious mental states. It follows that the doctrines of bad faith and pre-reflexive consciousness are incompatible.

Again, I do not think Sartre has a solution to this problem within his own philosophy. However, a solution may be constructed along the following lines. If a person holds a belief about one of their own mental states (even a subliminal belief) then it follows that to that degree they are aware of that mental state. It clearly does not follow from that that their belief is true and that leaves room for a kind of unconscious and a kind of bad faith which is compatible with a now weakened version of pre-reflexive consciousness.

Clearly, if Freudianism is true and if Sartre's thesis about pre-reflexive consciousness is inconsistent with Freudianism then Sartre's thesis is false. However, if the above argument is sound then Sartre's thesis is not inconsistent with Freudianism so even if Freudianism is true that cannot demonstrate the falsity of Sartre's thesis.

If Cartesianism is false and if Sartre's thesis is a version of Cartesianism then Sartre's thesis is false. However, if it is true that Sartre's thesis is an important departure from Cartesianism then the falsity of Sartre's thesis cannot be demonstrated by any demonstration of the falsity of Cartesianism.

With these threats to the plausibility of the view that pre-reflexive consciousness is consciousness of itself removed we may examine the doctrine in more detail.

Sartre says

> Consciousness is aware of itself in so far as it is consciousness of a transcendent object. (40)[64]

A transcendent object is an object which is not exhausted by the consciousness of it. It is an object for consciousness, something that consciousness is conscious of, but not an item within consciousness in the sense of a part of consciousness. A transcendent object is an object which transcends the consciousness of it.

In evaluating Sartre's claim we need to decide the force of his ' in so far as'. A plausible interpretation is this. If consciousness is conscious of a transcendent object then consciousness is conscious of itself, and if consciousness is not conscious of a transcendent object then consciousness is not conscious of itself. (It would follow from that that in Sartre's terms we had ceased to talk about consciousness because consciousness is essentially consciousness of itself.) On this reading, consciousness of a transcendent object is both necessary and sufficient for consciousness being conscious of itself.

The difficulty here is that 'necessary and sufficient' cannot mean 'logically necessary and sufficient'. This is because it seems not to be contradictory to maintain that consciousness is always conscious of a transcendent object but is either sometimes or never conscious of itself. Argument is required to show that it logically follows both that if consciousness is consciousness of a transcendent object then it is consciousness of itself and that if it is conscious of itself it is conscious of a transcendent object.

It is perhaps too strong a requirement on Sartre's thesis that it logically follow from supporting premises that consciousness of a transcendent object entails consciousness's consciousness of consciousness so I shall consider a weaker argument consistent with his phenomenology.

The objects of consciousness are transcendentally constituted by acts of consciousness. An object being just the sort of object it is for consciousness depends upon the possibility of certain acts of awareness being directed towards it. It depends in particular upon certain preconceptions being 'read into' the present perception of the object. Now, for this kind of procedure to be possible consciousness has to, so to speak, draw on its own resources or draw on itself to make intelligible its present object of awareness. If that is right then consciousness of transcendent objects does indeed depend upon consciousness of consciousness. Consciousness has to 'refer to itself' to be conscious of its transcendental object.

So, although it does not straightforwardly follow from the fact that there is consciousness of a transcendent object that there is thereby a consciousness of consciousness, this does follow, albeit rather loosely, if a premise is supplied about the possibility of transcendent objects.

However, this is not exactly the kind of consciousness of consciousness that Sartre has in mind. He puts his view as follows:

> All is therefore clear and lucid in consciousness: the object with its characteristic opacity is before consciousness, but consciousness is purely and simply consciousness of being conscious of the object. This is the law of its existence. (40)[65]

What Sartre needs is a reason for holding that consciousness is consciousness of being conscious of the object, and not purely and simply consciousness of the object. I see no reason forthcoming from Sartre's text. The claim is just baldly asserted.

There is one particular kind of consciousness which Sartre wishes to distinguish from pre-reflexive consciousness and this is any kind of consciousness where consciousness is its own object. So now we have two broad claims about pre-reflexive consciousness which need to be reconciled:

1   Consciousness is consciousness of itself.
2   Consciousness is not its own object.

On the face of it, if x is conscious of y then x takes y as the object of its consciousness so if x is conscious of x, or more paradoxically but more in keeping with Sartre's view, if x is x's consciousness of x, then x is its own object, or x is the object for x. Sartre must distance himself from this kind of thinking in his characterisation of pre-reflexive consciousness on pain of incoherence. He needs a way of reading (1) which allows (2) to be true. Is there such a reading?

We need, I think, to give 'object' a strong reading so that if consciousness is its own object then consciousness is presented to itself as an item for its own scrutiny. Arguably this cannot be what pre-reflexive consciousness consists in because it makes consciousness both subject and object in the same respect, and that is incoherent. *Qua* consciousness of consciousness consciousness cannot be what consciousness is of.

But if that is right, what are we to make of consciousness being a consciousness of itself? An inadequate model for understanding this is any kind of spatial image of consciousness arching towards itself or shining on itself. Sartre's image is 'clear and lucid' (40). The point is that there is no obstacle to consciousness's contents being immediately apparent to consciousness. This is not because there exist special or additional acts of consciousness which constitute consciousness's consciousness of itself. Rather, consciousness's nature is self-evident to itself. It knows what it is just by being what it is.[66] If there were *per impossibile* such an obstacle then we would have to give up talking about consciousness here because any such opacity is characteristic of the objects of consciousness, not of the consciousness of those objects.

If Sartre's view that pre-reflexive consciousness is consciousness of itself is open to question, the alleged translucency of consciousness bears on an interesting and important philosophical question: What is awareness?

Suppose a person is looking at a wall. We would want to say that it is at least true that two physical objects are involved in this situation: the person *qua* physical object and the wall. I am not suggesting that a person is just a physical object, but uncontroversially at least a physical description is true of both the person and the wall. Suppose further that we are acquainted with all the relevant physiological facts, and physical facts about the light-waves from the wall contacting the person's retina. The important residual issue is this: What is the person's awareness of the wall they are looking at?[67]

It will perhaps be objected that I have constructed this example in dualist terms, or made it rest on dualist assumptions. This might be true but I do not think so. Suppose materialism is true, then the relation called 'awareness' (if it is a relation) is a physical one. But what is the awareness *qua* awareness, the consciousness of the wall *qua* consciousness? To put it another way, even if the awareness is physical, what have we said about it when we have called it 'awareness'? What can we say about the awareness that is identified with the physical thing?

It might be that this awareness is nothing at all, or it might be that the awareness is something non-physical, or a non-physical property of a physical relation. These options seem to me entirely open.[68]

The interest of this problem for Sartre is that he talks about consciousness as clear and lucid, and so seems to capture the notion of the awareness of a physical object (or anything else) as opposed to that which is aware and that which the awareness is awareness of. Conceptual room is left for Sartre's developed view in *Being and Nothingness* that consciousness from the point of view of phenomenological ontology is a kind of nothingness.

11 Consciousness without the I

Sartre raises the question of whether pre-reflexive consciousness has an I as part of its structure. His answer is no. Pre-reflexive consciousness is consciousness without the I.

The structure of Sartre's argument that pre-reflexive consciousness is consciousness without the I is as follows. There are only two possible candidates for what an I might be: either the I is a subject or the I is an object. It is either that which is conscious or part of what consciousness is consciousness of. Sartre takes it that he has already shown that the I is not a subject, or at least that it is phenomenologically illegitimate to postulate the I as subject because no such I appears to consciousness. Second, Sartre wishes to make a distinction between moments of consciousness when there is consciousness of the I and moments when there is not. He calls the type of consciousness where no I appears 'pre-reflexive consciousness' thereby capturing, as he thinks, our intuitive or pre-philosophical belief that it is possible for there to be consciousness of an object without that which is conscious appearing to consciousness in that act.

If this seems a question-begging procedure we may plead in Sartre's defence that he is describing what appears to consciousness, not what actually might be the case non-phenomenologically, and it seems plausible to maintain that no I as subject appears to consciousness, and often no I as object appears either. Against Sartre, it could be argued that the precondition for anything appearing to consciousness is the I as subject, and therefore the I as subject is shown to exist by a phenomenological argument without having to be an object of awareness. From the point of view of strict phenomenological description, however, Sartre would seem to be correct.

Given this non-appearance of the I in consciousness, Sartre thinks no room is left for an I in pre-reflexive consciousness:

> Now we ask, is there room for an I in such a consciousness? The reply is clear: evidently not. Indeed, such an I is not the object (since by hypothesis the I is inner); nor is it an I of consciousness, since it is something for consciousness. (41)[69]

What is for consciousness is the me. By this Sartre means that the only self which appears to consciousness is oneself as a psycho-physical whole – that person who I am. Sartre draws an interesting analogy to illustrate this point. He says that the transcendental ego bears the same relation to the psycho-physical me as a mathematical point does to three dimensions. The force of this is that mathematical points are not real in the sense that they have no real empirical or spatio-temporal reality and ascribing them such reality would interfere with geometrical models of three-dimensional objects. Similarly, ascribing reality to the transcendental ego as the irreducibly subjective ground of experience interferes with a phenomenologically correct account of consciousness. Much as a mathematical point as something extended rather than ideal would disrupt our understanding of three-dimensional solids, so a transcendental ego as a subjective item within consciousness would interrupt the understanding of consciousness as the pure awareness of its objects.

To make the subjective source of consciousness something also available to consciousness, as Husserl does by the transcendental reduction, is incoherent.

Either the transcendental ego is irreducibly subjective, and so cannot be an object for consciousness, or else the transcendental ego is an object for consciousness and so cannot be irreducibly subjective. If it does not appear to consciousness then within the phenomenological framework we are not entitled to claim that it exists. If we are to claim that it exists then this can only be because it is an item for consciousness, and it is this that Sartre claims is true. If this is right then there is little point in continuing to talk of a transcendental ego at all. Transcendental facts are facts which are necessary conditions for experience and it is indeed the role of the transcendental ego, according to Husserl, to ground consciousness transcendentally. But it can hardly be the role of the transcendental ego to ground consciousness if it is amongst the objects for consciousness. This is not only because if something is that which is conscious then to that extent it is hidden from consciousness, but also because the conditions for consciousness are not empirical. If x is a condition for consciousness then the existence of x may not depend upon the existence of consciousness epistemologically or ontologically, even if the existence of consciousness should turn out to be a condition for the individuation of a condition for consciousness *qua* condition for consciousness. So even if the existence of consciousness is necessary for a condition for consciousness being what it is under that description, the existence of that condition cannot depend upon consciousness.

Still less can a condition for consciousness be an object for consciousness because objects of consciousness depend upon consciousness for their existence *qua* objects of consciousness. In general there is no logical obstacle to its being the case that if A is a condition for B then B is a condition for A, so in that case a certain condition for consciousness would itself be possible only if consciousness exists. The dependence would be, so to speak, reciprocal.

But this cannot possibly be the case with the Husserlian transcendental ego. In the strongly Kantian tradition within which Husserl writes, transcendental conditions are, *qua* transcendental, not empirical, and it is anyway independently the case that for Husserl the transcendental ego is the ground or condition for everything and nothing grounds it even if it only exists when its intentional acts exist.

I adduce these points in substantiation of Sartre's claim that Husserl is wrong to suppose a transcendental ego could be a part of consciousness.

Sartre has another argument against Husserl which goes like this. Consciousness according to Sartre is a 'spontaneity' (41). Again, the word is Kant's and is intended to draw attention to the agency of consciousness.[70] Within the Kantian tradition the activity or spontaneity of the understanding is contrasted with the passivity or receptivity of the senses. Sartre accepts at least half of this picture because it is his view that the individual consciousness is inherently free. But consciousness could not be free if there existed a Husserlian transcendental ego. Consciousness is free, therefore there exists no Husserlian transcendental ego.

However, the relation between freedom and Kant's doctrine of spontaneity is more complex than this. There is a distinction between 'absolute' and 'relative' spontaneity. If a subject's thoughts and experiences are regarded as relatively spontaneous, they would require some external causal input to set them going. But, once started, they would be irreducible to a purely causal story about the sensory reception of material and its series-processing as information. If the subject's thinking were absolutely spontaneous, it would ultimately have been instantiated outside the causal order. It would seem open to the Husserlian to reply to Sartre that absolute spontaneity is a property of the transcendental ego itself: it freely produces its thoughts and experiences and is not caused to do so.

There is also a distinction between freedom as it pertains to the necessary conditions for experience (implying independence from causality) and freedom as it pertains to the necessary conditions for agency (implying autonomy in its practically relevant sense). The one need not be regarded as either necessary or sufficient for the other. Sartre overlooks this distinction, but again, it would seem open to the Husserlian to ground both experience and agency in the freedom of the transcendental ego and not in consciousness itself.

If we accept that in at least some sense consciousness is free, we still need grounds for accepting Sartre's second premise. Why would a transcendental ego preclude the freedom of consciousness?

Sartre's comment on this is *prima facie* not terribly revealing:

> Consciousness is then no longer a spontaneity; it bears within itself the germ of opaqueness. (41–2)[71]

To use Sartre's metaphors, if consciousness were, *per impossibile*, an opaqueness, then consciousness would no longer be consciousness because consciousness is essentially transparent. Phenomenologically, it is possible to make sense of this.

Consciousness is pure awareness; awareness of the objects of consciousness. It would be an obstacle to this purity of consciousness for a transcendental ego to be present within it as one of its structures. But Sartre needs more than this. He needs to show that the existence of the transcendental ego is incompatible with the freedom of consciousness.

On at least one view of the transcendental ego its existence would not be incompatible with the freedom of consciousness, although I suspect Sartre would not share this view. I mean that there is a subjective source of consciousness, or something that is conscious, does not entail that consciousness is not free. We would have to say that the consciousness of the transcendental ego is free because the transcendental ego is free, as we might say the movements of someone's arm are free because that person is free.

But Sartre wants consciousness itself to be free, not that which is conscious (in this subjective sense) to be free. Now, it might well be that consciousness in that sense cannot be free if there is a transcendental ego because the operations of consciousness issue from a source which is free. They are, so to speak, dictated, constrained or determined by that source, much as someone's arm is not free if the movements issue from the whole person who nonetheless might be free.

If consciousness itself is free then it cannot be operated by anything else. It has to be a kind of pure agency and I think this is what Sartre tries to capture using 'spontaneity' (41). If we accept this interpretation as plausible and meaningful then we should accept Sartre's thesis that the Husserlian transcendental ego is incompatible with the freedom of consciousness.

There is perhaps another reason which could be brought in support of Sartre against Husserl here. If consciousness is a pure spontaneity then the transcendental ego as an 'inhabitant' or structure of consciousness would inhibit or intrude into this freedom. Consciousness itself would have a self-constraining structure. Its putative transcendental ground would appear within itself and subject and object would in a sense collapse into one. This is incompatible with Sartre's view of the 'play' of consciousness in *Being and Nothingness* – its being just or only the free awareness of its objects.[72]

To pursue my analogy, suppose the brain moves the arm. As things are, this presupposes that the brain is not part of my arm and no part of my brain is part of my arm. In general, if A acts on B then A is not B, and no part of A is a part of B. For this not to be the case would inhibit agency.

Sartre rejects the idea that consciousness is a substance, so his philosophy of mind is incompatible with traditional idealism and dualism. If consciousness is not a substance then *a fortiori* it is not a mental substance. If Husserl's transcendental ego existed then consciousness would be a substance, but consciousness is not a substance, so Husserl's transcendental ego does not exist. As Sartre puts it:

> We would be forced to abandon that original and profound view which makes of consciousness a non-substantial absolute. (42)[73]

Sartre does not say why the adoption of the transcendental ego would have this effect but an argument for that conclusion may be adduced. The transcendental ego, whatever it is, if it exists is something rather than nothing. However, consciousness is a 'nothingness', a pure awareness of objects. If it became something, some-thing, it would cease to be that pure awareness.[74] It would have in its structure a substance in the quasi-Aristotelian sense of an entity which has properties – the operations of consciousness – but does not itself stand in need of anything else in order to exist, and which is not itself a property. The presence of such a being in the midst of consciousness is incompatible with Sartre's phenomenology of consciousness, his description of how consciousness appears, in that consciousness itself would become a substance; the transcendental ego would be its essential structure.

If we accept that consciousness is not a substance, but Husserl's transcendental ego is, then I think Sartre is entitled to his conclusion.

There are in fact good grounds for saying that Husserl's transcendental ego is a substance, Husserl's disclaimers notwithstanding. The transcendental ego for Husserl is the ground of the world but is not grounded by anything else. This logically entails the Aristotelian view of a substance as that which makes properties possible but exists independently of other things. Clearly, if Husserl's transcendental ego is not grounded by anything else it does not depend upon anything for its existence and in that sense it is a substance. For this reason I think Sartre is correct to say that the transcendental ego is incompatible with the non-substantial view of consciousness.

Husserl has in fact missed an opportunity, the opportunity to describe consciousness as a pure phenomenon:

> A pure consciousness is an absolute quite simply because it is consciousness of itself. It remains therefore a 'phenomenon' in the very special sense in which 'to be' and 'to appear' are one. It is all lightness, all translucence. This it is which differentiates the *cogito* of Husserl from the Cartesian *cogito*. (42)[75]

There is much insight in this passage. The claim that to be and to appear are one may be taken in two ways, one Hegelian and one Berkleyan.

On the Berkleyan reading, to be and to appear are one and the same because *esse est percipi* (in the case of physical objects).[76] There is no difference between an appearance's appearing and it being perceived. Clearly, if something is an appearance then it is perceived, because all appearing is appearing to.

We can push this reading still further. Not only is Berkeleyan idealism thinkable but solipsism is thinkable.

On one sort of solipsism there is no difference, or at least no phenomenological difference, between what is, and what appears (to or within my consciousness). Whatever the philosophical merits or demerits of solipsism, this variety is thinkable because of certain phenomenological facts, viz. that it can seem as though my experience ('now') is all there is.

On the Hegelian reading a certain insight about consciousness is being expressed. This is: there is no difference between consciousness being what it is and consciousness knowing what it is. This is constitutive of Hegel's Absolute Knowing.[77] The Hegelian reading of Sartre is given some plausibility by the fact that Sartre uses the Hegelian term 'absolute' to describe consciousness in so far as consciousness is consciousness of itself.

Husserl's mistake is to fail to realise that implicit in his phenomenology is a quasi-Hegelian view of consciousness free from a particular Cartesian tenet, the tenet that consciousness is a substance. If the transcendental ego is subtracted from Husserl's phenomenology then the residue approximates more closely to this Hegelian picture.

Hegel's phenomenology of consciousness is more complex, sophisticated and subtle than that of either Husserl or Sartre but the Sartrean point is nevertheless a valuable one. If the transcendental ego is something rather than nothing and if it appears within consciousness, then at least one element of consciousness is reified into something over and above a pure awareness.[78]

This idea of consciousness is in one sense accurately described as 'Cartesian' because Descartes thought a mind is not exhausted by its acts of awareness. For Descartes, there not only exist the various thoughts of a mind but there exists that mind itself; that which has them. That much would seem to be common between Husserl and Descartes on consciousness, and so to that extent Husserl and Descartes are a common target for Sartre.[79]

Where there is a clear dissimilarity between Descartes and Husserl is that for Husserl the transcendental ego is available to consciousness through the transcendental reduction. For Descartes, a mind is not directly aware of itself – I mean aware of itself *qua* mind or soul. A mind is only directly aware of its own operations. In that sense the Cartesian view of the mind is much nearer to Sartre's than to Husserl's.

Whatever the philosophical merits and demerits of Sartre's critique of Husserl here, I think there is much intuitive plausibility in the idea that there is a kind of consciousness without an 'I'. Much of the time, in our daily preoccupations, our attention is absorbed (as the metaphor has it) with what we are preoccupied with, and not with ourselves as that which is preoccupied. Indeed, it could be plausibly maintained that to the extent that a sort of consciousness is a reflection on the self or itself it cannot be a consciousness of the objects of day-to-day awareness. On this view we are only intermittently conscious of ourselves. Most of the time we are unreflectively aware of the objects and people around us.

12 Consciousness with the I

Phenomenology is the description of what appears to consciousness just as it appears, without any assumption about the objective reality or causal properties of what does so appear. A phenomenology of consciousness is a description of how consciousness appears to consciousness. A clear and adequate phenomenology requires a correct account of the nature of consciousness. Sartre sees the Husserlian transcendental ego as precisely a threat to such an account, and so as an obstacle to a proper phenomenology. Phenomenology requires that the I not be an irreducibly subjective source of consciousness. Nor can it be something which appears within or to consciousness as part of its structure. The I must be an object for consciousness: something that consciousness is a consciousness of, or one of the intentional objects towards which consciousness is directed. So Sartre writes:

> All the results of phenomenology begin to crumble if the I is not, by the same title as the world, a relative existent: that is to say, an object for consciousness. (42)[80]

By a relative existent Sartre means something which depends upon the existence of something else for its existence. In his view, the I depends upon the existence of consciousness. Unless the I were amongst the intentional objects of consciousness the I would not exist, or what amounts to the same thing, the I *per impossibile* would not be the I.

This idea of the I as a relative existent is fully consistent with Sartre's earlier claim that the I is not a substance. If *x* is a substance then there is nothing else that needs to exist in order for *x* to exist, but if *x* is a relative existent then if *x* exists then there also exists at least one item numerically distinct from x upon which the existence of x depends. So, if x is a substance then x is not a relative existent, and if x is a relative existent then x is not a substance. It follows that if Sartre can show that the I depends upon consciousness for its existence then he will thereby have shown that consciousness is a relative existent. It will further follow that Sartre has brought another argument against the thesis that the I is a substance or that consciousness, because it includes the I as one of its structures, is substantial. If it is true that Husserl's phenomenology of consciousness implies that the I is a substance, and if Sartre's argument is sound, then Sartre will have refuted that implication of Husserl's phenomenology.

The question we need to address is whether the I depends upon consciousness for its existence. Sartre has already argued that there is a kind of consciousness without the I: pre-reflexive consciousness. He now distinguishes this from reflexive consciousness, a kind of consciousness to which the I does appear. He develops the idea of reflective consciousness in the context of some remarks about Descartes, Kant and Husserl.

Sartre draws a distinction between Kant's view of the self and those of Husserl and Descartes as follows:

> The Kantian I think is a condition of possibility. The *cogito* of Descartes and Husserl is an apprehension of fact. $(43)^{81}$

The distinction between these three theorists is not as clear as Sartre would have us believe. It is true that Kant's 'I think' (*Ich denke*) is a condition for the possibility of experience. Unless any of the experiences which take place in a self-same mind called 'mine' could in principle be prefaced by the thought 'I think ... ' then it would not make sense to say that they belong to a unified consciousness at all. It is the possibility of the 'I think' accompanying any of my experiences which makes them mine. A putative experience only counts as such if it is an episode in a mind, so in that sense it cannot be that there are experiences without a subject or experiencer. It is just that point that is accepted by Descartes and Husserl, however. The self which they each postulate is a condition for possibility, because for Descartes it is true that there are no thoughts without a thinker – no thinking without a thing that thinks – and for Husserl the transcendental ego is the transcendental ground of consciousness. For these reasons, saying that the Kantian 'I think' is a condition for possibility fails to draw any contrast between Kant on the one hand and Descartes and Husserl on the other.

Despite this, Sartre is correct to maintain that the *cogito* of Descartes and Husserl is apprehended as a fact, and that of Kant is not. The fact that I think is introspectively available to Descartes, and for Husserl it is disclosed by the phenomenological reduction. In contrast to this, although one's empirical thinking is available through the exercise of inner sense according to Kant, the transcendental unity of apperception – which is the unity of consciousness as constituted by the possibility of the I think accompanying any of my perceptions – is established by philosophy. Kant may well think independently of this that if

I am thinking 'I think' then I may be aware of that as a fact but that will just be another empirical fact; a fact about my occurrent psychology. No introspective scrutiny or consciousness of consciousness will reveal the 'I think' as a transcendental condition for experience because no transcendental condition is empirical. To this extent, then, Sartre does succeed in drawing a contrast between Kant on the one hand and Descartes and Husserl on the other.

Sartre's strategy in developing his own phenomenology of the self is to accept from Descartes and Husserl that the I think is given as a fact, yet repudiate the view that the I is a condition for the possibility of consciousness. On the contrary, consciousness will turn out to be the condition for the I. Sartre's agreement with Descartes that the apprehension of the I think is a fact may be seen here:

> We have heard of the 'factual necessity' of the *Cogito*, and this phrase seems to me most apt. Also, it is undeniable that the *Cogito* is personal. (43)[82]

The 'factual necessity' ('nécessité de fait') of the *cogito* is the putative necessary truth of 'I think' as thought by the thinker. Whether 'I think' could in some sense be a necessary truth, for example, as Descartes thought, when it is thought, is an unsolved philosophical problem.[83] I should say 'I think' is true just on condition it is thought, although the ontological status of the I in that case remains obscure.

Sartre is concerned only that we should accept a minimal phenomenological fact: If I think it is possible for me to be aware of that fact. Although Sartre clearly thinks 'I think' has the status of a necessary truth, he does not need that as a premise in the present argument. He wishes us to accept that there are moments of consciousness with the I, just as he earlier wished us to accept that there are moments of consciousness without the I. 'I think' does not have to have the status of a necessary truth for that conclusion to go through. The premise 'I think' is sufficient for that.

If it is true that there is a kind of consciousness with the I, it will follow that such a consciousness is personal. By 'personal' Sartre means 'someone or other's', so any consciousness that is owned by some subject of awareness, or any consciousness which includes experiences which are had or undergone by some subject will count as a personal consciousness. Clearly, then, a consciousness which involves an I in any of these senses is personal.

To this extent Sartre's phenomenology of the self is strongly Cartesian. He is not saying there is no consciousness without a subject. Clearly this is in a sense possible for Sartre. The Cartesianism is in the claim that in at least some forms of consciousness there is both an I and a consciousness and these are not the same. He is thus at variance with the tradition stemming from Hume, where the ontological status of the self is exhausted by the existence of a set of experiences. In the type of consciousness under consideration, there is not only consciousness but a subject of consciousness:

In the *I Think* there is an *I* who thinks. (43)[84]

The crucial departure from Cartesianism lies in the fact that the I denoted by the first person singular pronoun in the 'I think' is produced by conscious reflection.[85]

Sartre straightforwardly assumes that 'I' is a referring expression, even though this issue is controversial. For example, Sartre's view could not be correct if the grammatical grounds Wittgenstein adduces in *The Blue and Brown Books* for denying that 'I' is any kind of referring expression were conclusive. My view is that 'I' is a referring expression albeit of a special sort. 'I' is the nominative pronoun each person uses only to refer to himself. Although 'me' is also a pronoun that each person only uses to refer to himself, it differs from 'I' in being an accusative and dative pronoun with no grammatically well-formed nominative use. My use of 'I' differs from my use of 'Stephen Priest' because while I may use 'Stephen Priest' correctly to refer to someone other than myself, viz. someone else whose name is 'Stephen Priest', I cannot correctly use 'I' to refer to someone else. In my grammatically well formed uses of 'I' I cannot fail to refer to myself, even though I might misascribe properties to myself. Not only is 'I' a referring expression, when it is used grammatically its user always succeeds in referring.

For these reasons Sartre is right in his assumption that 'I' is a referring expression. In these passages Sartre uses 'I' to refer to the I and this appears only in certain sorts of consciousness. It is itself the product of a certain sort of consciousness: self-conscious reflection. It follows that Descartes' thinker/thought distinction can only serve as Sartre's starting point:

> The fact that can serve as a start is, then, this one: each time we apprehend our thought, whether by an immediate intuition or by an intuition based on memory, we apprehend an I. (43)[86]

Descartes does not think that the soul can directly intuit itself. Although the soul is what thinks, there is no direct introspective acquaintance with the soul. However, it is clear that Descartes thinks there is no thought without a thinker and that we are introspectively acquainted with our thoughts *qua* ours. Both Descartes and Sartre hold that we are not identical with any one of our thoughts. It is to this extent common to Descartes and Sartre that an I appears to consciousness in reflection. The difference is that Descartes assumes that there is an I whether we introspect or not (even though he accepts the logical possibility that should he cease to think he should cease to exist) while Sartre does not make the assumption that there is an I when there is no conscious reflection. He leaves open the possibility he wishes to argue is real: that the I is created by reflection.

To illustrate the kind of Cartesian starting point he is adopting Sartre provides this example:

If for example I want to remember a certain landscape perceived yesterday from the train it is possible for me to bring back the memory of that landscape as such. But I can also recollect that I was seeing that landscape. (43)[87]

Here Sartre distinguishes two kinds of remembering. It is possible to remember something or to remember oneself perceiving that thing. This seems a genuine distinction.

Suppose some person A perceives some object, x, at time t. Two possible modes of recollection of x then seem possible. Either A simply remembers x or else A both remembers x and remembers perceiving x, or even that it was he himself that perceived x.

These possibilities remain open, I think, whether or not it is the case that if A perceives x then A is conscious of perceiving x or whether if A perceives x A is not conscious of perceiving x in perceiving x. This is because if A is conscious of perceiving x in perceiving x then it is uncontroversially possible for A to both remember x and remember that they perceived x.

Even if it is the case that in perceiving x A was not conscious of perceiving x it remains logically possible that A should remember x but not thereby remember perceiving, or themselves perceiving x. I do not mean by this that they forget the perception, or that they themselves perceived, or assume that someone else perceived x, but merely that there is no contradiction in the supposition that there should be a mental act of remembering x which is not partly constituted by a recollection of perceiving, or of oneself perceiving x, even if the perception of x was a self-conscious one. Although A does not remember A perceiving x or remember the perceiving of x in recollecting x, A does not forget this either.

If, conversely, A was not conscious of perceiving x in perceiving x then it is equally open for A to remember x but not remember that it was they that perceived x, or for them to both remember x and remember that it was they who perceived x.

In the first case, if A remembers x then A remembers x *tout court*, and it is reasonably uncontroversial that a recollection of the object of an experience that was not self-conscious need not itself be self-conscious. At least, there is no logical reason why such a recollection should be partly a recollection of oneself.

Perhaps more controversially, it is possible to remember that it was in fact oneself who perceived x in one's recollection of x even if one was not self-conscious in the perception of x. This is because of the mode of presentation of x in memory. By 'mode of presentation' here I mean that the memory of x is phenomenologically similar to x as x would be presented to A were A perceiving x. Now, from the fact that the memory of x exhibits such a mode of presentation it does not logically follow that the memory that it was oneself, A, who perceived x is veridical. There is no contradiction in supposing that such a memory is non-veridical no matter what the mode of presentation of its intentional object. Or, to put it another way, nothing logically follows from the phenomenology of memories about their truth values.

However, I am only arguing that it is possible that A should remember that it was himself who perceived *x* even if they were not conscious of perceiving *x* in perceiving *x*. This possibility exists because of the peculiar mode of presentation of memories of intentional objects of experiences truly denoted by first person singular expressions. By making these distinctions I hope to have removed logical obstacles to Sartre's distinction between remembering something and remembering that it was oneself who perceived that thing.

Sartre's view that memories do not come tagged with the I is consistent with remembering a past experience without knowing who had that past experience; as long as the experience occurred, and the memory is dependent on this kind of experience in the right kind of way – and that this is correct. This makes Sartre an early exponent of 'quasi-memories'.[88] The non-tagged view faces several problems however. It appears to violate the application of the Kantian 'unity' requirement to memory: that unless one can ascribe concurrent and successive experiences to something that is, at least potentially, one and the same I, one cannot make genuine judgements or acquire knowledge of the world based on memory. (In so far as Sartre violates this Kantian view he escapes the Kantian framework in another respect.) If the non-tagged view is true, the subject could not conclude that 'I do not remember experiencing *x*' from the premise 'I never experienced *x*'; but being able to draw such conclusions and make such judgements is necessary to distinguishing between memories and false memories, illusions, fantasies, passing images, and so on. We can distinguish between them; and if a precondition for doing so is indeed that memories come tagged, then *pace* Sartre, memories do come tagged.

Further, if the non-tagged view is true, then subjects who engage in ordinary inferential reasoning using various memories are guilty of systematic enthymeme (which is most implausible); for if memories are not tagged, the subject cannot trade on any identity between the referents of the different memories; but in ordinary inferential reasoning using various memories we do trade on such identities (i.e. without ascertaining whether we are using each memory involving premise to think of ourselves in the same way). If Sartre's view of memory is wrong, then he has lost a vital premise in his argument for the conclusion that not all consciousness is accompanied by an I. Even if his non-tagged view is right, it needs to be supplemented by a plausible account of quasi-memories such as that provided by Parfit in *Reasons and Persons*.

Sartre thinks drawing the distinction between remembering something and remembering that it was oneself that percieved that thing guards us against making a mistake about the self. From the fact that we may remember ourselves experiencing, or that it was onself who perceived, we may be tempted to conclude erroneously that all consciousness is accompanied by an 'I', a Husserlian transcendental ego. This mistake may be thought of as thinking a logical inference is possible from the first of these two sentences to the that clause of the second:

1   'I can always perform any recollection whatsoever in the personal mode, and at once the I appears.' (44)

2   'Thus it seems that there is not one of my consciousnesses which I do not apprehend as provided with an I.' (44)[89]

Clearly, from that fact that it was possible for me to remember that it was I who perceived *x*, it does not logically follow that a transcendental I accompanies all my perceptions. If I veridically remember that I perceived *x*, what does logically follow is that I perceived *x*, but this does not of itself commit us to the existence of a Husserlian transcendental ego. However, if I veridically remember that I perceived *x* it does follow that there existed a quasi-Kantian but purely formal I at the time that I perceived *x*: myself whatever I am. My perceiving *x* is fully consistent with my being a Sartrean psycho-physical 'me' – a whole person. So, the inference fails even in those cases where I do in fact remember myself perceiving *x*.

The inference fails in any case because from the fact that something may be the case it does not logically follow that it is the case. The fact that I may apprehend my consciousness as accompanied by an I does not entail that I do so. From the fact that I do sometimes apprehend my consciousness as accompanied by an I, it does not logically follow that I always do so. Nor does it follow that my consciousness is always accompanied by an I.[90]

So far I have interpreted Sartre as guarding against a certain kind of philosophical mistake; postulating a metaphysical self by taking an invalid inference as valid. It is possible to read him too as providing a psychological explanation of our coming to believe in a metaphysical self, if and when we do.

It is at least sometimes the case that if I remember something I remember that it was I who perceived that thing. Then an I does appear to memory, a remembered I. This entails a tripartite structure to what is remembered: the remembered object of perception, the perception, and the I as subject of that perception. It is tempting to then conclude that, always, if there is consciousness then there is an I that is conscious in the Husserlian sense. If we ask: Why in the Husserlian sense? then I think an answer is implicit in what Sartre has argued so far.

The I as recollected is, *qua* intentional object of memory a psychological I, and not a whole person – that human being who I am. Naturally, it is possible to remember oneself as the human being who one is perceiving some object, but this need not be the case. If I remember 'that it was I' who perceived the object then this memory may be, for example, an image of that person who I am perceiving that object, but this is not necessarily the case. I may just, for example, remember the fact that it was I who remembered the object. In that case no image of the whole person need appear to consciousness, and room is left for the thought of me as the truncated object of thought to be identified with the subjective Husserlian transcendental ego. I do not know how sympathetic Sartre would have been to this account but it is at least consistent with his view of how the mistake is made.

Sartre's argument here is essentially a Kantian one. Indeed, Sartre's comment on sentence (1) above is:

Such is the guarantee of the Kantian claim concerning validity. (44)[91]

(Sartre's 'droit' is better translated as 'right' here, rather than 'validity'.) Kant's doctrine is that the 'I think' must be capable of accompanying all of my experiences as a condition of their being mine. Sartre is claiming that if I remember that I perceived some object, then that memory is in the 'personal mode' (43). There is an ambiguity here. Sartre wishes to maintain that memories in the personal mode are Kantian cases – cases of the 'I think' accompanying experiences. This claim may well be true, but it has not been established by the argument so far. We need to draw a distinction between a memory and what that memory is a memory of, and, in addition to that, between the act of remembering and the content of the memory. All that has been established so far is that if I remember myself perceiving something then an I appears to memory. We could interpret this I in two ways. We could say it is a part of the content of the memory, part perhaps of its occurrent phenomenological content, or we could say that it is oneself that is the I that is remembered. But, whichever of these we choose, it does not follow that the act of remembering is itself accompanied by an I. Clearly it is to Sartre's purpose in any case to deny that the memory is accompanied by an I in Husserl's sense. But then it cannot be the act of remembering which is in the 'personal mode' or is actually accompanied by an 'I think' in the Kantian sense.

It may be independently true that there is a distinction between self-conscious and non-self-conscious memories: I can remember and in doing so be conscious of remembering, or I can remember *tout court*. This distinction is consistent with the Kantian 'I think' doctrine, and is one Sartre would wish to maintain. However, it is not established or refuted by the appearance of an I to consciousness in memory. It is quite neutral with regard to that. I do not need to be conscious of remembering in order to remember myself perceiving, and I do not need to be conscious of myself as perceiving in order to remember myself perceiving, or remember *tout court*.

Nevertheless, Sartre's claim reconstrued as: that memory's content or object may appear in the personal mode, does substantiate the quasi-Kantian position he wishes to adopt. From the fact that such a content does include an I it logically follows that such a content may include an I because actuality implies possibility. Clearly, this is rather a revised Kantian position which does not establish that the 'I think' may (still less 'must be able to') accompany any of my mental acts, because Sartre wishes to deny that an I *qua* subject does accompany any of my mental acts in a transcendental sense.

Sartre will argue that there is a difference between conscious and self-conscious states but this distinction does not rely on the postulation of a Husserlian I.

13 Sartre's *cogito*

Sartre says that

All the writers who have described the *Cogito* have dealt with it as a reflexive operation, that is to say, as an operation of the second degree. (44)[92]

If we consider the work of Descartes, Kant and Husserl this claim seems justified. When Descartes concludes that he thinks because he doubts the *cogito* is a kind of reflection on the doubting. When Kant says the 'I think' must be capable of accompanying all my experiences the 'I think' is prefaced to the experiences as a kind of consciousness of them. When Husserl claims the discovery of the transcendental ego, as revealed by the transcendental reduction, it is as that which is the owner of the various mental acts opened up to phenomenological description. In each case, the *cogito* is a kind of reflection on, or consciousness of, consciousness. Sartre is therefore correct when he claims:

> Such a *Cogito* is performed by a consciousness directed upon consciousness, a consciousness which takes consciousness as an object. (44)[93]

The point here is not just that there has to exist a meta-consciousness which ascribes the *cogito* to consciousness, it is also that the *cogito* is assumed to itself possess the status of a meta-consciousness, or a consciousness of consciousness. Sartre wishes to break decisively with this view by claiming that the *cogito* belongs not to reflecting consciousness, the consciousness which is consciousness of consciousness, but to pre-reflective consciousness, the consciousness which is the object of reflexive consciousness, and, as such, it is falsely believed to exist as the transcendental subject of all consciousness. In fact, according to Sartre, reflexive consciousness is not characterised by the *cogito* and the *cogito* only belongs to pre-reflective consciousness in so far as it is an object of reflective consciousness. This is a central step in Sartre's argument that the I exists only as the object and not as the subject of consciousness.

Sartre makes this point explicitly when he says

> Now, my reflecting consciousness does not take itself for an object when I effect the *Cogito*. What it affirms concerns the reflected consciousness. (44)[94]

The claim that reflecting consciousness does not take itself for an object is part of Sartre's thesis that there exists consciousness without an I, and in order to be conscious I do not have to be self-conscious.

In general, consciousness of some intentional object does not presuppose consciousness of oneself as being conscious of that intentional object. Sartre introduces the special (or particular) case of reflective consciousness where the intentional object of reflective consciousness is pre-reflective consciousness. Reflexive consciousness of pre-reflexive consciousness does not presuppose consciousness of reflexive consciousness nor consciousness of being conscious in a reflexive way, nor consciousness of oneself being conscious in a reflexive way. So, although reflexive consciousness is a consciousness of consciousness, it is not a consciousness of itself in so far as it does not take itself as its own intentional object.

This leaves conceptual room for Sartre to deny that the *cogito* is a structure of reflective consciousness, but assert that the *cogito* is produced by reflective consciousness as a structure of pre-reflective consciousness – as a structure of the object of reflective consciousness. The *cogito* is ascribed to the pre-reflective consciousness by the reflexive consciousness, and its existence consists in its being so ascribed.

This in turn allows Sartre to maintain that pre-reflexive consciousness is only accompanied by the I *qua* object of reflective consciousness. Without reflection there is no I.

If these arguments are sound then Sartre has shown that it is at least true that pre-reflexive consciousness, *qua* intentional object of reflexive consciousness, is accompanied by an I. What he has not yet shown is that this is at most what is true of a personal consciousness. Before deciding whether Sartre succeeds in this we should briefly consider certain tenets of the Cartesian–Husserlian philosophy he wishes to retain.

Sartre's retentions

Sartre wishes to retain the incorrigibility of the *cogito*:

> Let us agree: the certitude of the *Cogito* is absolute. (44)[95]

That 'I think' is true if and only if it is thought is not entailed by Sartre's doctrine of the translucence of consciousness, because even if consciousness is a consciousness of itself it is not necessarily a consciousness of the subject of consciousness, and Sartre wishes in any case to deny that in the case of pre-reflective consciousness in so far as it is not an object of reflexive consciousness. Nor, indeed, does the reverse entailment hold. If it follows from the fact that 'I think' is thought that 'I think' is true – because if a thought is thought then it is thought by some subject – that does not imply that all consciousness is consciousness of consciousness. It does follow that 'I think' is a self-conscious thought, because of the indexicality of the first person singular pronoun, but from the fact that that thought is a self-conscious one it does not follow that all thinking is self-conscious. This is because indexicality cannot be bestowed on any non-indexical thought by what follows from the indexicality of any indexical thought.

Nevertheless, the certainty of the *cogito* is fully consistent with the translucency of consciousness, as is Descartes' incorrigibility thesis about the mental. Descartes thinks that all first person singular psychological ascriptions are incorrigible. This means that if I believe I am in a mental state then that belief is true, and if I believe I am in a mental state of a particular kind then that belief is true, and, it is not possible for me to be in a mental state without my knowing that I am in that mental state. (It is not clear that the historical Descartes did subscribe to the theses of the incorrigibility and translucency of the mental in the stark way that I have just described. John Cottingham argues in his *Descartes* that Descartes at least did not argue for these views. I therefore use 'Descartes' ahistorically as a label for a cluster of views.)

There is a sense in which, despite the incorrigibility thesis, even for Descartes there is consciousness without the I. Descartes thinks that the soul is never directly acquainted with itself, only with its own operations. From a phenomenological point of view then, Descartes' idea of thinking and Sartre's idea of pre-reflective consciousness are similar, indeed, logically equivalent: Consciousness's contents appear to consciousness but the subject *qua* subject does not appear. This is what Sartre retains from the Cartesian picture.

Descartes assumes that the soul as subject continues to exist throughout the operations of thinking, but Sartre wishes to maintain that there is only a subject *qua* object of reflexive consciousness. This allows Sartre to accept both the certainty of the *cogito* (it is certain when and only when thought) and the incorrigibility thesis (if I am in a mental state then I know that) without subscribing to the idea of the perennial subject. Descartes, Husserl, and in a complex sense Kant think there is no consciousness without a subject. Sartre thinks there is.

Clearly, there is no contradiction in the supposition that it is both true that if 'I think' is thought then it is true, and consciousness is consciousness of itself. Equally, there is no incoherence in holding that if I am in a mental state then I know that, and consciousness is an awareness of its own contents.

If it is objected to this that Descartes' postulation of the I and Sartre's unwillingness to postulate an I are mutually inconsistent then it should be remembered that for both Descartes and Sartre (for Descartes always, for Sartre sometimes) no I appears to consciousness. Also, for each of Descartes and Sartre there is another sense in which the subject does exist. For Descartes the soul exists (during the time between God's creation of it and God's possible annihilation of it) and, for Sartre, that psycho-physical whole person who I am exists (between the time of my birth and the time of my death). But equally clearly, for Descartes the soul never appears to consciousness and, for Sartre, I frequently do not appear to my consciousness either.

Sartre wishes to retain the certainty of the *cogito* for a special reason. This is what he calls the 'unity' of reflecting and reflected consciousness:

> As Husserl said, there is an indissoluble unity of the reflecting consciousness and the reflected consciousness (to the point that the reflecting consciousness could not exist without the reflected consciousness). (44)[96]

There are at least two complementary ways of understanding what Sartre wishes to retain from Husserl here. Reflecting and reflected consciousness are mutually dependent in the sense that *qua* reflecting consciousness reflecting consciousness is necessarily a reflecting on reflected consciousness, and *qua* reflected consciousness reflected consciousness is necessarily reflected on by reflecting consciousness. We could say this is a conceptual truth, depending on the semantics of 'reflecting' and 'reflected' and 'consciousness', or, we could say reflecting and reflected consciousness are dialectically antithetical (and so mutually dependent) in the

Hegelian sense.[97] It does not seem to me to matter much which of these two ways we choose in reading Sartre here. In either case it comes out in a strong sense as impossible that there should exist either a reflecting or a reflected consciousness in abstraction from one another.

It is important to note, however, that Sartre privileges the conceptual or dialectical dependence in one direction. He says reflecting consciousness could not exist without reflected consciousness. This asymmetry is maintained on phenomenological grounds. Although pre-reflexive consciousness does not exist *qua* reflected consciousness without reflecting consciousness, clearly pre-reflexive consciousness may and does exist without being reflected upon by reflecting consciousness. (Think of ordinary cases where one is aware but not directly aware of oneself: taking a shot in billiards, repairing a tyre, typing on a word processor.) There is no equivalent of unreflected pre-reflexive consciousness in the case of reflecting consciousness – reflecting consciousness only exists as reflecting consciousness, but reflected consciousness exists as pre-reflexive consciousness when not reflected upon.

That much is conceded by Sartre to Husserl. The question now is how the certainty of the *cogito* is derived from the unity of reflecting and reflected consciousness. Sartre uses the Hegelian term 'synthesis' to describe this unity:

> The fact remains that we are in the presence of a synthesis of two consciousnesses, one of which is consciousness of the other. (44)[98]

It seems to me the derivation cannot be a deductive one. From the fact that one consciousness is consciousness of another it does not deductively follow that it is also or thereby a consciousness of the subject of that consciousness. So, the problem is why the reflected consciousness is accompanied by an I. I do not see any argument forthcoming from Sartre here and I take it that Sartre's view is that the I of reflected consciousness is simply phenomenologically given to reflecting consciousness. In a sense this is still unsatisfactory because it is not an explanation of the appearance of the I, but we should remember that phenomenology does not deal in explanations, only descriptions, so if Sartre is writing a phenomenology book there is no onus on him to provide such an explanation.[99]

I think a quasi-Hegelian answer could be constructed (to which Sartre might be sympathetic). This would make the I of reflected consciousness into a social construct. Hegel thinks it is a necessary condition for any conscious being becoming self-conscious that they encounter another conscious being. In a complex struggle for mutual recognition, each takes the other as a model for the object of his self-awareness.[100] Although this Hegelian theme is apparent in Part Three of *Being and Nothingness*, where Sartre deals with the existence of others, the body, and concrete relations with others, the most Sartre offers us in *The Transcendence of the Ego* is a way in which the certainty of the *cogito* is made possible.

If an I appears to reflecting consciousness as a structure of reflected consciousness then reflecting consciousness is consciousness of such an I. To that extent it is not possible for reflecting consciousness to exist without being a consciousness of the I and the reflected consciousness and, in an obvious sense, this is a consciousness of the *cogito*. This amounts to the fact that 'I think' is true at least so long as it is reflected upon. It is just that that Sartre wishes to retain of the Cartesian *cogito*.

Sartre's final retention is the intentionality of consciousness;[101] the important tenet of phenomenology, from Brentano, through Husserl, to Sartre that consciousness is consciousness 'of' some object:

> The essential principle of phenomenology 'all consciousness is consciousness of something' is preserved. (44)[102]

Why is Sartre entitled to this? He has already argued that pre-reflective consciousness exhibits intentionality. This is a condition of its being what it is. Now, it is necessarily true that reflecting consciousness too exhibits intentionality because it is a consciousness of consciousness. Reflecting consciousness is a consciousness of reflected consciousness so reflecting consciousness always takes reflected consciousness as its intentional object. So it is logically impossible that reflecting consciousness should not be intentional. That is a condition of its being what it is. In this way, the intentionality of consciousness is retained in the synthesis of reflecting and reflected consciousness.

15 Positional consciousness

Pre-reflexive consciousness is non-positional because it has no I as subject. To the extent that a consciousness takes an I as intentional object, and to the extent that consciousness has an I as subject, the consciousness counts as positional.

Saying what a positional consciousness is is partly done by mentioning an I. It has a source, or somewhere from which it seems to emanate in the Husserlian sense.[103]

'Positional' contains the term 'posit'. The crucial difference between Husserl and Sartre on the self is that for Sartre but not for Husserl consciousness posits the I. Nevertheless, phenomenological appearances are retained by its seeming as though the I posits consciousness. Indeed, this is how Husserl's mistake of postulating the I as perennial subject of consciousness is possible: because it appears as though the I posits consciousness.

Sartre says:

> In so far as my reflecting consciousness is consciousness of itself, it is non-positional consciousness. It becomes positional only by directing itself upon the reflected consciousness which itself was not a positional consciousness of itself before being reflected. (44–5)[104]

This passage taken in isolation is inconsistent with the following view of positional consciousness. A consciousness is 'positional' if and only if it either is a reflecting consciousness or is a reflected consciousness. This, however, omits mention of the I in constituting a consciousness as positional, so I prefer: a consciousness is positional if and only if it takes an I either as subject or as object. If we do not adopt that interpretation then the scope of 'positional' is too wide.

Clearly, the intentionality of consciousness is not of itself sufficient for the positional nature of consciousness, or else all consciousness would be positional and that is something Sartre explicitly denies, and there seems no good reason to say that a consciousness counts as 'positional' if its intentional object happens to be consciousness. It is the appearance of the I which makes both reflecting and reflected consciousness positional.

We cannot correctly say against this that it is consciousness's consciousness of itself which makes consciousness positional. For Sartre all consciousness is consciousness of itself but only some consciousness is positional. Being conscious of itself and being positional cannot be the same property of consciousness, nor can any putative dependence be always and everywhere reciprocal.[105]

Positional consciousness depends upon consciousness being a consciousness of itself, because that is part of the essence of consciousness. Consciousness could not exist unless it were consciousness of itself. Positional consciousness is a kind of consciousness, so clearly, positional consciousness depends upon consciousness being a consciousness of itself.

The reverse does not obtain, however, because consciousness may be a consciousness of itself without being a positional consciousness. For Sartre, this is the case for example with unreflected consciousness. Indeed, Sartre explicitly says that reflecting consciousness, although it is positional *qua* a consciousness directed towards reflected consciousness, it is non-positional *qua* consciousness of itself.

For these reasons it is not a viable interpretation of 'positional consciousness' that it denotes what consciousness's consciousness of consciousness consists in.

Sartre draws an important conclusion from the distinction between reflecting and reflected consciousness. The *cogito* belongs to the reflected consciousness, not to the reflecting consciousness:

> Thus the consciousness that says 'I think' is precisely not the consciousness which thinks. Or, rather, it is not its own thought which it posits by this thetic act. (45)[106]

So when within the Cartesian framework I think 'I think' I make a judgement about my occurrent thought. But this judgement is not a thought about itself. It is about a thought of mine other than that judgement itself. To put it in Sartre's terms, the reflecting consciousness's thinking of 'I think' is a thought about the thinking of the reflected consciousness, not a thought about itself.

Sartre's hesitation or revision introduced by 'or rather' in the passage above is to be explained as follows. Of course the reflecting consciousness thinks – it at least thinks 'I think' for example – so it is not true that the reflecting consciousness is not the consciousness that thinks. But it is true that the reflecting consciousness is not the consciousness that the 'I think' is thought about or refers to. Although reflecting consciousness thinks the 'I think' this thought is about the thinking reflected consciousness which has an I as part of its structure.

If we make a distinction between a thought and its truth conditions then we may say that the thought 'I think' belongs to reflecting consciousness – it does think that thought – but the truth conditions of 'I think' belong to reflected consciousness.

Sartre now addresses a question which may be raised about his account. How do we know whether the reflecting consciousness has an I as structure? Might it not even be the case that the I of reflected consciousness exists also as the I of reflecting consciousness? If, after all, we are in the last resort talking about two structures of one and the same consciousness, what is to prevent our maintaining that one and the same I exists as subject of both structures?

> We are then justified in asking ourselves if the I which thinks is common to the two superimposed consciousnesses, or if it is not rather the I of the reflected consciousness. (45)[107]

Sartre's answer is that the I belongs only to the reflected consciousness and not also to the reflecting consciousness. There are two grounds for this reply.

First, from the fact that reflected consciousness has an I as part of its structure it does not follow that the consciousness which reflects upon this consciousness also has that (or any) I as part of its structure. Sartre is correct in thinking that no such inference obtains. The onus would be on the person who thinks that there is no impersonal consciousness to show that reflecting consciousness is personal.

Second, it is a part of Sartre's phenomenology of consciousness that there are moments of consciousness without the I. From a phenomenological point of view it is extravagant to postulate an I where none appears to consciousness. Indeed, this is phenomenologically illegitimate. Arguably, if an I appeared to consciousness as part of its own structure then all the objections about consciousness dividing and destroying itself would apply in the case of reflecting consciousness. It is a condition of reflecting consciousness existing as reflecting and not reflected consciousness that it have no I as any part of its structure. So, again, the onus is on Sartre's opponent to show that reflecting consciousness has an I as its subjective source.

It would be question-begging to bring against Sartre the objection that an I must exist as subject or condition for reflecting consciousness, even if it is true that reflecting and reflected consciousness are parts of one and the same consciousness. Sartre wishes to maintain that the I is a posit of consciousness and not the reverse. Sartre has not proved this but the contrary, Husserlian, position has not been proved either. The question is open.

Within the Sartrean framework so far established it is legitimate to suppose that reflecting consciousness is a consciousness without an I as subject, and that reflecting consciousness is not itself the object of its own reflection:

> All reflecting consciousness is, indeed, in itself unreflected, and a new act of the third degree is necessary in order to posit it. (45)[108]

From the fact that reflecting consciousness is a reflecting on consciousness it does not follow that it is a reflecting on itself. *Qua* reflecting consciousness it is not that, but a reflecting on reflected consciousness.

There seems no logical objection to some reflecting consciousness being a reflecting on itself, but Sartre wishes to describe the reflecting on reflected consciousness in a different way. If there is a consciousness of reflecting consciousness then this is a new sort of consciousness; a meta-meta-consciousness. It is perhaps the kind of consciousness necessary to write or understand *The Transcendence of the Ego*, in general, to be aware of the fact that one is self-conscious.

Sartre now adds a third kind of consciousness to the two he has already distinguished:

1   Pre-reflexive consciousness
2   Reflexive consciousness
3   Consciousness 'of the third degree'

Consciousness of the third degree is reflection on reflective consciousness. Reflexive consciousness is consciousness of pre-reflexive consciousness, which thereby counts as reflected consciousness, and pre-reflexive consciousness is our ordinary, non-self-conscious awareness of objects and persons.

Sartre is concerned to dispel the danger of an infinite regress of postulated consciousnesses here. The regress threatens and at two levels, one epistemological and the other ontological, but Sartre really only deals with the second of these:

> Moreover, there is no infinite regress here, since a consciousness has no need at all of a reflecting consciousness in order to be conscious of itself. It simply does not posit itself as an object. (45)[109]

It is true that consciousness does not presuppose self-consciousness, despite Lockean and Kantian arguments to the contrary. But Sartre, *prima facie*, faces a special difficulty. For him consciousness is consciousness of itself, so consciousness being a consciousness of consciousness is not simply a presupposition of consciousness, it is constitutive of consciousness.

The objection that Sartre wishes to guard against is that this picture of consciousness makes all consciousness depend upon reflecting consciousness. This clearly would generate an infinite regress because reflecting consciousness is a kind of consciousness and if all consciousness presupposes a reflecting consciousness then reflecting consciousness presupposes a reflecting consciousness (other than itself).

Sartre deals with this threat of an ontological regress by saying that there is a distinction between consciousness being consciousness of itself and consciousness being an object for a reflecting consciousness. Putatively, all consciousness is a consciousness of itself (including reflecting consciousness) but consciousness is only sometimes an object for reflecting consciousness (when it is reflected consciousness).

I take it the distinction is as follows. If consciousness is always and everywhere a consciousness of itself only one, or one kind, of consciousness is involved, but in the case of reflecting consciousness two, or two kinds, of consciousness are involved: the consciousness which reflects and the consciousness which is reflected on.

If this is right then consciousness being a consciousness of itself cannot possibly be identical with reflecting consciousness being a consciousness of reflected consciousness. If there is a problem here it is guaranteeing that if consciousness is a consciousness of itself it is thereby only one kind of consciousness and not two. What Sartre has to deny is that consciousness's being conscious of itself consists in consciousness directing some reflexive or meta-conscious act of consciousness towards itself. Sartre does deny this, or at least does not assert it, but, as we have seen (p. 50 above) his positive characterisation of consciousness being a consciousness of itself is largely in metaphorical terms. If we try to unpack these, then I think something close to the Cartesian incorrigibility thesis emerges: If I am in a mental state then I know I am in that mental state, and if I believe I am in a mental state then that belief is true, and if I believe I am in a mental state of a particular kind then that belief is true. 'I know I am in a mental state' between knowing the intentional modality of a mental state (whether it is desire, belief, intention, etc.) and knowing its content (that p, that q, that r, etc.). Sartre has a grasp of the distinction between a psychic act and its content because he is familiar with Husserl's *noesis/noema* distinction. The fact that he deploys no such distinction here suggests that he does not think it important to make it. If that is the case, then we may suppose that if Sartre holds that I know I am in a mental state then I know both the state's intentional modality and what its content is.

Nevertheless, two reservations need to be made about talking about Sartre's incorrigibility thesis in this way. First, to say that I believe such and such must not be taken to imply the postulation of a meta-act of consciousness directed towards consciousness. Some other account of what believing is needs to be given.[110]

Second, this characterisation does not capture the particular phenomenology of consciousness Sartre intends us to adopt. To put it rather paradoxically, it is as though consciousness counts as consciousness of itself just in virtue of being consciousness; as though being conscious were sufficient for the knowledge of the contents of one's own consciousness in the sense of logically sufficient. To put it another way, consciousness having a certain content implies consciousness of that content.

If we allow that Sartre has arrested the threatened ontological regress by denying that reflexive consciousness is necessary for consciousness of consciousness, the possibility of an epistemological regress still remains.

The problem is how we may know that pre-reflexive consciousness exists without an act of reflective consciousness, how we may know that reflexive consciousness exists without a meta-reflexive act of consciousness which takes reflexive consciousness as its object and so on *ad infinitum*.

The solution, I think, is to concede that reflective consciousness must indeed be the object for some kind of meta-reflexive act of consciousness, but deny that the existence of such a meta-reflexive consciousness may only be known by some act of meta-meta-reflective consciousness. A plausible alternative is simply to postulate the existence of such a meta-meta-reflexive consciousness to account for our knowledge of the existence of reflexive consciousness. This of course cannot be a phenomenological solution to the problem because something non-phenomenological will be necessary for, but always escape, phenomenological characterisation.

In any case, from a phenomenological point of view it is extremely unlikely that such a meta-meta-act of consciousness is available to consciousness.[111]

I take it that if Sartre's account of consciousness's being a consciousness of consciousness is both coherent and true, then he has brought a convincing objection to the epistemological regress (at least implicitly) by denying that reflexive consciousness is needed for the Cartesian incorrigibility thesis to be maintained. To allow this we need to allow that I can know that I am in a mental state without consciously reflecting on that state. I must be able to know that I am in it just in virtue of being in it. This would seem a logical possibility only relative to certain accounts of what 'knowing' means – ones that exclude the plausible notion that I cannot know that *p* without, at least, being consciously aware of *p*. If this requirement on knowing is dropped then it is not incoherent to maintain that someone knows they are in a mental state yet is not directly acquainted with that state even though they are in it. It clearly would be incoherent to maintain that they had this knowledge but were not in that state. Although it is uncontroversial that being in a state is a necessary condition for knowing one is in that state, it requires argument to establish that being in a state is sufficient for knowing one is in that state. Sartre provides no such argument. We have to assume that one comes by the knowledge by some other route than being directly acquainted with the state. For example, my knowledge that I am in a mental state might eventually be found to have neurologically sufficient conditions. (Though this is not to say that neurological evidence is likely to persuade someone that they have knowledge of one of their own mental states when they do not think they do.) This possibility supplements Sartre's phenomenology but could not be endorsed from within it.

Sartre does not say exactly what the relationship is between me and my mental state if I know I am in it but am not directly conscious of it. I have used the locutions 'just in virtue of being in it', 'without consciously reflecting on that state' and 'without being directly acquainted with that state' to try to capture his meaning but these are not synonymous. In particular, I may consciously reflect on a state of my mind without having been immediately presented with it (the exact intentional modality, say, has been brought to my attention by someone else).

16 The me

Sartre has so far argued that it is at least true that reflected consciousness is a personal consciousness – consciousness with an I. He now wishes to substantiate two of his earlier claims: that unreflected pre-reflexive consciousness is consciousness without an I, and that the I of reflected consciousness is produced by reflecting consciousness.

That the I is a product of reflection would solve two philosophical problems, and for Sartre, that is the reason for believing it is such a product. It would account for the fact that when I think about my thoughts I think of them as mine, and yet it avoids the incoherence that Sartre thinks is caused by the postulation of the transcendental ego:

> But is it not precisely the reflective act which gives birth to the me in reflected consciousness? Thus would be explained how every thought apprehended by intuition possesses an I without falling into the difficulties noted in the preceding section. (45)[112]

It is clear that one possible explanation of why an I appears to reflecting consciousness is that that I is produced by reflecting consciousness. But from the fact that such an explanation is internally consistent it does not follow that it is true, so Sartre needs to provide further argument to demonstrate this. Also, from the fact that some putative solution to a philosophical problem fails to generate further philosophical problems to which other putative solutions are prone it does not logically follow that that solution is the correct one.

For these reasons we need to examine Sartre's grounds for holding that pre-reflexive consciousness is impersonal, and personal consciousness depends upon an act of reflection. It is, after all, consistent with the phenomenology so far described that pre-reflexive consciousness is perennially characterised by an I and that this I is discovered by reflecting consciousness. How can Sartre rule this out?

His tactic is to outline a phenomenology of pre-reflexive consciousness. Now, there might seem to be something paradoxical or inherently self-defeating about such a project. After all, pre-reflexive consciousness is by definition a kind of consciousness not open to conscious reflection and so *a fortiori* not open to conscious phenomenological reflection. The project is made doubly difficult if *qua* reflected consciousness pre-reflexive consciousness automatically appears with an I as subject. It would then be impossible to be conscious of consciousness without either supplying consciousness with an I or discovering an I in consciousness. Sartre needs a mode of access to pre-reflexive consciousness which will reveal whether it has an I as subject or not, and this in complete abstraction from the deliverances of reflecting consciousness. The project is made even more intractable because Sartre accepts from Husserl what might be true: that the act of reflection transforms consciousness as the object of reflection.

Sartre's solution is to try to remember pre-reflexive consciousness. It is precisely because consciousness is a consciousness of itself in which it does not present itself to itself as an object that a memory of that consciousness is possible which in turn does not present that consciousness as an object.

What Sartre tries to do is to reconstruct in his present consciousness as accurately as he can what it was like to be in a non-reflexive state of consciousness a few moments earlier. To do this he tries to suspend, so far as he can, philosophical and phenomenological preconceptions about the structure and content of the earlier consciousness.

The example Sartre chooses is that of reading. He has just been reading, and he now tries to imaginatively reconstruct the lines he has been reading and the pre-reflexive consciousness of those lines. It is as though Sartre imaginatively places himself in the role of the remembered pre-reflexive consciousness and so remembers both that consciousness's consciousness of itself and its directedness towards its intentional objects.

This rather hermeneutic procedure does not present the remembered consciousness as an object for reflection, for two reasons. It is not a reflecting on the past consciousness because the past consciousness does not exist, and, it is not a reflecting in any case because it is an imaginative substitution of one's present consciousness for a past one. Sartre is confident about the result:

> There is no doubt about the result: while I was reading, there was consciousness of the book, of the heroes of the novel, but the I was not inhabiting this consciousness. It was only consciousness of the object and non-positional consciousness of itself. (46–7)[113]

So certain phenomenological structures are preserved. The intentionality of pre-reflexive consciousness appears to Sartre's phenomenological remembering, as does pre-reflexive consciousness's being a consciousness of itself. Precisely what fails to appear is the Husserlian transcendental ego.

It seems to me that there is both something tendentious and something plausible about Sartre's procedure here. If I remember some conscious state that I was in then there would seem to be three possible levels of remembered content:

1   I remember what I was conscious of: the objects of my consciousness.
2   I remember what I was conscious of plus my consciousness of those objects.
3   I remember what I was conscious of, my consciousness of those objects, and myself as conscious of those objects.

What is tendentious about Sartre's account is that he arrests the level of phenomenological remembering at level (2). There seems no *a priori* justification for this, and the procedure itself seems consistent with a phenomenological revealing of (1), (2) or (3). It is after all the case that I often remember objects or people I have perceived without remembering my consciousness of them – even though there was no doubt I was conscious of them, and even though the mode of presentation of those people and objects in memory may well depend upon a certain mode of presentation of them in my perception of them.

Similarly, it is often the case that I not only remember objects and people, but I also remember that it was I who was conscious of them. Indeed, Sartre has already allowed that this happens. The fact, if it is a fact, that I was not self-conscious in the perception of certain objects or people is not a compelling ground for saying that I do not remember that it was I in that case that did that perceiving.

Given these alternative phenomenological findings, what is Sartre's justification for claiming (2) as the finding in his particular example? Sartre gives no argument. A weak reply in Sartre's favour would be to say: this is how it seemed to Sartre. The problems with this are that the fact that it seemed this way to Sartre does not preclude its seeming otherwise to other people (for example Husserl), or otherwise to Sartre on other occasions. Suppose Husserl phenomenologically remembers a transcendental subject and Sartre remembers none. Suppose Sartre has simply forgotten his transcendental ego. Memory is not infallible.

Sartre says:

It suffices to try to reconstitute the complete moment in which this unreflected consciousness appeared. (46)[114]

The problem is however that it does not suffice to try to do this, but it would suffice to succeed if the phenomenological findings were then an intentional pre-reflexive consciousness with an object but no subject.

The fallibility of memory, even careful phenomenological remembering, implies that it is always logically possible that the complete moment of some past consciousness has not been recollected. There is always logical room for some structure to be present in the original consciousness but omitted in the remembering of that consciousness. (Conversely, it is equally possible that some extraneous structure or content be imaginatively imposed by the remembering consciousness which was not a part of the original remembered consciousness.)

To a certain extent Sartre is aware of these difficulties. He partly addresses them when he draws a distinction between the incorrigibility of reflecting consciousness and the findings of phenomenological remembering:

This non-reflective apprehension of one consciousness by another consciousness can evidently take place only by memory, and [...] therefore it does not profit from the absolute certitude inherent in a reflexive act. (47)[115]

For sake of argument let us grant Sartre the contentious Cartesian incorrigibility thesis alluded to here. We may then understand his dilemma as follows:

1   An I is incorrigibly given to reflection.
2   No I is corrigibly given to memory.

(2) is ambiguous between 'No I is given to memory at all' and being consistent with 'An I is given incorrigibly to memory'. It is the first sense that captures Sartre's view. Sartre concedes that incorrigible claims are clearly to be preferred to corrigible claims, and that, *prima facie*, this threatens his view that pre-reflexive consciousness has no I as subject.

Sartre is clearly right to prefer incorrigible claims to corrigible claims. Assuming we wish to maximise the number of our true beliefs and minimise the number of our false beliefs, then clearly incorrigible claims are to be adopted wherever possible. The epistemological difficulty is in deciding which beliefs are true and which false.

Sartre presents his dilemma as between:

1   'an absolutely certain act which permits the presence of the I in the reflected consciousness to be affirmed' (47)

and

2   'a questionable memory which would purport to show the absence of the I from the unreflected consciousness' (47–8)[116]

The problem is that by the preference of incorrigibles, thesis (1) is to be preferred to thesis (2) but *prima facie* that does not yield the conclusion Sartre thinks avoids Husserl's difficulties.

Sartre's solution is to point out that the two claims are not in conflict so there is no compulsion to choose between them. (He cannot choose neither.) To put it clearly, if we read (1) and (2) as a disjunction then we should read the disjunctive connective inclusively (*vel*) and not exclusively (*aut*).

Sartre is correct in adopting this solution because from the fact, if it is a fact, that an I is incorrigibly given to some reflecting consciousness it does not follow that an I 'inhabits' the consciousness reflected upon when that consciousness is not reflected upon. Indeed, this does not logically preclude other modes of access to such a consciousness which may either fail to disclose an I or even establish that no I is present in it when it is not reflected upon, for example phenomenological remembering.

The question still remains, however, of how Sartre may make the inference from:

1   No I is given to phenomenological remembering of pre-reflexive conscious-
    ness.

to

2   No I 'inhabits' pre-reflexive consciousness.

The form of Sartre's epistemological difficulty is: From the fact that it has not
been shown that p it does not follow that not-p, and, in particular, from the fact
that some procedure has failed to demonstrate that p it does not logically follow
that not-p. Indeed, the possibility of either p or not-p is logically consistent with
any number of failures to demonstrate that p.

Sartre's attempt to deal with this difficulty has two parts. First, he claims that
an I is never given in phenomenological remembering of pre-reflexive consciousness:

> All the non-reflective memories of unreflected consciousness show me a
> consciousness without a me. (48)[117]

The trouble with this is: from the fact, if it is a fact, that no I has ever appeared
to non-reflective memories of unreflected consciousness, it does not follow that
this is impossible, nor indeed that some future exercise of phenomenological
remembering will not disclose an I. Also, it has already been allowed by Sartre
that some remembering is remembering that I did such and such. So at least
some remembering (if veridical) is remembering of the I.

Finally, even if an I is never remembered, it does not follow that it did not
exist as part of the structure of the otherwise remembered consciousness. The
exercise of phenomenological remembering therefore provides at most weak
inductive grounds for the absence of the I from pre-reflexive consciousness.

The other part of Sartre's attempt to meet the difficulty is to assume independently that it is incoherent to suppose that an I inhabits pre-reflexive
consciousness. He takes it he is entitled to this assumption because of the arguments treated above (pp. 51–64). If those arguments are sound then Sartre has
ideed proved that no I inhabits pre-reflexive consciousness because if it is impossible for the I to exist as transcendental subject of consciousness then *a fortiori* it
does not. In that case, however, it is not so much an independent assumption
which is invoked here as an independent proof – one which makes the exercise
of phenomenological remembering superfluous.

Despite this, Sartre presents his conclusion as following from the conjunction
of the findings of phenomenological remembering and the incoherence of
postulating a transcendental ego. The conclusion is:

> There is no I on the unreflected level. (48)[118]

Sartre presents us with an interesting phenomenological description of what does appear on the unreflected level. This, I think, supports his case in a new way:

> When I run after a streetcar, when I look at the time, when I am absorbed in contemplating a portrait, there is no I. There is consciousness of the streetcar-having-to-be-overtaken, etc., and non-positional consciousness of consciousness. In fact, I am then plunged into the world of objects: it is they which constitute the unity of my consciousness; it is they which present themselves with values, with attractive and repellent qualities – but me, I have disappeared; I have annihilated myself. There is no place for me on this level. And this is not a matter of chance, due to a momentary lapse of attention, but happens because of the very structure of consciousness. (48–9)[119]

Taken out of the context of Sartre's phenomenology the first sentence of this passage is *prima facie* incoherent. It both affirms and denies that there is an I, but, for Sartre, the sense in which there is an I is not the same as that in which there is no I. It was true of me – that psycho-physical whole that I am – that I ran for the streetcar, but no transcendental ego appeared as the subject of the consciousness of the streetcar. This supports Sartre's case because if it is true that there are veridical memories of moments of consciousness without the I then it follows that there are moments of consciousness without the I. Indeed, I think it is possible to do more than Sartre suggests. It is of course possible to reflect consciously on oneself, to present oneself to oneself as the object of one's own consciousness, but it is also possible to cease doing this. There is such a thing as beginning and ending being self-conscious. I can reflect upon the fact that I am now writing, and in some sense an I appears. Or I can stop doing this and simply concentrate my attention on this pen and these words. The psycho-physical whole who I am presumably continues to exist throughout this process but the self as object of awareness ceases to exist. As Sartre puts it:

> I am plunged into the world of objects. (49)[120]

If we take seriously Sartre's claim that the consciousness of a self would interrupt the consciousness of other objects then the whole account begins to look more convincing.

This passage is notable in other ways. The description of the streetcar as having-to-be-overtaken is highly Heideggerian. Heidegger distinguishes two modes in which objects may be presented to *Dasein* (the kind of being a human being fundamentally is): In the mode *Zuhandenheit*, objects have instrumental usefulness for *Dasein*, but objects can also be 'there' for *Dasein* in the mode *Vorhandenheit* – the mere theoretical, uninterested contemplation of the spectator.[121] Sartre describes the streetcar in the mode *Zuhandenheit* as to-be-overtaken. What a streetcar is for Sartre is what it is for and this, for Sartre (but not Heidegger) is an achievement of consciousness.

Sartre has already argued that not only are the intentional objects of consciousness constituted by the consciousness of them but the unity of consciousness is due to several acts of consciousness being implicated in the constitution of a single intentional object. If it is true that there are moments of consciousness without the I, the I cannot be the owner or unifier of such consciousness. If we then ask 'What is?' then a highly plausible candidate, perhaps in the last resort the only candidate, is the objects of consciousness.

If we conjoin the various claims Sartre has made about the I and pre-reflexive consciousness I do not think the result is a deductive argument, with premises all guaranteed to be true, yielding as conclusion the fact that there is no transcendental subject of pre-reflexive consciousness. Nevertheless, Sartre has at least succeeded in casting extreme doubt upon the existence of such a subject.

17 The phenomenology of the I

To substantiate the view that pre-reflexive consciousness is without an I Sartre presents a phenomenology of the self. In this Sartre defines his own position in relation to Husserl.

Husserl is committed to a strong contrast between the way in which a physical object is presented to consciousness and the way in which consciousness is presented to consciousness in reflection. Importantly, a physical object appears under distinct 'aspects', 'perspectives' or 'profiles' (*Abschattungen*), but an act of consciousness, in contrast, is grasped 'all at once' or in a wholly unperspectival way. A physical object is in fact an 'ideal unity' constructed out of the various perspectives on it, but consciousness is given as a unity directly to reflexive consciousness.

Sartre accepts this contrast from Husserl, and argues that the incorrigibility of the findings of reflection depends upon the non-perspectival nature of the apprehension of consciousness by consciousness. Because physical objects are not given phenomenologically *qua* physical objects there is always logical room for a set of phenomena not to be the appearances of a physical object. To put it another way, the having of any particular set of sense experiences is logically consistent with either the truth or the falsity of the claim that they are experiences of a physical object.

In the case of consciousness's reflection upon consciousness the situation is quite different. If there is putative conscious reflection on consciousness then this is allegedly never consistent with the falsity of the claim that this is consciousness of consciousness. Nor does Sartre seem to leave room for the possibility that it appears to someone that there is reflective consciousness of consciousness but there is no such consciousness. Although this is not countenanced by Sartre it would seem to be at least a logical possibility.

In either case, this asymmetry between the perception of physical objects and conscious reflection on consciousness is adduced by Sartre as support for his corrigible/incorrigible distinction. Reflection is incorrigible but sense perception is corrigible.

Sartre offers a tripartite taxonomy of the findings of consciousness from a phenomenological point of view:

1   Physical objects
2   (Reflected) consciousness
3   'Eternal truths'

Physical objects, although they are ideal unities of their (infinite number of) aspects, manifest themselves as spatio-temporal particulars. Their temporality implies that, at least in a sense, they transcend the perception of them – a physical object is nothing over and above, or is not exhausted by, the set of perceptions of it. They do not transcend time. Similarly, with any conscious content as the object of reflection, although the content of reflected consciousness is not to be identified with the conscious reflection on it, it too is something temporal. In the case of 'eternal truths' however:

> As for meanings, or eternal truths, they affirm their transcendence in that the moment they appear they are given as independent of time, whereas the consciousness which apprehends them is, on the contrary, individuated through and through in duration. (49–50)[122]

I take it the notion of an 'eternal truth' subsumes not only traditional *a priori* certainties such as definitions, logical truths and the truths of mathematics, but also Husserlian meanings. An eternal truth, therefore, is not only transcendent in the sense that what it is is not specifiable in terms of the consciousness of it, but also in the sense that it transcends time; temporal predicates are not applicable to it. It follows that an eternal truth has no temporal parts. Consciousness, in contrast, changes in content, and the discrimination of one kind of consciousness from another depends upon an awareness of such changing content.

Sartre now poses the central question of his phenomenology of the self: Is the I given to reflective consciousness like an eternal truth, or like the content of consciousness? Is it a transient item to be discriminated as one content amongst others in the flux of one's mental life, or is it non-temporal, an entity which transcends all consciousness of it?

> The reply is clear; the I is not given as a concrete moment, a perishable structure of my actual consciousness. On the contrary, it affirms its permanence beyond this consciousness and all consciousness, and – although it scarcely resembles a mathematical truth – its type of existence comes much nearer to that of eternal truths than to that of consciousness. (50)[123]

What the I has in common with an eternal truth is its transcendent atemporality. The I is not given as a changing and so temporal structure, nor is it given as part of the content of consciousness. On the contrary, it transcends all consciousness of it. Sartre thinks this is how the I is phenomenologically given: that is how it appears to consciousness when consciousness is stripped of preconception. There is, I think, much intuitive or pre-phenomenological plausibility in this. After all, we all, rightly or wrongly, draw a distinction between on the one hand the changing flux of one's experience and, on the other hand, the relatively enduring subject of those experiences: that which has them. This pre-phenomenological view does not imply the non-temporality of the self, only the duration of the self through its experiences. But Sartre is saying more than this. He is not claiming that the subject of consciousness endures at least as long as the set of experiences of which it is the owner. He is saying that in some strong sense the self is independent of the kind of temporality which pertains to the contents of consciousness. It is as though the temporality of experience is so pervasive of experience that the only temporality with which we are directly acquainted is the temporality of experience. So if we are acquainted with a self then this cannot be something temporal, or at least, cannot be temporal in the same sense. If it were it would perhaps count as part of the content of experience.

So far I have accepted Sartre's claim that a certain temporality pertains to the contents of consciousness. It may be doubted, however, that all the contents of consciousness are temporal. Temporality pertains to those contents with the character of occurrent thoughts, certainly events or processes with a definite start and stop, duration, mutability, etc., but being in certain moods, believing that p, reflecting, intending, or meaning that q do not straightforwardly occur 'in time', where criteria for their doing so would include being able to be slowed down, reversed, left unfinished, interrupted, spot-checked, observed continuously, given a determinate duration, etc. If this is correct, then the temporality argument only shows that the self is 'beyond' certain of the contents of consciousness; others of those contents are as atemporal as the self. It follows that Sartre has not shown that the self is distinct from consciousness, but his concern, after all is to show that the self is not subject to that temporality that does pertain to consciousness. The fact that some of consciousness's contents are atemporal does not preclude this.

We may unpack the notion of the self being 'beyond' consciousness – any actual or possible consciousness – as follows. The self is given phenomenologically as the subject of consciousness, as that which is conscious, so, take any consciousness you like, to the extent that it is an object for reflection an I appears as its subject. This is analogous to the Kantian thought that the I think must be capable of accompanying any of my perceptions. It is in a sense independent of them. It is not to be identified with any or all of them, yet it is what their being 'mine' consists in.

18 The ego and the *epoché*

The next phase of Sartre's phenomenology of the self is the ironic invocation of a central phenomenological device against a mistake Sartre perceives as common to Descartes and Husserl. The mistake is the reification of the subject, and the device is the phenomenological *epoché*, or reduction of the world of the natural attitude to that of transcendental subjectivity.

As we saw in the first chapter, the *epoché* essentially entails suspension of belief in the objective reality of the objects of experience. It is employed in Husserl's phenomenology to facilitate the description of the objects of consciousness *qua* objects of consciousness. If something does not appear as an object of consciousness it is not postulated within the descriptions of transcendental phenomenology.

Now, Sartre's point is precisely that the transcendental ego does not appear as an object for consciousness except in reflection, hence it must fall by the *epoché*. The irony of this criticism of Husserl is that the transcendental ego is the cornerstone of Husserl's 'transcendental phenomenology' yet it is precisely that which is phenomenologically illegitimate.

It seems to me that Sartre is entirely correct in this aspect of his critique of Husserl. There is a tension between on the one hand the employment of the *epoché* and on the other hand the postulation of a transcendental I. Husserl faces a dilemma. Either an exception has to be made to the thoroughgoing use of the *epoché*, or else the transcendental ego must be abandoned in so far as it does not appear to consciousness. Sartre does not consider the first option, and I think rightly not. Some good argument would seem to be needed to justify witholding the *epoché* in the case of the I but not in the case of, say, physical objects, and no such argument would seem to be available. This leaves only the option Sartre advocates: the abandonment of the transcendental ego.

Sartre resumes his attack on the Cartesian–Husserlian error of reifying the self, as follows:

> Indeed, it is obvious that Descartes passed from the *Cogito* to the idea of thinking substance because he believed that *I* and *think* are on the same level. We have just seen that Husserl, although less obviously, is ultimately subject to the same reproach. (50)[124]

As we have seen, the mistake common to Descartes and Husserl is to assume that because there is consciousness there is an irreducibly subjective psychic I that is conscious. There is no phenomenological warrant for such a postulation because an I exists only in so far as it is an object for reflection.

Although Sartre assimilates Husserl's transcendental ego to Descartes' thinking substance, there are obvious disanalogies between the two concepts. For example, Descartes' subject is the immortal soul of Platonic Christianity, but Husserl's subject is a quasi-Kantian transcendental ground of experience. However, the two concepts of the subject are much closer than this disanalogy would suggest. Both are subjects of consciousness. Both are immaterial. Both are substances, in the sense that they are not properties and stand in no need of anything else in order to exist (with the important qualifications that the Cartesian soul depends upon God for its existence and the transcendental ego only exists when its experiences exist). Both are discovered partly by an introspective scrutiny of thinking, partly by the exercise of pure reason. Both are a condition for experience. Descartes' *cogitationes* are operations of the soul. Husserl's acts of consciousness are emanations from the transcendental ego.

To understand the origin of this mistake we need to unpack the spatial metaphor 'level' (30) ('plan' TE 34). This cannot mean that what the Cartesian and Husserlian ego have in common is that they both appear to consciousness, because, clearly, the Cartesian soul has no direct acquaintance with itself, only with its operations. What Sartre means, I think, is that within the Cartesian–Husserlian framework it is equally self-evident that there is thinking and that I am a thing that thinks. Neither claim is more or less certain than the other.[125] It is not clear that this is true but it is the most plausible reading of Sartre's metaphor.

For Sartre it is by no means self-evident that there is an I if there is thinking. The I is not an entity given directly to consciousness whenever there is thinking, nor is there any logical compulsion to derive the existence of a mental subject from the fact that there is thinking. In this sense the I and thinking are on different 'levels'.

There is another interpretation of 'levels' here, which is highly Sartrean. Sartre distinguishes between the reflective and the pre-reflective levels of consciousness. It is the failure to make that distinction which misleads Descartes and Husserl into postulating an I wherever there is thinking.

At work in these passages are three kinds of method, each of which may yield a different notion of the self. Sartre calls them:

1   Metaphysical
2   Critical
3   Phenomenological[126]

We could represent Sartre's location of the thinkers he considers in this section of *The Transcendence of the Ego* as follows:

1   Metaphysical – Descartes, Husserl
2   Critical – Kant, Husserl
3   Phenomenological – Kant, Sartre

Descartes does not engage in either phenomenology or critical philosophy in proving that he is a thing that thinks. Clearly, there are close analogies between the method of systematic doubt in the first two *Meditations* and Husserl's transcendental reduction but the soul is not proved to exist by any such quasi-phenomenological manoeuvres. It is not as though, for example, the soul is an indubitable residue given directly to consciousness, for Descartes. On the contrary, the soul is postulated as a metaphysical entity, as Descartes as he really is, and this is supposed to be established by rational argument.

Similarly, Descartes is not a critical philosopher of the self. Within the critical post-Kantian method adopted by Sartre, the self as soul is an extravagant rationalist postulate. Descartes is not trying to answer the question of how experience is possible even if it is true that there could be no thought without a thinker for him. Even if he decides on the limits of what may be known (with certainty), he draws those limits much more broadly than Kant or any post-Kantian critical philosopher.

Husserl does not count as a phenomenologist of the self for Sartre. (Indeed in *Being and Nothingness* Sartre argues that Husserl is not a phenomenologist but a phenomenalist: someone who thinks that any claims about physical objects may be translated into claims about actual or possible perceptual contents without loss of meaning.) He thinks Husserl has no genuine phenomenology of the self because, as we have seen, the transcendental ego must fall before the *epoché*. The failure to realise this precludes Husserl from engaging in a phenomenology of the subject. Rather, Husserl's transcendental ego is a metaphysical postulate like the Cartesian soul. It is not in the world – it is not an item falling within possible experience – it grounds the world. For Sartre, no one can be a phenomenologist and maintain this.

Kant has the merit of avoiding the metaphysical trap which Descartes and Husserl succumb to. Indeed, it is possible to read *The Transcendence of the Ego* as the pushing of Kant's theory of the self to some of its logical conclusions, even though Sartre's depiction of the self as an object is un-Kantian.

Sartre is, in his own estimation, the true phenomenologist of the self who avoids any metaphysical mistakes about its existence and nature. Sartre, perhaps, would not accept this, but his critique of Husserl falls under the heading 'critical philosophy' as well as 'phenomenology'.

One final, but complementary, reading of 'level' rests on this:

> If the I in the I think affirms itself as transcendent, this is because the I
> is not of the same nature as transcendental consciousness. (51)[127]

The I and the 'I think' are on different levels because that I think is directly given to consciousness, but the putative I that thinks is given to only one sort of consciousness: reflective consciousness. In the absence of reflection no such I is given.

Sartre uses Kant's distinction between 'transcendent' and 'transcendental' to clarify this claim. If *x* is transcendent then *x* is not a possible object of consciousness, at least *qua x*, but if *x* is transcendental then *x* is a condition for consciousness and, even though not empirical, may be coherently thought of as *x*. The I of the 'I think' is transcendent because it is not given to consciousness (except as a product of reflection) but consciousness is transcendental as described phenomenologically because it is a condition of our everyday empirical consciousness.

19 Consciousness and the I

If Sartre's arguments so far are sound then Husserl's transcendental ego falls by the *epoché*. Its postulation from a phenomenological point of view is quite illegitimate.

However, although the I is not a transcendental ego according to Sartre, it is something rather than nothing even within the horizon of phenomenology. This means that there is a difference – a phenomenological difference – between the appearance of consciousness with the I and the appearance of consciousness without the I. Further, there is a distinction between consciousness and the I such that the I is not, and is not any part of, consciousness, even if it is not a transcendental ego:

> Let us also note that the I think does not appear to reflection as the reflected consciousness: it is given through reflected consciousness. (51)[128]

In reflection, then, there are two objects for the reflecting consciousness: the consciousness which is reflected upon, and the I which accompanies that reflected consciousness. I take it Sartre thinks this distinction is phenomenologically given. It is simply self-evidently not the case that the I that is reflected on is, or is a structure of, the consciousness which is reflected on.

What does it mean to say that the I is given 'through' reflected consciousness? Sartre provides us with a simile to help us understand this. He says that the I appears through reflected consciousness like a pebble at the bottom of water (51–2). Again, the appositeness or otherwise of this image may only usefully be appraised phenomenologically. Husserl employs alternative images: that of the I as 'behind' consciousness, or the sun emanating rays of sunlight as the I as the source of acts of consciousness. It seems difficult to find good philosophical grounds for preferring Husserl's similes of Sartre's or *vice versa*.

The images are presumably mutually inconsistent. If the I is sufficiently like a pebble in water for Sartre to be right, then it is sufficiently unlike the sun as a source of light for Husserl to be wrong. It does not seem logically impossible that the two images should be consistent but Sartre at least conceives of himself as providing an alternative model to Husserl's.

Suppose A appears phenomenologically through B. It follows that A is not B, (so) B is not A, A is not any part of B, and B is not any part of A. It follows also *ceteris paribus* that unless B appeared then A could not appear. What is not entirely clear is whether if A appears through B then if B appears then A appears. I see nothing in Sartre's text to commit him to that as a general principle, even if when reflected consciousness appears an I is given to reflecting consciousness. Aside from these logical points we have to be content with the image presented by 'through'. It is of course a spatial metaphor. It is reasonably clear what it means for a face to be visible 'through' a pane of glass, less so what it means for the I to appear 'through' reflected consciousness. The unclarity in the second case arises through thinking of the mental in spatial terms.

Although the I is given 'through' consciousness, it is not the 'source' of consciousness according to Sartre. Sartre provides us with two reasons for doubting this tenet of Husserlian transcendental phenomenology, even though it may seem to be true:

> To be sure, the I manifests itself as the source of consciousness. (51)[129]

If '*x* manifests itself' implies '*x* appears phenomenologically' then it is doubtful whether Sartre's position may be understood consistently. After all, he has argued so far that the phenomenological findings are incompatible with the Husserlian view of the ego as the 'source' of consciousness. For this reason it is better to read 'manifests itself' as something like 'is easily taken as' or 'is easily believed to be'. Then we may read Sartre as criticising a recurrent tendency in modern philosophy to reify the self into a subjective source of consciousness despite the fact that this is not how the self is directly given to consciousness. Not only Husserl, but Descartes, and on certain readings Kant, are guilty of this reification.

Sartre does not produce a reason why philosophers have been systematically misled into postulating an irreducibly subjective ego as the 'source' of consciousness. If that is not how the ego appears to consciousness then it is puzzling that the mistake should have been made.

Sartre's account is however easily supplemented by linguistic considerations adduced by Kant, Wittgenstein and Ryle. The public use of 'I' by whoever uses it to denote whoever uses it is carried over into a private metaphysical use as the name of a purely psychical 'owner' of consciousness, as though because no physical self appears as the subject of consciousness there must exist a non-physical self as a kind of proxy. Because the self is not a physical object it must be a non-physical object.[130] It is argued by Ryle in *The Concept of Mind* that Cartesian dualism does not have to be true in order for our ordinary psychological vocabulary to be meaningful.[131]

20 Why the I is not the source of consciousness

Sartre reiterates two of his grounds for doubting that the I is the source of consciousness:

i   'Nothing but consciousness can be the source of consciousness.' (52)
ii 'If the I is a part of consciousness, there would then be two I's.' (52)[132]

I shall treat each of these in turn.

i Consciousness as the source of the self

That there may exist no source of consciousness other than consciousness itself is implied by two characteristically Sartrean doctrines: Consciousness is an absolute, like a Spinozistic substance, and consciousness is free.

If something is a substance then although other things may depend upon it for their existence, it does not depend upon anything else for its own existence. It follows that if consciousness is a substance, or like a substance in this respect, then consciousness may have no source. This is because if A is the source of B, then A depends upon B for its existence but if B depends upon nothing for its existence then *a fortiori* B does not depend upon A for its existence.

Equally, if something is free then it is a cause but not an effect, but if A is the source of B then A may be the cause of B or the cause of some part of B. This is precluded if B is free, because if B is free then nothing is the cause of B so *a fortiori* A is not the cause of B.

Sartre does not offer independent arguments here (52) for consciousness's being both a Spinozistic substance and free but I take it these doctrines are already established to his satisfaction.

Clearly, if we allow that consciousness is a free substance, and if being a free substance is inconsistent with having a source other than itself, then consciousness has no source other than itself. Sartre's argument is valid because if p and q are mutually inconsistent, and if p is true, then q must be false, but it is only sound if, in addition, both its premises are true.

The possibility of consciousness being the source of itself is consistent with consciousness being a free substance. If A is a free substance then A is free and one way of reading 'free' here is 'cause of itself' or 'cause of its own actions' so if A is free then A is the cause of what A does. Similarly, if A is a free substance then A is a substance, so if A has a cause then A is the cause of itself. Nothing causes A to be other than A, so A is the cause of its own existence. Here I am taking it that if something is the source of something it is at least the cause of that thing.

ii The impossibility of two I's

If the I of reflected consciousness existed as the source of that consciousness, then a single psyche would include two I's as its subject. Sartre assumes here that consciousness is a unity; the existence of two I's in one and the same consciousness is inconsistent with that unity, so if consciousness is a unity then it is impossible that there should be two I's. Consciousness is a unity, the Husserlian phenomenology of the self generates two I's and so is incompatible with the unity of consciousness. Therefore the Husserlian phenomenology of the self is false.

This is a valid argument and is also sound if the two premises, that consciousness is a unity and Husserl's phenomenology implies the existence of two I's, are true. We may assume that if some putative consciousness in fact had two I's as subjects then that putative consciousness could not turn out to be a unity. It would in fact have to turn out to be two consciousnesses if consciousnesses are individuated through their subjects.

What are the two I's? Sartre identifies them as the I of reflexive consciousness and the I of reflected consciousness. In a sense for Sartre both these I's exist. The problem of the two I's only arises if we take the I of reflected consciousness to be a transcendental ego: the subject of reflected consciousness. Reflexive and reflected consciousness form a unity but this unity would be impossible if the subject of reflective consciousness were numerically distinct from the subject of reflected consciousness. Sartre's solution is to abandon the Husserlian idea that the I exists as subject of reflected consciousness. The existence of the problem on Husserl's account is taken by Sartre as confirmation of the cogency of his own phenomenology of the self.

21   Sartre's conclusions on 'The I and the Me'

Sartre ends the chapter of *The Transcendence of the Ego* called 'The I and the Me' with a summary of his four principal conclusions so far:

i   The I is an existent.
ii   The I is open to a special kind of intuition.
iii The I only appears to reflexive consciousness.
iv   The I must fall by the *epoché*.

I shall examine each of these in turn.

i The I as an existent

Sartre says:

> The I is an existent. It has a concrete type of existence, undoubtedly different from the existence of mathematical truths, of meanings, or of spatio-temporal beings, but no less real. The I gives itself as a transcendent. (52)[133]

To say that this I exists or is an existent is to say that the I is something rather than nothing. Husserl's mistake is not to postulate an I when in fact no I exists but to misunderstand the nature of the I. In other words, Husserl's mistake is about essence not about existence. Husserl thinks the I is the transcendental ego, but for Sartre the I has a kind of permanence analogous to but not identical with that of mathematical truths.

Not only does the I exist according to Sartre but the I is real. Existence is to be contrasted with non-existence or absence of being, but being real is to be contrasted with being artificial or fictitious. The I is not artificial or fictitious for Sartre because it is not simply an invention of consciousness, or exhausted by our belief in its existence. Its reality consists in its independence of our belief in it, and its independence of particular conscious thoughts about it. What its reality does not consist in is being the transcendental subject of pre-reflexive, or reflected consciousness.

Sartre also claims that the I is given as a transcendent. In terms of the Kantian distinction between the transcendent and the transcendental, the I is not transcendental because it is not a condition for consciousness, but it is transcendent because what it is is not exhausted by the consciousness of it. It is, to put it metaphorically, 'beyond' consciousness, not in the sense that it is inaccessible to consciousness (clearly it is not or a phenomenology of the self would be impossible) but in the sense that its reality is not wholly apprehended by any particular act of consciousness. In this respect, if few others, the I is rather like a physical object.

ii The I as open to intuition

Here Sartre is drawing our attention to a certain kind of mistake:

> The I proffers itself to an intuition of a special kind which apprehends it, always inadequately, behind the reflected consciousness. (53)[134]

Clearly, Sartre has made room for a kind of intuition distinct from both the intuition of mathematical truths and the intuition of physical objects, which is the intuition of the I. He does not differ from Husserl in precisely that respect, but over what the intuition of the I is an intuition of. The notion of an intuition is one the phenomenologists inherit from Kant, and it denotes the direct apprehension of some object by consciousness.

However, more than that is implied here. The intuition of the I is such as to easily mislead us into the Husserlian view that the I is a transcendental ego. Although Sartre has no account of how this error is possible, one possibility must be expressly excluded. It must not be the case that the I is phenomenologically given as a transcendental ego. If this were the case Sartre would have conceded to Husserl precisely the point he wishes to repudiate.

iii The I only appears to reflective consciousness

The nearest Sartre comes to offering an explanation of the error is:

> The I never appears except on the occasion of a reflective act [...] there is an unreflected act of reflection, without an I, which is directed on a reflected consciousness [...]. At the same time a new object appears which is the occasion for an affirmation by reflective consciousness. (53)[135]

The 'new object' which appears is the I, but the I must appear in such a way that it is (incorrectly) taken for a Husserlian ego or (correctly) taken for a Sartrean 'me'. In that sense the I is the occasion for all affirmation by reflective consciousness. It may, for example, be affirmed to be Husserlian or Sartrean. We need to know in virtue of exactly which phenomenological features the I may be misconstrued on the Husserlian model. Sartre gives us no clue to that, even though in the remainder of the book he develops his own positive phenomenology of the I.

iv *The I must fall by the* epoché

The final irony Sartre has brought against Husserl is this:

> The transcendent I must fall before the stroke of the phenomenological reduction. The *Cogito* affirms too much. The certain content of the pseudo 'Cogito' is not 'I have consciousness of this chair', but 'There is consciousness of this chair'. (53–4)[136]

Sartre's critique of Husserl and the post-Cartesian phenomenological techniques is suggestive of the criticism Russell and Lichtenberg brought against Descartes' *cogito*. From a phenomenological point of view, from the fact that consciousness appears to consciousness it does not follow that any I appears to consciousness, or exists as either subject or object of that consciousness. Indeed, from a logical point of view, from the fact that there exists consciousness it does not logically follow that something is conscious. No contradiction would seem to be involved in the supposition that there is consciousness without a subject.

The I falls before the *epoché*. Like any other object of consciousness, its objective taken-for-granted reality must be suspended in the interests of phenomenological description. In this sense, Sartre considers himself a stricter and more thoroughgoing phenomenologist than Husserl.

3 The theory of the material presence of the me

Summary

Sartre reiterates his rejection of any unconscious mind and argues for his identification of the psycho-physical whole person with 'the me'. He describes the phenomenological relations between the ego and its actions, states and qualities and analyses the concept of action. After a discussion of the relations of any object to its properties Sartre rejects the view that the ego is a thing, or like a physical object. Instead he compares the ego–states relation to the world–objects relation. Sartre describes phenomenologically the 'poetic' production *ex nihilo* by the ego of its states and argues that the ego is constituted by reflective consciousness. The ego has a pseudo-interiority which it borrows from the real interiority of consciousness. Sartre shows himself to be anti-Cartesian on self-knowledge in refusing to privilege first person psychological ascriptions over third person ones. The ego is mistakenly taken as real but is the ideal unity of states and actions.

1 Sartre's criticisms of La Rochefoucauld

Sartre identifies La Rochefoucauld as an early anticipator of two related movements in modern European thought: the so-called 'self-love' moralists and those psychologists who make use of the concept of an unconscious. The self-love moralists thought that a self-reflexive act was implicit in any act of consciousness whatsoever so that if a person is conscious of something, then that person implicitly desires that object for himself. Indeed, the object is really desired by that person's psychic 'me', and all acts of cognition are implicitly referred back to such a psychic me. Sartre wishes to refute this kind of psychology because it seems to make a mistake closely analogous to Husserl's postulation of the transcendental ego.

It is well known that Sartre denies the existence of an unconscious mind, at least in the sense advocated by classic Freudian psychology. Indeed, the idea that consciousness is implicitly a consciousness of itself is a residual Cartesian strain in Sartre's essentially anti-Cartesian phenomenology. If someone believes in an unconscious then they believe that a person may be in a mental state without knowing that they are in that state. In particular, there exist psychological drives which motivate or determine the person's behaviour in ways of which the person is ignorant. One reason why Sartre wishes to repudiate this view is that it seems to present an insuperable barrier to a thoroughgoing phenomenology of consciousness. Another is that it is incompatible with his doctrine of human freedom.

The theories of the 'self-love' moralists and the Freudians are closely related in that the psychologies of both logically entail the existence of an unconscious. The self-love moralist is committed to an unconscious because the 'me' which is the reflexive object of psychic acts is usually not available to introspection. It is concealed by emotion. Similarly, the Freudian is committed to the view that an agent *qua* psychic agent is not fully available to his own introspection. Indeed, his own true motives or drives are not available for conscious scrutiny (except under Freudian analysis).

Sartre's characterisation of these two theories, as they originate in La Rochefoucauld, is riddled with Husserlian themes:

> La Rochefoucauld was one of the first to have made use of the unconscious without naming it. For him, self-love conceals itself under the most diverse forms. It must be ferreted out before it can be grasped. In a more general way, it has been admitted as a consequence that the me, if it is not present to consciousness is hidden behind consciousness and is the magnetic pole of all our representations and all our desires. The me seeks, then, to procure the object in order to satisfy its desire. (55)[137]

For example, Husserl's transcendental ego is hidden from consciousness, at least until the transcendental field is opened up by the phenomenological reduction. Further, Husserl refers to the transcendental ego as the subjective 'pole' of consciousness. It is common to La Rochefoucauld, the self-love moralists and to Husserl that a hidden 'me' is the source of all one's acts of consciousness. This 'hidden subject' is clearly present in Freud's psychology in a parallel way. Sartre's aim in these passages is nothing less than the demolition of this entire idea of the self.[138]

There is, according to Sartre, a fundamental methodological error which unites these traditions. It is the failure to recognise the distinction between reflexive and pre-reflexive consciousness. The consequence of this is a confusion of the structures of pre-reflexive consciousness with those of reflexive consciousness. In particular, what belongs to acts of reflection is mistakenly ascribed to the objects of reflection. It is a central task of Sartre's phenomenology of consciousness to clearly separate these two sorts of structure, and point out cases where what belongs to reflexive consciousness has been ascribed to pre-reflexive consciousness.

There is a second, and related, confusion. Sartre thinks what belongs to the objects of consciousness is misidentified as a structure of consciousness itself. What consciousness is of is confused with what consciousness is. Again, it is a task of his phenomenology to make a clear distinction between consciousness and its intentional objects. The ascription of the ego to pre-reflexive conscious-ness is a special case of the confusion between an object of consciousness and a structure of consciousness.

Sartre provides us with an example of the separation of the object of consciousness from the consciousness of it. ('Separation' means the distinction Sartre makes between the two in his phenomenological description of their rela-tionship.) Suppose, Sartre says, that you pity your friend Pierre and you go to help him. Pierre is presented to your consciousness as having to be helped. This is how Pierre appears to you, and it is a property of Pierre, a phenomenological property, which appears to you. This property of Pierre is not a property of your consciousness but a property of Pierre as the object of your consciousness. Sartre is engaged in phenomenology here and not psychological explanation. Sartre's view is quite consistent with either a realist or an anti-realist explanation of perception at this point. For example, it would be no objection to Sartre's thesis to say that the appearance of Pierre as having to be helped, or needing assis-tance, is the result of a quasi-Kantian imposition of preconceptions on Pierre as intentional object. The revelation that being-in-need-of-help is a property of Pierre within the framework of the phenomenological description is consistent with a variety of explanations of how that appearance is possible.

A hint of the kind of explanation with which Sartre would wish to supple-ment his phenomenology is given when he tells us that Pierre's appearance acts on one 'like a force' (56). This is an analogy to help us understand the phenomenology, but the appropriateness of the analogy depends upon our seeing the logical possibility of a causal relation running from the appearance to one's own consciousness. This cannot be construed literally by Sartre of course because nothing can act on consciousness. Consciousness is free.

This example illustrates the distinction between consciousness and its inten-tional object. That is part of the phenomenological framework Sartre needs to retain in his critique of Husserl and the broadly Husserlian position of La Rochefoucauld.

There is another consequence of the Pierre example which is to Sartre's purpose. No 'me' is present to one's consciousness of Pierre:

> There is no me: I am in the presence of Pierre's suffering just as I am in the presence of the colour of this inkstand: there is an objective world of things and of actions, done or to be done, and the actions come to adhere as quali-ties to the things which call for them. (56)[139]

We see now, with new impact, why there must be moments of consciousness without the I. All there is for consciousness is Pierre's suffering, or Pierre as having to be helped. Consciousness of self – even of the unconscious but puta-tively perennial kind advocated by La Rochefoucauld, the self-love moralists, and the Freudians – would interfere as a barrier, as a distraction, to the possibility of Pierre's suffering being presented as an object for consciousness.

This does not mean that one is not conscious of Pierre. One is conscious of

Pierre but not thereby conscious of oneself. Similarly, this does not mean that your consciousness of Pierre is not a 'consciousness of itself' (to use Sartre's turn of phrase). It simply means that the 'me' does not exist as an intentional object in addition to Pierre's appearance as suffering.

Sartre's analogy between Pierre's suffering and the colour of the inkwell is designed to reinforce the claim that the properties of both are objective or mind-independent qualities of objective or mind-independent objects. This is true within Sartre's phenomenological description. It is how they are given to consciousness.

Just as it was open to a quasi-Kantian to claim that the appearance of Pierre as suffering is due (or partly due) to the imposition of *a priori* structures of consciousness on Pierre, so it is open to a quasi-Lockean to say that the colour of the inkwell is a secondary quality – that it does not belong to the object (except as a power or disposition) independently of the perception of that object. Sartre could allow this as consistent with his phenomenology. His point is that the colour of the inkwell is given to consciousness as a property of the inkwell and not as a property of consciousness. It is given as mind-independent whether or not it is mind-independent. It will be an important part of his phenomenology of the self that the 'me' is given as an object for consciousness in a parallel way; and not as any kind of structure of consciousness.

Sartre has two objections to any account of an example of the 'Pierre's suffering' type which makes it dependent upon an unconscious or on a self-reflective desire. They are phenomenologically redundant and they turn out to be incoherent.

Sartre considers the view that I go to Pierre's assistance in order to terminate an unpleasant state of mind that I am in as a result of perceiving Pierre suffer. Sartre agrees that this may happen but it is something distinct from the sponta-neous act of assisting Pierre based on the simple perception of his suffering. If I am in an unpleasant state as a result of seeing Pierre suffer then I can know I am in that state. It could be objected that Sartre begs the question against his opponents here, but a reply on Sartrean lines could be constructed: If I am moti-vated by an unpleasant state of mind I must feel this unpleasantness for it to motivate me. To the extent that I feel it I am aware that I am in it. To the extent that I am aware that I am in it, it cannot be an unconscious state.

The postulation of such a state is in any case phenomenologically redundant. It is the intuition of the unpleasant quality of Pierre which motivates the action of helping him. The quality is, phenomenologically speaking, on the side of the object and not on the side of consciousness. Indeed, even if the consciousness of Pierre includes a desire, that desire is to remove the unpleasant property of the object. The desire is not directed against itself, nor against oneself as the subject of desire.

For a desire to motivate my action I must feel it and for a mental state to motivate my action I must know that I am in it. What the Freudians and the self-love theorists are explicitly committed to, and what La Rochefoucauld is implicitly committed to, is a confusion of reflected and unreflected acts of consciousness. In order for a putatively unconscious act of consciousness to play a role in one's psychology it must in fact be reflected, and thereby turn out not to be unconscious at all. Sartre asks rhetorically:

> Even if the unconscious exists, who could be led to believe that it contains spontaneities of a reflected sort? Is it not the definition of the reflected that it be posited by a consciousness? But, in addition, how can it be held that the reflected is first in relation to the unreflected? (57)[140]

Clearly, it is contradictory to maintain that an unconscious contains reflected acts of consciousness because, necessarily, if a state is unconscious it is not the object of an act of consciousness, but if a state is reflected then, necessarily, it is the object of an act of consciousness. Sartre thus condemns the Freudians, the self-love theorists, and La Rochefoucauld for implicitly maintaining that a person may be in a mental state but both be aware and not be aware that they are in that mental state. This argument goes through so long as Sartre is entitled to maintain that the respect in which one is putatively aware one is in a mental state is just the respect in which one is unaware one is in that mental state.

There is an additional reason why Sartre thinks allegedly unconscious states must be unreflected. If a state were thoroughly unconscious we could not know of its existence. It might be thought that this is not a sound objection for Sartre to bring on his own terms. After all, he maintains that there exist unreflected mental states: those of pre-reflective consciousness. However, even those, although unreflected, include an implicit awareness of themselves. From the standpoint of his thoroughgoing Cartesianism about the transparency of the mental he may consistently ask the epistemological question of the Freudian: How do you know the unconscious exists? If the Freudian replies that it is postulated to explain actions then Sartre may reply that his own philosophy shows that this postulation is redundant. If the Freudian replies that the unconscious is revealed under therapy, Sartre may reply that it is then no longer an unconscious.

Sartre is at pains to persuade us that his critique of the unconscious is consistent with the reflected/unreflected distinction. The reflected depends upon the unreflected, but the unreflected is not to be identified with the unconscious. In particular, there is no unconscious self. Phenomenologically, the unconscious and the Husserlian transcendental ego are equally unwarranted postulations.

2 The autonomy of unreflected consciousness

Unreflected consciousness's autonomy consists in its acting but not being acted upon. This idea is facilitated by the critique of: the unconscious, the self as agent but object of desire, and the transcendental ego. For Sartre unreflected consciousness is consciousness without a subject. If consciousness did have a subject it would not be autonomous. Acts of consciousness would not have quasi-Kantian spontaneity. Rather, acts of consciousness would be performances by an ego, an unconscious or some other irreducibly subjective source of mental life. This would mean they are not free, but rather the determined result of some subjective but hidden agent.

Sartre takes it that the refutation of the idea of the subject implies the freedom of unreflected consciousness:

> We arrive then at the following conclusion: unreflected consciousness must be considered autonomous. (58)[141]

From the fact that no subject of consciousness performs the acts of consciousness it cannot be validly concluded that acts of consciousness are not causally determined. That is the conclusion Sartre desires, so for it to go through we need to conjoin the present critique of the self with the earlier argument that consciousness is a Spinozistic substance. It is a cause but not an effect. If that is true then nothing acts on consciousness and *a fortiori* no subject acts on consciousness.

It might be objected that the fact that *x* is uncaused does not entail that *x* is free. I agree that this inference does not go through as it stands but Sartre's characterisation of consciousness includes (perhaps uncontentiously) the idea that consciousness is composed of mental acts. If *x* acts but is not caused to act that is arguably what is meant by *x* being free on at least one plausible construal of 'free'. It is this particular construal Sartre wishes to capture by the term 'spontaneity'. Something acts (absolutely) spontaneously if and only if it acts but is not acted upon, *a fortiori* its acting is not caused by its being acted upon.

Sartre is not even prepared to concede that the object of consciousness has an effect on consciousness. This is ruled out because there is not anything that determines consciousness. Instead, Sartre says it is phenomenologically *as if* the objects of consciousness determine consciousness. Consciousness itself retains its autonomy:

> Everything happens as if we lived in a world whose objects, in addition to their qualities of warmth, odour, shape, etc., had the qualities of repulsive, attractive, delightful, useful, etc., and as if these qualities were forces having a certain power over us. (58)[142]

'As if' is the crucial expression in this passage. Sartre's point is that this is not in fact true. Consciousness is a free spontaneity which perpetually chooses its objects. This idea is crucial to the development of Sartre's existential phenomenology. It is a premise for the controversial thesis of *Sketch for a Theory of Emotions* that we choose our own emotions and it anticipates the definition of 'consciousness' in terms of freedom in *Being and Nothingness* according to which there is no situation in which a consciousness does not have a choice. Freedom for Sartre is a disposition to make choices and consciousness possesses this disposition so long as it exists. Because consciousness is not subject to exterior causation, consciousness's choices are not determined but genuinely spontaneous.

No such real 'forces' as those mentioned in the passage just quoted are revealed by phenomenological investigation. One is reminded of Wittgenstein's insistent advice to 'look and see' in philosophy, rather than accept generalisations in a preconceived, taken-for-granted way.

Sartre says pre-reflective consciousness is a 'totality' (58) which has no need of being completed. Two items sometimes thought by philosophers and psychologists to be 'inside' consciousness, or to be part of its structure, lie 'outside' it: the 'me' and the objects of consciousness. The 'me' is one object of consciousness amongst others.

In this way the critique of psychology leads Sartre to the same conclusion as his phenomenology of the self:

> The me must not be sought in the states of unreflected consciousness, nor behind them. The me appears only with the reflective act. (59–60)[143]

The me is called by Sartre a 'noematic correlate' (60). As we have seen (p. 3 above) the noema, or noematic correlate, in Husserlian phenomenology is the intended content of an act of consciousness. So Sartre, in these pages, is standing Husserl on his feet. Far from the me being a subject or source of consciousness, the me is an object for consciousness of a particular type: reflective consciousness.

Sartre conceives of himself as having effected a radical shift in phenomenology: the abolition of the transcendental ego and its replacement by the me as object. The implications of this shift, if Sartre has been successful, are very great. The transcendental ego was after all the ground of consciousness and of the world according to Husserl. It remains for Sartre to say what sort of object the me is, and for us to evaluate that positive account.

3 The constitution of the ego

The ego for Sartre is essentially a unity. The fundamental error of Husserl's phenomenology of the self is that, when pushed to its logical conclusions, it bifurcates the ego into subject and object. In a sense there is an I and a me, but the I and the me are not subject and object. Rather, they are both objects but the appearance of their being two is an illusion. They are in fact two aspects of one reality: the psycho-physical whole which each of us essentially is:

> We begin to get a glimpse of the fact that the I and the Me are only one. We are going to try to show that this ego, of which I and Me are but two aspects, constitutes the ideal and indirect (noematic) unity of the infinite series of our reflected consciousness. (60)[144]

We have not yet reached the stage of the argument where the me is identified with the psycho-physical whole that I am. Here the me as it appears to me depends upon the unity of consciousness. Sartre draws from the fact of the unity of consciousness the conclusion that there can be only one self per consciousness. In this he is right if consciousnesses are individuated through their owners.

Nevertheless, the psycho-physical me is already implicitly introduced in the way Sartre draws the I/me distinction. He says:

1   'The I is the ego as unity of actions' (60).[145]

but also

2   'The me is the ego as the unity of states and qualities' (60).[146]

'Ego' here is Sartre's word for that human being who each of us is. A kind of dualism is being retained here but it is hardly Husserlian, still less Cartesian. It is the minimal intuitive psycho-physical dualism which makes the posing of the 'mind–body problem' possible. 'I' is the name of the human being *qua* agent and 'me' is the name of the human being *qua* thinker. The two personal pronouns may be given this use because one and the same human being may be understood under two sorts of description: physical descriptions which imply agency and psychological descriptions which imply mentality. Sartre is aware that there exists a variety of dependencies between the possibility of each of these descriptions, and perhaps for that reason he says the I/me distinction is at root 'functional' or 'grammatical':

> The distinction that one makes between the two aspects of one and the same reality seems to us simply functional, not to say grammatical. (60)[147]

Wittgenstein and Ryle could readily agree that a grammatical distinction between 'I' and 'me' could lead to a mistaken ontological distinction between the human being who one is and a hypostatised subjective ego. Indeed, Sartre's replacement of the Husserlian subject by the human being is highly suggestive of the neo-Aristotelian advocacy of the whole person as the subject of thought and action by Merleau-Ponty, Wittgenstein, Ryle, Strawson and others. Strawson for example thinks when I talk about myself I am not talking about my self.

When Sartre says the distinction is functional he means we have it because it is useful to us. Human beings both think and act so it is useful to be able to distinguish a person *qua* thinker from that person *qua* agent.

The problem that runs through this account, however, is that the 'I'/'me' grammatical distinction does not coincide with the thinker/agent distinction or ordinary (French or English) language. I can say 'I am running' and 'I am thinking' or I can reply 'Me' to 'Who was the runner?' or 'Who was the thinker?' If Sartre is using the terms stipulatively, his substantial point may still stand. 'I' and 'me' are used to refer to a unitary human being. They are used to refer to the human being who uses them by the human being who uses them when he knows who he is referring to.

4 Consciousness and the ego

Sartre's account of the relationship between consciousness and the ego is highly Kantian. Sartre distinguishes two kinds of unity which consciousness possesses (which should not be confused with the view that consciousness is two unities or anything of that sort). These are:

1   The immanent unity of consciousness.
2   The transcendent unity of consciousness.

These correspond roughly to what Kant calls the transcendental unity of consciousness and the empirical unity of consciousness. Sartre's transcendent unity is close to Kant's empirical unity, and Sartre's immanent unity is close to Kant's transcendental unity.[148] Sartre defines the immanent unity of consciousness as follows:

> [This is] the flux of consciousness constituting itself as the unity of itself. (60)[149]

and the transcendent unity of consciousness in this way:

> states and actions (60–1)[150]

So by 'immanent unity of consciousness' Sartre means what has traditionally counted as the unity of consciousness. The expression designates consciousness as a unity irrespective of the changing states of consciousness. By 'transcendent unity of consciousness' Sartre means the set of states of consciousness and actions which form a unity by being the states and actions of one and the same person. The first kind of unity counts as immanent because consciousness is immanent to itself. It constitutes itself as a unity and is directly aware of all of its own states. The second kind of unity counts as transcendent because a person is not directly aware of all of his or her past, present and future states (at one time). In this sense the transcendent unity of consciousness transcends the consciousness of it. It is possible to grasp Sartre's meaning intuitively or pre-philosophically here. There is a distinction between, on the one hand, one's own present consciousness, which is a unity in the traditional sense – it is necessarily not more than one – and on the other hand the unity of oneself as a person constituted by all the states one is ever in and all the actions one ever performs. If these are all performed by one and the same person then they too form a unity.

We need to raise now the question of the ego's relations to these two kinds of being. Sartre says:

> The ego is the unity of states and actions. (61)[151]

Prima facie this is straightforwardly to identify the ego with the transcendent unity of consciousness, but this appearance is misleading. It is possible to think of one's states and actions in two ways. They can be thought of as a unity *tout court* or they can be thought of as a unity *qua* mine, and it is this second sense which Sartre is trying to capture by calling them the 'ego' and not simply a 'transcendent unity'. Indeed, Sartre says of the ego:

> It is the unity of transcendent unities and transcendent itself. (61)[152]

It might be objected to Sartre that one's states and actions always form a unity, so why invoke the ego to be the unity of unities? An argument may be constructed to give point to Sartre's distinction.

Consider any two states (or actions). If they are both states of one and the same person then they thereby form a unity, and so on for any such states. However, now consider the unity of all such unities; the set of all sets of states of one and the same person. Sartre uses the term 'ego' to designate precisely that set of sets, or unity of unities.

The ego is thus transcendent (but not transcendental) because it is the unity of transcendent unities. Sartre provides no argument for this, but it could be plausibly maintained that any unity of transcendent entities would itself have to be transcendent. If some states transcend consciousness, then the set of such transcendent states transcends consciousness.

Am I an ego? Reasons are available for answering positively and negatively. I am not my ego because my ego is only how I appear to myself or how I think of myself. I seem to myself to be an ego in reflecting consciousness. I am my ego because as Sartre famously maintains, a person is the sum of their actions, and my ego is the unity of my actions. It would seem to follow that I am my ego to the extent to which I think of myself as I am.

Sartre draws an analogy between the ego and the objects of pre-reflective consciousness. Just as pre-reflective consciousness achieves its synthetic unity through being a set of acts directed towards an intentional object, so reflective consciousness achieves its unity by being a set of acts directed towards the ego. The ego is an intentional object of reflective consciousness:

> It is a transcendent pole of synthetic unity, like the object pole of the unreflected attitude, except that this pole appears solely in the world of reflection. (61)[153]

There is a further point to this analogy. Just as the retention of the perception of a series of 'aspects' of an object has to be 'read into' the perception of some present consciousness of an intentional object of pre-reflective consciousness to make that object into a unity truly called 'a physical object', so my states and actions are synthesised by reflective consciousness into a consciousness of myself. Both the intentional object of pre-reflexive consciousness and the ego of reflexive consciousness are object poles of consciousness. Their role is in the achievement by consciousness of the experience of objectivity.

That, in outline, is Sartre's positive account of the ego, but more remains to be said. Sartre provides us with considerable phenomenological description of the nature of the unity of the ego. We may consider this under three headings: (i) states, (ii) actions, (iii) qualities.

i States

Implicit in Sartre's account is a distinction between four sorts of mental state. To use a partly non-Sartrean vocabulary, we may mark these categories: corrigible and incorrigible mental states, and dispositional and occurrent mental states. I define them as follows:

1   A person is in an incorrigible mental state if, and only if, that person is in that state then that person knows they are in that state.
2   A person is in a corrigible mental state if and only if, if that person is in that state then that person may or may not know they are in that state.
3   A person is in an occurrent mental state if and only if there is some datable period t1 … t2 during all of which time some event is happening which constitutes that person's being in a mental state.
4   A person is in a dispositional mental state if and only if there is some datable period during which they have a tendency to be in an occurrent mental state irrespective of whether they are in that occurrent state.

Sartre says:

> The state appears to reflective consciousness. (61)[154]

which does not entail that if S is a mental state then S always appears to reflection but does entail that if S is a mental state then S is a possible object of reflection. The non-entailment is to Sartre's purpose because he maintains that there are pre-reflexive states. That if S is a mental state then S may appear to conscious reflection is also to Sartre's purpose because Sartre repudiates the classic notion of the unconscious. If for any S, S is a possible object of reflection then it is impossible that there are states in principle inaccessible to conscious reflection.

Sartre maintains that in reflection it is possible to be directly aware of a mental state one is in:

> The state is given to it, and is the object of a concrete intuition. If I hate Pierre, my hatred of Pierre is a state that I can apprehend by reflection. (61)[155]

So a state may be given phenomenologically to perception in an immediate or direct way. It is possible to apprehend it, in at least some respect, just as it is. As Sartre puts it, the state is 'real' (61). This is not to suggest that no preconception is brought to bear on one's mental states in reflection on them, but to point to the fact that phenomenologically there is no appearance/reality distinction in the apprehension of a mental state. For example, if I consciously pay attention to my pain then what I apprehend is my pain as I experience it.

That phenomenologically there is no appearance/reality distinction does not entail that I cannot be mistaken about what kind of mental state I am in, because some of my mental states are dispositional. Being given phenomenologically as it is does not imply being given incorrigibly in any other way:

> Is it therefore necessary to conclude that the state is immanent and certain? Surely not. We must not make of reflection a mysterious and infallible power, nor believe that everything reflection attains is indubitable because attained by reflection. (61)[156]

Reflection suffers from two sorts of fallibility according to Sartre: fallibility with regard to 'validity' (61–2) ('droit' TE 45) and with regard to 'fact' (61–2) ('fait' TE 45). Sartre does not spell out the distinction but it amounts to this. If I make a mistake of *validity* in the exercise of reflection then I either ascribe to my state properties which it lacks or fail to ascribe to the state properties which it possesses. It is consistent with my making this kind of mistake that I nevertheless judge correctly that it is that mental state that I am in. However, if I make a mistake of *fact* in the exercise of reflection then I think I am in one kind of mental state when I am in another and so misidentify the mental state that I am in. Whether this distinction is tenable depends *inter alia* upon the criteria for the individuation of mental states. They must not depend upon the phenomenological properties of a mental state, or neither kind of mistake could be made.

Sartre supplies a case where I may be mistaken about the kind of mental state that I am in. It rests on the distinction between an occurrence and a disposition. Here is the occurrence:

> I see Pierre, I feel a sort of profound convulsion of repugnance and anger at the sight of him (I am already on the reflective level): the convulsion is consciousness. (62)[157]

The phenomenological content of this occurrent anger is given incorrigibly as an object of reflection. I cannot be mistaken about the existence and nature of its felt qualities. However, here is the disposition:

> But is this experience of repugnance hatred? Obviously not. Moreover, it is not given as such. In reality I have hated Pierre a long time and I think that I shall hate him always. An instantaneous consciousness of repugnance could not, then, be my hatred. (62)[158]

Anger and hatred are not the same. Anger, or at least the feeling of anger, is an occurrent experience, but hatred is a long-term disposition. Hatred is a disposition to anger. Although I cannot be mistaken about the nature of my feeling of anger when I reflect on it consciously, I may mistake it for hatred. I may mistake a single occurrence of anger for the disposition of hatred. However, if I conclude from my feeling anger that I hate Pierre, I may or may not be correct in that. This is what the corrigibility of the state consists in. Clearly, this leaves room for my being correct in judging that I hate Pierre on the basis of feeling anger towards him. This is precisely because hatred is a disposition to feel anger. As Sartre puts it, the disposition is given through the occurrence. It is through the occurrence that epistemological access to the disposition is possible:

> My hatred appears to me at the same time as my experience of repugnance. (62)[159]

Two related conclusions follow. Hatred is not a content of consciousness, as, say, a feeling of anger is, and hatred is not an incorrigibly known mental state, but a feeling of anger is. The first is presented here:

> Hatred is not of consciousness. (63)[160]

The corrigibility of first person singular ascriptions of anger is implicitly suggested by Sartre when he says this about anger:

> It overflows the instantaneousness of consciousness, and it does not bow to the absolute law of consciousness for which no distinction is possible by appearance and being. (63)[161]

So, is Sartre here abdicating his rather Cartesian view about the incorrigibility of the mental? I think not. He retains the incorrigibility thesis about occurrent mental states but rejects it about dispositional mental states. For Sartre, only occurrent mental states belong to consciousness, so the traditional Cartesian view of the incorrigibility of mental states is to that extent retained. As Sartre puts it:

> It is certain that Pierre is repugnant to me. But it is and always will remain doubtful that I hate him. (64)[162]

We may leave on one side the objection that it might not be Pierre who is the object of repugnance, even though the misidentification of the intentional object makes the judgement that I am in a state of being angry at Pierre a corrigible state.

ii The constitution of actions

Understanding Sartre on action requires an appreciation of a pair of distinctions which he draws between

1   'active consciousness' (68)

and

2   'spontaneous consciousness' (68)

and between

1   'actions [...] in the world of things' (69)

and

2   'psychical actions' (69).[163]

Sartre does not say what these two distinctions consist in, but it is important to find ways of making them more precise because in their application they mark an important departure from Husserl. Husserl includes no account of physical action in his description of the ego so, *a fortiori*, no account of what Sartre calls 'actions in the world of things'. Of course, Husserl's human being of the natural attitude is an agent, but a phenomenology of action is not taken up into Husserl's transcendental phenomenology of the self. Bodily actions are suspended by the *epoché*.

Sartre says drawing the distinction between active and spontaneous consciousness is one of the most difficult tasks of phenomenology. It is perhaps made peculiarly difficult for Sartre because he is unwilling to allow that acts of consciousness have causes. The distinction has to be made out in terms of the properties of the acts of consciousness themselves. In devising a theory of action, if not a phenomenology of action, it is important to distinguish between on the one hand pure randomness and on the other hand acting freely. If my actions were utterly random events with no causes then arguably we should have to give up calling them 'my' actions at all, or at least 'free' actions. This is because acting freely partly consists in being the cause of one's own actions. An account of the agent is needed which allocates the agent a strong causal role in the occurrence of their own actions.

It is partly possible to construct the notion of such an agent by mentioning only items to be met with in consciousness of the sort Sartre describes. For example, suppose *reasons* are items which exist within consciousness. Then it would be possible to distinguish spontaneous mental acts from active mental acts as follows:

1   A mental act is spontaneous if and only if it has an effect but no cause.
2   A mental act is active if and only if it has an effect and has a cause of a special type, viz. a reason.

Whether Sartre may consistently accept this depends upon whether what reasons are may be specified entirely by talking about consciousness. That may be doubted. If reasons exist wholly or partly outside consciousness then Sartre cannot consistently mark the distinction in this way because such a reason is a cause of a mental act outside consciousness and he thinks there is none.

Sartre's second distinction presents less of a problem. We may say:

1　An action is an action in the world of things if and only if it is physical.

and

2　An action is a psychical action if and only if it is mental.

This distinction uses a physical/mental distinction in an unexplicated way. Phenomenologically a physical/mental distinction may be drawn between what is presented through *Abschattungen* and what is not. There is an intuitive but phenomenologically complex difference between, say, moving one's arm and thinking. From now on I shall call actions in the world 'physical' actions and psychical actions 'mental actions' or 'mental acts'.

Sartre argues that both mental and physical actions are transcendent. If x is transcendent then x has at least the following property: x is not exhausted by the consciousness of it. So if x is the intentional object of some act of consciousness, x is not just an intentional object. Sartre thinks we will be more readily convinced that physical actions are transcendent than that mental actions are. He claims about physical actions:

> We would like to remark that concerted action is first of all [...] a transcendent. That is obvious for actions like 'playing the piano', 'driving a car', 'writing', because the actions are 'taken' in the world of things. (68–9)[164]

Sartre is right to designate action of this sort 'transcendent' because unless some strong idealism is true then my playing the piano is not nothing over and above my consciousness of playing the piano. If the intentional object of my consciousness at that time is my playing the piano then there is more to my action of playing the piano than being the intentional object of my consciousness. To put it in phenomenological terms, my action transcends the horizon of my consciousness. Sartre's account is true of physical actions. They transcend consciousness.

However, Sartre wishes to persuade us that mental actions are transcendent in a parallel sense. As he puts it:

> But purely psychical actions like doubting, reasoning, meditating, making a hypothesis, these too must be conceived as transcendences. (69)[165]

Again, Sartre is right about this. The act of reasoning or doubting is not exhausted by one's consciousness of it, and there is more to such actions than being intentional objects.

This is not to suggest that there are properties of either mental or physical acts which are in principle inaccessible to phenomenological description (though that may be independently true). It is to suggest that there is more to both kinds of action than may be apprehended in a single act of awareness of them. What they are cannot be grasped directly all at once. This is what Sartre means when he says:

> What deceives us here is that action is not only the noematic unity of a stream of consciousness: it is also a concrete realisation. (69)[166]

The *noema* is the intentional content of an act of consciousness; that which is meant or intended by that act. Mental and physical actions are not identifiable with any single noematic correlate of consciousness. They are constructed out of them.

Indeed, actions for Sartre have the following phenomenological components:

1   'noematic unity' (69)
2   'concrete realisation' (69)
3   'time' (69)
4   'articulations' (69)
5   'moments' (69).[167]

Each of these needs defining in relation to action:

1   An action is a noematic unity if and only if it is an intentional object.
2   An action has a concrete realisation if and only if there is something which it consists in for that action to occur.
3   An action is temporal if and only if it endures through some finite duration t1 ... t2.
4   An action has articulations if and only if it has empirical properties.
5   An action has moments if and only if it has essential properties.

Even though in any act of awareness of an action not all the properties of that action are given to consciousness, the action is apprehended as the whole action that it is. Consciousness grasps the action as the unity that it is without apprehending all its properties. Sartre thinks a necessary condition for this holistic achievement of consciousness is that there be several acts of consciousness (directed either towards that action or to others of the same type) each of which is the direct apprehension of at least one of the moments of that action. This facilitates the consciousness of that action as a unity for consciousness:

To these moments correspond concrete, active consciousnesses, and the reflection which is directed on the consciousnesses apprehends the total action in an intuition which exhibits it as the transcendent unity of the active consciousness. (69)[168]

This account takes Sartre some way towards distinguishing spontaneous occurrences within consciousness from mental actions. For example, catching a glimpse of something in the shadows is a momentary occurrence in consciousness. It is not the reflected unity of an action. But the methodical doubt of Descartes in the *Meditations* is a series of mental actions.

Mental and physical actions are partly constitutive of the ego for Sartre. This is a decisive break with Husserl, whose transcendental ego is by no means constituted by actions. It is their subject.

iii *Qualities as facultative unities of states*

The ego according to Sartre is not transcendental but transcendent. It is not a subjective, contentless, pole of consciousness but a unity constituted by states and actions. Sartre also insists that the ego is partly constituted by dispositions so he reintroduces the idea of a disposition in his explanation of what a quality is. Sartre tries to treat a quality as 'an intermediary between' (70) states and actions, but in fact much of what he discusses under 'qualities' is not distinct from what he discusses under 'states'. Indeed, mental qualities are identical with those mental states which are dispositional. Sartre says:

The ego [...] is directly the transcendent unity of states and actions. Nevertheless there can exist an intermediary between actions and states: the quality. (70)[169]

A quality is made up of the following phenomenological components for Sartre:

1 'an intermediary' (70)
2 'a disposition' (70)
3 'a transcendent object' (70)
4 '[a] substratum' (70)
5 'a relation of actualisation' (70)
6 'a potentiality' (70)
7 'a virtuality' (70)
8 '[a] unity of objective passivities' (70).[170]

Each of these needs defining as a putative property of a quality:

1 A quality is an intermediary between an occurrent state and an action if and only if it is not identical with either that state or that action and it makes possible both.

2   A quality is a disposition if and only if it is a tendency or a propensity for a certain state to obtain or for a certain action to occur.
3   A quality is a transcendent object if and only if it is not exhausted by the consciousness of it (i.e. it is something over and above an intentional object).
4   A quality is a substratum if and only if it is both an intermediary and a disposition.
5   A quality enters into a relation of actualisation if and only if it is a disposition realised by at least one state or at least one action.
6   A quality is a potentiality if and only if it is logically possible that it enters into a relation of actualisation.
7   A quality is a virtuality if and only if it admits of an appearance/reality distinction.
8   A quality is a unity of objective passivities if and only if it is a mind (consciousness)-independent potentiality which admits of more than one realisation.

I assume that each of (1)–(8) is singularly necessary for x's being a quality, and that (1)–(8) are jointly sufficient. Sartre provides us with the following examples of kinds of quality:

> Naturally, faults, virtues, tastes, talents, tendencies, instincts, etc., are of this type. (71)[171]

So the ego is the unity not only of (occurrent) states and actions but of qualities too. This marks a significant departure from the Husserlian phenomenology of the self because Husserl's transcendental ego and the transcendental field of consciousness opened up by the *epoché* contain no dispositions.

5 The ego as the pole of actions, states and qualities

Sartre's phenomenology of the self entails a description of the relation of the ego to its actions, states and qualities which putatively eschews any commitment to the doctrine that the ego is the transcendent subject of these.

Sartre draws a distinction between the psychic and consciousness. Consciousness is a series of mental acts unified by their intentional objects. The psychic in contrast lies entirely on the side of the intentional object. The psychic for Sartre is not a constituent of consciousness but an object for consciousness. It lies outside consciousness and consciousness is directed towards it. Indeed,

> The psychic is the transcendent object of reflexive consciousness. (71)[172]

Crucially, Sartre claims the ego belongs to the psychic, not to consciousness. The ego is not a part of consciousness, nor is it the subject of consciousness – that which is conscious. On the contrary, amongst the transcendent objects given to consciousness there exists the ego. Indeed, it is that which makes possible the synthetic unity of the psychic. The question now arises of the relation of the ego to the synthetic unity of the psychic. There is a particular account which could be invoked here which Sartre is keen to avoid. It is one derived from Husserl's account of synthetic unity. Sartre quotes from Husserl's *Ideas* I:

> Predicates, however, are predicates of 'something'. This something also belongs to the nucleus in question and obviously cannot be separated from the nucleus. It is the central point of unity of which we were speaking earlier. It is the point of attachment for predicates, their support. But in no respect is it a unity of the predicates in the sense of some complex, in the sense of some linkage of predicates, even if one cannot set it beside them, nor separate it from them: just as they are its predicates, unthinkable without it and yet distinguishable from it.
>
> (*Ideas* §131)(72–3)[173]

There is a drastic mistake which runs through Husserl's thinking here which needs to be rectified before we are in a position to examine Sartre's criticisms. Husserl has failed to distinguish between predicates and properties. A property is something that pertains to something, so something's properties are its characteristics, but a predicate is not that. A predicate is a word sense or set of word senses which may be used to ascribe a property to something. Paradigmatically, a predicate is an indicative sentence minus its grammatical subject. It therefore makes no sense at all for Husserl to say predicates are 'of something' or for there to be 'a point of attachment for predicates' or 'a support' for them.

However, what Husserl wants to say is clear enough. He is presenting a neo-Lockean account of the relationship between an object and its properties. Properties, logically, are properties of something and Husserl calls this something a 'nucleus'. The nucleus is the bearer of properties or what the properties are properties of. Husserl expressly excludes from his account the possibility that what makes the properties of an object a unity, properties of one and the same object, is their relation to one another. Even if the nucleus *qua* nucleus depends on its properties, and even if the properties *qua* properties depend upon the nucleus, any properties and any nucleus are distinct from one another. In particular, it is not possible to correctly regard the nucleus as any kind of 'construction' out of its properties. It is Husserl's view that properties would be unthinkable as such without the existence of a nucleus as their bearer (and presumably the nucleus would be unthinkable without properties to bear).

Sartre thinks this whole account of the relationship between an object and its properties is mistaken, and may lead us into a mistaken account of what synthetic unity is. Sartre's answer to the question: In virtue of what is a set of properties properties of one and the same object? is that they are properties of each other and it does not make sense to talk about an object as something over and above its properties. He thinks it both false and phenomenologically illegitimate to postulate a nucleus or substratum as that which bears properties but which is not itself a property. At best, the postulation of such a nucleus is redundant:

> An indissoluble synthetic totality which could support itself would have no
> need of a supporting X. (73)[174]

Sartre says for a set of properties to be properties of one object they must be
concretely analysable, that is, it must not in reality be possible to separate one
property from another. It is no obstacle to the unity of the properties as the
object that they be analysable in thought. Indeed any synthetic unity may be
intellectually analysed by a process of abstraction: thinking of one property or
sub-set of properties of an object without thereby thinking of other properties of
that object.

To emphasise that there is no need to postulate an unknowable 'X' or nucleus
for the properties to inhere in Sartre invites us to consider the case of a melody.
The suggestion is that we will perhaps be more tempted to postulate the existence of a substratum in the case of a physical object than in the case of a
musical object. In the case of a melody, something's being a melody depends
upon the real inseparability of its notes and other musical properties. Sartre says
it would be useless to postulate a nucleus in such a case. He does not say why, but
I think a reason may be adduced.

Although both melodies and physical objects endure through time, a melody
typically changes its properties (at least its macroscopic properties) more rapidly
than a physical object. One note, for example, is replaced by another. Because
the notes are not sustained throughout the melody we are not as tempted to
postulate something which sustains them as we are in the case of the compara-
tively enduring properties of a physical object, its shape, size, or even colour for
example.

It is by reference to the melody as a whole that we recognise a particular note
as part of the melody, and not by reference to some unknowable nucleus which
supports all the notes. The melody consists in the notes in the relations in which
they stand to one another.

Sartre takes it then that there are severe philosophical objections to the notion
of a nucleus, substratum or object 'X' which bears the properties of an object.
As the account of the object–property relation offered by Husserl is mistaken,
Sartre is unwilling to extend it to the particular case of the ego's relation to its
actions, states and qualities:

> For these very reasons we shall not permit ourselves to see the ego as a sort
> of X-pole which would be the support of psychic phenomena. (74)[175]

The relation of the ego to its states, actions and qualities may be described in
this way: Ontologically it is nothing over and above them, but phenomenologically it is their unity. It is them considered as a unity.

Sartre amends the metaphor of the ego being a 'support' of its states by
saying:

The ego is nothing outside of the concrete totality of states and actions it supports. (74)[176]

Clearly there is a paradox here, but one Sartre intends. If A supports B then it is *prima facie* incoherent to suppose that A does not exist outside B or is nothing over and above B. But this is to assume A is not partly or wholly self-supporting. (After all, pillars may support a building but be part of it, and a building may be architecturally self-supporting like the beehive tombs near Mycenae.) Sartre invites us to relinquish the metaphor of the ego as an external 'support' of its states, to leave room for his positive account of the ego as that which the unity of actions and states consists in. A philosophical anticipation of the difference between Husserl and Sartre on the ego is the difference between Locke and Hume on the self.

6 The ego–world analogy

Not only is Husserl's account of the object–property relation mistaken, but any analogy between the ego and a physical object is a poor one. According to Sartre, the best analogy to illustrate the relation of the ego to its states is with the world and the objects in it.

Rather as Heidegger understands the world as the totality of significance within which *Dasein* understands itself, by 'world' Sartre means the synthetic totality of what exists, not the mere aggregate of existing things:

> If we were to seek for unreflected consciousness an analogue of what the ego is for consciousness of the second degree, we rather believe that it would be necessary to think of the world, conceived as the infinite synthetic totality of all things. (74)[177]

The world is for the unreflected consciousness what the ego is for reflected consciousness. Unreflected consciousness is directed towards objects united by and into a world. Reflected consciousness is directed towards actions, states and qualities united into the ego. The world is the synthetic totality of things. The ego is the synthetic totality of actions, states and qualities. The world is not a nucleus supporting the things in it, it is the synthetic unity of those things. The ego is not a nucleus supporting its states, it is the synthetic unity of those states:

> The ego is to psychical objects what the world is to things. (75)[178]

Sartre considers this analogy most apposite. The phenomenological structure of the world–things relation is of the same type as the ego–states relation. The common and neo-Kantian name for both is 'synthetic unity'.

However, there is an important disanalogy between the two which Sartre wishes to warn us of. It is psychologically rather rare for the world to appear as the synthetic unity of things, but the ego invariably appears as the synthetic unity of states. Sartre does not mean that it is only, say in philosophy, that the world is conceived in this way. He means that the world is typically not given to us as that kind of unity. We are usually engaged with particular objects. However, in reflection we are always aware of the unity of states:

> But the appearance of the World in the background of things is rather rare: special circumstances, described very well by Heidegger in *Sein und Zeit*, are necessary for it to 'reveal' itself. The ego, on the contrary, always appears at the horizon of states. (75)[179]

Heidegger's point is each object is what it is in virtue of internal relations to everything else. Appreciation of the world as this totality of significance is not at all common.

Sartre's analogy is apposite. The world is the 'horizon' of things as the ego is the 'horizon' of states. The thought of a thing existing independently of the world, the totality of things related *qua* significant totality, is just as much an intellectual abstraction as the thinking of a state of consciousness which is mine as something existing independently of me as the totality of my states, actions and qualities. Both kinds of abstraction are possible. I can think of this object as just this object – this peculiar unique one – without thereby thinking of it as a member of the totality of things which give it significance. I can analogously think of one of my mental states as just this peculiar unique mental state without thereby thinking of it as one of the synthetic totality of mental states truly called 'mine'.

Sartre describes the relation of the ego to its states pursuing further the parallel with objects and the world:

> Each state, each action is given as incapable of being separated from the ego without abstraction. (75)[180]

Equally, each thing is given as incapable of separation from the world without abstraction.

It is possible to abstract a mental state from the ego, but it is also possible, according to Sartre, to abstract the ego from its mental states. I can think of myself as separate from my mental states. Sartre says an example of this is the making of the judgement 'I am in love' (75) 'Je suis amoureux' (TE 58). However, I can never truly think of myself as separate from my mental states. It is presumably precisely this kind of abstraction which enables Husserl to mistakenly postulate the transcendental ego as the subject of consciousness.

In at least one sense it is possible to think of the world in abstraction from the totality of objects which comprise it. Then 'world' would either mean 'being' or 'existence'; the being of what is in abstraction from what it is, or else 'what is' but not 'what is' in the sense of what actually is but 'what is' in the sense of whatever is. It is not even clear that the idea of what is in this sense is epistemologically parasitic upon the possibility of the world as it is: the totality of actual things.

Sartre thinks both ego and world are given as transcendent. Ego and world are not nothing over and above the consciousness of them, nor are they exhausted by being the intentional objects of pre-reflexive and reflexive consciousness respectively.

7 Sartre and the Evil Genius

How Cartesian is the relation between the ego and its states as described by Sartre? Clearly, the self is the soul for Descartes and for Sartre the soul does not exist. *Prima facie*, the existence of the soul is open to at least the objections that Sartre has brought against Husserl's neo-Lockean account of the relation between an object and its properties. Descartes would be the last to concede that the soul is nothing over and above its conscious states. So, ontologically, Sartre is much more like Hume than Descartes on the self.

What of the knowledge each of us has of our own ego and its states? Descartes thinks such knowledge both indubitable and incorrigible and Sartre, up to a point, shares this picture. But only up to a point; to construe Sartre as a Cartesian about self-knowledge it is not sufficient to point out that he regards first-personal access to one's occurrent mental states as being privileged over third-person access or asymmetrical to that access (which he clearly does). By that criterion Wittgenstein and Davidson come out as Cartesian, which is grossly implausible. The point is that there is a logical gulf between the views of these philosophers and the Cartesian claims of infallibility and absolute transparency. Sartre, like Davidson, can claim, in general, that I grasp my conscious states fully and correctly and immediately (i.e. without need of empirical evidence). But I may deceive myself; I may be wrong about whether any two thoughts of mine have the same content; about whether, on expression, they have an ambiguous meaning; about whether the intentional modality of a thought is correctly expressed in 'achievement' terms or not (Do I perceive that p, or does it merely seem to me that p?).

In many respects Sartre is not only non-Cartesian but resolutely anti-Cartesian. In the developed philosophy of *Being and Nothingness* he rejects 'ideas', the notion that the mind is a substance, the notion that minds could continue to exist, just as they are, whether or not any surrounding material world or environment existed, indirect realism in perception and so on.

Admittedly, Sartre has already claimed that 'the certitude of the *Cogito* is absolute' (44) and this would make Sartre a kind of Cartesian if by 'cogito' he means Descartes' argument 'I am thinking; therefore I exist' but there is no textual evidence in the accompanying passage that he does mean this. If he did mean this, he would be undermining his own argument by dealing with the *cogito* as a 'reflective operation', giving priority to reflection over the consciousness reflected on; and there is evidence elsewhere that he does not mean this, for example: '[...] there is a pre-reflective cogito which is the condition of the Cartesian cogito'.[181]

We need to examine further an important departure by Sartre from

Cartesianism. It has already been partly anticipated in the discussion of the corrigibility of first person singular claims about dispositions (section 4.i above), but we need to follow Sartre in his further applications of the notion of corrigibility.

Sartre remarks about the ego:

> This transcendent totality participates in the questionable character of all transcendence. This is to say that everything given to us by our intuitions of the ego is always given as capable of being contradicted by subsequent intuitions. (75)[182]

It is one of Sartre's principles that if x is a transcendent object then any claim about the nature of x *qua* transcendent object is in principle falsifiable. This is because only descriptions of the phenomenological properties of what is directly given to consciousness are incorrigible, and it is part of the concept of a transcendent object that what it is is never entirely and directly given to consciousness. If this general principle is true, and if the ego as the unity of states is a transcendent object, then it follows that claims about the ego are corrigible. Sartre states the corrigiblity thesis in terms of intuitions. For any claim about the ego based on an intuition it is always in principle possible for there to exist some further intuition which would falsify that claim.

Clearly, from the corrigibility thesis it does not follow that knowledge of the nature of the ego is impossible (so long as knowing that one knows is not a condition of knowing). From the fact that I believe that p it does not follow that p is true, for most values of p, but this does not disqualify me from knowing that p. Also, the fact that any proposition is in principle revisable does not entail that one specific currently believed proposition is false. From the fact that any proposition may be reallocated a truth value it does not follow that it will be. In other words, Sartre's corrigibility thesis is consistent with the truth or falsity of any of our current beliefs about the ego (where 'or' is clearly to be read as in 'either p or not p but not both').

The corrigibility thesis applies only to our dispositional states. Sartre remains thoroughly Cartesian about our occurrent states. In other words, he thinks that all first person singular psychological ascriptions about dispositional states may be true or false if believed, but all first person singular psychological ascriptions about occurrent states are true if believed.

There is another respect in which Sartre breaks with Cartesianism. Sartre thinks that the clarity of a first person singular psychological judgement is no guarantee of its truth.

> For example, I can see clearly that I am ill-tempered, jealous, etc., and nevertheless I may be mistaken. (75)[183]

So, no matter how persuaded I may be, or how evident it may seem to me that I possess certain dispositions, it does not follow that I have them. There is always logical room for error.

Whether this position may be sustained depends upon how it is construed. It is true that from the fact that *p* seems evidently true it does not follow that *p*. Sartre is right that from the fact that I know I am in a particular occurrent state it does not follow that I am in a particular dispositional state – even where that type of occurrent state may be constitutive of that type of disposition. However, I may be sequentially acquainted with a series of qualitatively similar mental states in such a way that it logically follows that I am in a particular dispositional state. For example, as Sartre says, from the fact that I am angry it does not logically follow that I hate (if we follow Sartre in maintaining that being angry is an occurrence but hating is a disposition). Nevertheless, if hatred is a disposition to be angry then if I am angry at the same object a sufficient number of times then it will follow that I hate the object of my anger. (I leave aside the question of how many times I have to be angry for the disposition of hatred to be realised.)

Suppose I am directly and incorrigibly acquainted with a series of angry states directed towards a common object. Suppose I conclude on that basis that I hate that object. Arguably, then my belief that I hate that object is thereby true. It is not clear that knowledge of one's dispositions is logically incorrigible: that it would be contradictory or incoherent to deny one's beliefs about one's own dispositions.

Despite this reservation, it is clear that in many cases we are mistaken about our dispositions. From the fact that I feel tired it does not follow that I am tired. From the fact that I believe I am polite it does not follow that I am polite, and so on.

It follows that the nature of the ego, in so far as the ego is constituted by its dispositions, is dubitable. Any of us may be quite mistaken as to our natures in fundamental respects. However, Sartre does not wish us to conclude from this that each of us has a 'real me' or a 'true self'. On the contrary, we make ourselves what we are by our choices and actions. Our dispositions are themselves constantly open to revision by the thoughts and actions we commit ourselves to:

> This questionable character of my ego – or even the intuitional error that I commit – does not signify that I have a true me which I am unaware of, but only that the intended ego has in itself the character of dubitability (in certain cases, the character of falsehood). (76)[184]

Sartre's reluctance to postulate a 'true self' has two philosophical motivations. First, it would commit him to a notion of the unconscious: oneself as one really is, yet oneself as inaccessible to one's own acts of consciousness. Second, at least the existence of an immutable true self possessed of fixed traits of character would be inconsistent with the Sartrean thesis that each human essence is freely determined by that human being. Sartre wishes to repudiate any theory of the person on which personality is not determinable and revisable by the person. This repudiation is prerequisite to the self-defining humanity of *Being and Nothingness* and the public lecture *Existentialism is a Humanism*.

Descartes' Evil Genius may deceive me as to the contents of my memory, and this is a further reason why I may be mistaken about my dispositions. I conclude that I have a certain disposition by consulting my memory about certain occurrent states which would imply the existence of such a disposition. Memory is fallible so the claim that I have the disposition is fallible. Sartre agrees with Descartes therefore that I may not be mistaken about the phenomenological properties of my occurrent mental states, but remains thoroughly committed to the anti-Cartesian view that I may be systematically mistaken about my dispositions. As he puts it:

The power of the *malin génie* extends so far. (76)[185]

8 The certainty of the *cogito*

There is one respect, however, in which it is impossible for a person to be mistaken about their mental states, even those which are dispositional. This is with regard to whether they are that person's own mental states. If I am in a mental state and if I know that that mental state exists then I cannot be mistaken in my belief that it is mine.

This thesis of Sartre's is a conjunction of an incorrigibility thesis and an inalienability thesis. If p is incorrigible then if p is believed then p is true, but inalienability is a thesis about states: a state 'S' is inalienable if and only if it is necessarily a state of the person in that state, so that if a person is in a state of anger, for example, it is necessarily that person who is in that state and not another. The force of this rather tautological thesis is that no person may be in the mental state of someone else. The thesis must be construed as about the numerical and not the qualitative identity of mental states (or about token states not state types) because although 'if I am in a mental state that state is mine' is analytic, clearly it is logically possible that another person should be in a qualitatively similiar yet numerically distinct state.

Sartre's claim is that for any person and for any state for which the inalienability thesis is true, that person knows the inalienability thesis is true of him. We have to construe Sartre as holding that a person cannot consistently doubt the inalienability thesis in their own case, otherwise we ascribe to him the rather implausible view that each person mentally entertains the inalienability thesis.

Sartre advocates the conjunction of the incorrigibility and the inalienability theses by saying that the ego is not 'hypothetical' (76). He means: that I am the owner of my mental states is not a hypothesis. This is supposed to carry the implication that the proposition is not contingent and not empirical. If p is not contingent then p is necessary, and if p is not empirical then p is *a priori*, so it follows that the inalienability thesis is necessary and *a priori*.

Sartre is not committed to the view that the whole of his phenomenology of the ego is necessary and *a priori* but that the ego exists, and exists as the unity of one's mental states, would seem to have that status according to him:

In fact the ego is the spontaneous transcendent unification of our states and our actions. In this capacity, it is no hypothesis. I do not say to myself 'Perhaps I have an ego', as I may say to myself 'Perhaps I hate Pierre'. (76)[186]

Here Sartre makes the guarded claim that the ego is only inalienable and incorrigible under a certain description, viz. 'the spontaneous transcendent unification of our states'. This leaves room for knowledge of the ego to be corrigible under other descriptions of the ego. For example, it leaves room for me to be mistaken about my disposition to hate Pierre.

It follows that Sartre has retained two central components of the Cartesian conception of the person. I cannot be mistaken or consistently doubt whether I exist, and I cannot be mistaken about or consistently doubt what I am on a minimal psychological conception of my own nature. I am in fact an ego as the unification of a set of mental states. Descartes maintains a similar self-conception in this minimal respect: I am, he says, a thing that thinks.

Sartre and Descartes do, of course, offer radically dissimilar answers to the question: What thinks? For Descartes the thinker is the soul, but Sartre's rather Humean view of thinker makes the ego ontologically nothing over and above the set of its mental states: their unity. Unlike Descartes, Sartre offers no argument for this minimal incorrigibility thesis about the existence and essence of the ego but, clearly, Cartesian premises could be supplied.

That I am in a dispositional state is for Sartre a hypothesis (of mine). I take it there are two components in this claim. If I claim to have a certain disposition then this, if true, is contingently true, and is to be confirmed by experience. But even then any putative disposition may turn out not to obtain.

The ego has a rather Kantian and formal relation to its states for Sartre. Although ontologically the ego is exhausted by its states, formally it is what their being mine consists in:

I do not seek here a unifying meaning of my states. When I unify my consciousness under the title 'hatred', I add a certain meaning to them, I qualify them. But when I incorporate my states in the concrete totality me, I add nothing to them. (76)[187]

Sartre's point is that if I call one of my states 'hatred' then that is informative to me, because it could in principle turn out that a state of mine is not hatred. But if I call one of my states 'mine' then that is not informative because none of my states could turn out not to be mine.

If a state is hatred then something is true of it which does not obtain simply in virtue of its relations to other states. It has certain phenomenological properties constitutive of its being hatred. But if a state is one of mine then it has this status simply in virtue of its relation to other states of mine, that of being a member of that set. There is no additional phenomenological property which is constitutive of its being mine. A state of hatred *qua* hatred is phenomenologically distinct from states of mine which are not states of hatred, but a state of mine *qua* mine is not phenomenologically distinct from other states of mine. No new information is provided about one of my states (to me) by calling it mine. This is because the inalienability thesis is analytic.

Sartre considers three putative relations between an ego and its states. He rejects the first two and endorses the third. They are:

1   'emanation' (77)
2   'actualisation' (77)
3   'poetic production'. (77)[188]

Sartre says that emanation is the relationship of consciousness to emotion. Emanation is a spatial metaphor – for example the sun's rays may be thought of as 'emanating' from the sun. This is a metaphor which Husserl sometimes adopts in his descriptions of the transcendental ego's relations to its states. I take it that if B emanates from A then it is at least true that A is the source of B and B depends upon A for its existence.

Sartre says 'actualisation' is like the relation between a quality and a state. This means that the ego–state relation considered here is like the relation between an occurrent event and a disposition it realises. An ego may actualise or realise its states analogously.

Finally, by 'poetic production' is meant 'a relation of creation' (77). Normally, if A creates B then A is distinct from B but Sartre cannot intend this here because he is at pains to repudiate any view of the ego as distinct from its states. The 'creation' view of the ego is best viewed as the conjunction of four theses:

1   The ego is the unity of a set of mental states.
2   The ego is a spontaneity.
3   The ego is ontologically nothing over and above its states.
4   The ego is given as producing its states.

Sartre has provided sufficient argument against the idea that the ego is the subjective source of its mental states to feel entitled to reject the emanation view. It is less clear that the ego may not be a disposition for occurrent mental states to occur. Sartre supplies no direct refutation of this position, so one needs to be constructed from his views throughout the book.

The best Sartrean argument against the ego being a disposition relies on the premise that I am directly aware of my ego in reflexive consciousness, as the objective unity of my occurrent mental states. If Sartre is right about that, then it cannot be the case that the ego is a disposition realised by the obtaining of those states. The ego depends upon the states and the states depend upon the dispositions so the ego depends on the dispositions. If A depends upon B and B depends upon C then A depends upon C, but if A depends upon C, A cannot be identical with C unless 'depends on' is only the relation entailed by 'is identical with'. It follows that the ego is not a disposition.

Is the ego then a realisation of a disposition? The ego is the unity of states, both occurrent and dispositional. If an occurrent state is the realisation of a disposition, and if the ego is partly the unity of the dispositions themselves, then to that extent it makes sense to talk of the ego either as a complex of realisations of dispositions or as a unity of dispositions. In this sense Sartre has no good grounds for precluding the view that the ego is an 'actualisation'. This may all be consistent with his view of the ego's relation to its states as 'poetic production'.

9 Poetic production

Sartre says that the production by the ego of its states is a creation *ex nihilo*:

> This mode of creation is indeed a creation ex nihilo, in the sense that the state is not given as having formerly been in the me. (77)[189]

Sartre is making a phenomenological claim which is consistent with the states of the ego having causal conditions. He says the state is not given as present in the ego before its 'production'. This means that in reflexive consciousness of the ego and its states, if we are acquainted with one state we are not thereby acquainted with any cause of that state, for example, another state. One state, to use Sartre's quasi-Kantian term, exists 'spontaneously' and is then replaced by another state, so that any state is like, or appears as, a creation *ex nihilo*. For Sartre, this captures an important feature of how we appear to ourselves psychologically.

Sartre has already argued that there exists an epistemological gap between a disposition and its realisation, in the sense that, for example, I may be directly acquainted with my anger and not thereby acquainted with my hatred even if my anger is the occurrent realisation of my hatred as disposition. So I may know of the existence of my anger but be ignorant of or mistaken about the existence of my hatred. It follows that the anger is 'given as something new', or appears as a 'creation *ex nihilo*'.

This appearance depends upon my non-acquaintance with both the causal conditions of the state I am in and the disposition it realises:

> Even if hatred is given as the actualisation of a certain power of spite or hatred, it remains something new in relation to the power it actualises. (77)[190]

Given this spontaneity, or appearance of creation *ex nihilo* in the stream of one's mental states, the question arises of how the ego may exist and persist as the unity of such states over time. This, according to Sartre, is an achievement of reflexive consciousness. The ego is constituted or constructed out of states by reflexive acts of consciousness. I detect three stages to this process of ego-construction:

i   'the unifying act of reflection' (77)
ii   'a relation which traverses time backwards' (77)
iii   'the me (given) as the source of the state' (77)[191]

I shall say something about each of these in turn.

i The unifying act of reflection

Sartre explains this as follows:

> The unifying act of reflection fastens each new state, in a very special way,
> to the concrete totality me. (77)[192]

So, if I perform a unifying act of reflection I reflect on one of my states, but
reflect upon it as mine: that is, as a member of the set of mental states which *qua*
ego I am. The thought that this state is a member of that set called 'me' is read
into the apprehension of that state, or, to put it another way, the state is reflected
on under the description 'one of mine'. Clearly, either the recollection of
previous states of the set, or the anticipation of future states of the set or the
awareness of simultaneous but numerically distinct states of the set is implied by
the possibility of such a unifying act of reflection.

ii The relation traversing time backwards

Sartre realises this presupposition exists when he says:

> Reflection is not confined to apprehending the new state as attaching to this
> totality, as fusing with it: reflection intends a relation which traverses time
> backwards. (77)[193]

If some act of consciousness is the apprehension of some state at some time as a
member of some sequence of states then that act, or some subject of that act,
includes the knowledge or the belief that the series of states exists, and exists
over any time which includes the time of the apprehension of the state.

The account of the constitution of the ego Sartre offers is no different in
essentials from the account he gives of the constitution by consciousness of any
of its intentional objects. The ego is an object of consciousness, albeit consciousness of a special sort, viz. reflective consciousness. He says that consciousness
'intends' (77) the relation traversing time that constructs the ego. It is equally
clear that reflective consciousness 'intends' the ego, in the further sense that the
constructed ego is itself the intentional object of reflexive consciousness.

iii The me as the source of the state

Sartre says

> (the) relation [...] gives the me as the source of the state. (77)[194]

The result of the apprehension of a state as one of a set constitutive of 'me' or that is 'mine' is that I, as ego, appear as the source of my states. This appearance must be illusory or an important component of Husserl's doctrine of the transcendental ego would be true. Although states are the 'poetic production' of the ego, the ego is ontologically nothing over and above those states, or those states as a unity.

An important question arises here to which, so far as I can see, Sartre has no answer. If the ego is not the subjective source of my states but their unity, why should it appear as their source? If I am really the sum of my mental states why should I mistakenly take myself to be their subjective origin? This is an important question to answer not only for understanding the difference between Husserl and Sartre on the self but also for settling the difference between Descartes and Hume.

One possible answer, within the Sartrean framework, is that I mistakenly identify my previous mental states with myself as the ego-source of my present mental state. The force of this quasi-Humean construal of Sartre is that I am acquainted with a series of states S1 … Sn over time t1 … tn, but in the apprehension of, say, S2, the memory of S1 is retained. S1 no longer exists but in reflection it is tacitly assumed that I am in some sense the subject of my mental state and that my current state has an origin. If these two thoughts are not clearly distinguished, then, room is left for me to be assimilated to the states preceding S2. Just as Husserl's transcendental ego does not appear directly to present consciousness, so past states do not appear directly to present consciousness. This common property leaves open their assimilation, or the mistaking of one's past states for a transcendental ego. Sartre does not claim this, but it would not be inconsistent with his position to supplement it in this way.

In what sense exactly are mental states the poetic production of the ego? To understand this we need to clarify further the ontological status of the ego. By talking of the ego and its states we may be misled into thinking that the ego exists in addition to its states, which is false, and we must be careful that talking about the ego's states as its properties does not mislead us into taking the ego to be the subject or substantial bearer of those states, which is also false.

More misleading spatial metaphors are at work in our thinking about the ego. We may think of it as beside its states, or behind its states, or beneath its states, or visible through its states. Each of these tendencies needs to be resisted:

> The ego maintains its qualities through a genuine, continuous creation. Nevertheless, we do not finally apprehend the ego as a pure creative source beside the qualities. (78)[195]

It is impossible for an apprehension of the ego not to be the apprehension of a mental state because the ego is constructed out of mental states. Phenomenologically, the ego is not given as existing in addition to a set of mental states, so it is not given as a source of mental states. This is plausible because if A is the source of B then B depends upon A causally. That presupposes that B is distinct from A, but if B is distinct from A then A cannot be a construction out of B. The ego is a construction out of states so it is not the source or the origin of those states.

Sartre presents a thought experiment designed to convince us that the ego is exhausted by the existence of its states. He invites us to imaginatively remove its states one by one, and draw the conclusion that the ego would not exist as an imaginative residue once the process of subtraction is completed:

> It does not seem to us that we could find a skeletal pole if we took away, one after the other, all the qualities. (78)[196]

As is usually the case with thought experiments of this quasi-Kantian type, there are no non-question-begging grounds for maintaining that the residual entity exists or does not exist. If I claim to be unable imaginatively to think myself away as subject of my mental states but you claim to be able to do this, then this would seem to be a psychological difference between us; a difference in our powers of imagination or perhaps our preferences. Even if such an imaginative power were universal, that fact could only feature as a premise in an argument against the transcendental ego. Even then, from the fact that it is conceivable (even by everyone) that not-*p* it does not follow that not-*p*. It is consistent with the thought experiment that Sartre is right; that the transcendental ego does not exist. What Sartre lacks is a true premise which would validly yield this as conclusion:

> At the end of this plundering, nothing would remain: the ego would have vanished. (78)[197]

It begs the question to say that the thought experiment must have this result because the ego is just the unity of its states.

Sartre draws a distinction between the spontaneity of consciousness and the spontaneity of the ego. The spontaneity of consciousness is genuine but the spontaneity of the ego is a *pseudo-spontaneity*. Consciousness erroneously ascribes its own spontaneity to the ego, but the ego, being a passive object for consciousness, cannot itself exhibit that spontaneity.

Many questions are left unanswered here. Perhaps the most fundamental is: Why should we make such a profound mistake about our own nature as to ascribe the spontaneity of consciousness to the ego? Sartre only describes the putative pseudo-spontaneity of the ego, he does not say why it exists:

> But this spontaneity must not be confused with the spontaneity of consciousness. Indeed, the ego, being an object is passive. It is a question, therefore, of a pseudo-spontaneity which is suitably symbolised by the spurting of a spring, a geyser, etc. This is to say that we are dealing here with a semblance only. (79)[198]

The difference between the pseudo-spontaneity of the ego and the spontaneity of consciousness rests on the difference between the incorrigibility of claims about consciousness and a certain kind of corrigibility about the nature of the ego. As we have seen (p. 81 above) Sartre thinks that if I am in an occurrent mental state then I know I am in that state. Nevertheless I may be surprised by myself. For example I may be surprised that I am capable of hating my father (80). In such case I am surprised that I am capable of such a thought or emotion. I did not realise that I am the kind of person who is capable of being in such a mental state.

If I can be surprised at myself, according to Sartre, there must be, or appear to be, some kind of distinction between the ego and its states. An anomaly is discovered between the sort of state preceding the current state and the current state. The taken-for-granted I is the unity of previous states. The I at which I am surprised is the I as current object of reflection.

However, no genuine spontaneity may possess the structure of 'source and state'. Acts of consciousness are spontaneous because they have no subject and no cause. They spontaneously exist. The ego, as a construction out of such states, is a pseudo-spontaneity exactly because it has the apparent structure of 'source and state'. But if states had even an apparent source they could not be genuinely spontaneous. A genuine spontaneity has no cause: not even an apparent one.

In this sense the ego's production of its states is a poetic production. Its causal efficacy is fictional not literal. The real author of the states of the ego is consciousness. Indeed, consciousness is the author of the ego itself:

> The ego is an object [...] constituted by reflexive consciousness. (81)[199]

10 Interiority

If A constitutes B then A makes B what it is. Consciousness stands in two relations to the ego, one of them real, one of them illusory. The real relation is:

1   Consciousness constitutes the ego.

The illusory relation is:

2   The ego constitutes consciousness.

It is consciousness itself that is subject to the illusion. Consciousness takes itself to be constituted by the ego because:

> The order is reversed by a consciousness which imprisons itself in the world in order to flee from itself, consciousnesses are given as emanating from states, and states as produced by the ego. (81)[200]

In so far as Sartre is engaged in phenomenology there is no onus upon him to offer explanations, only descriptions. However, from a philosophical point of view we need to know how and why we come to be so systematically mistaken about our own nature, and why in particular consciousness wishes to flee from itself and imprison itself in objects. Sartre provides no answers to these questions. He merely contrasts what he takes to be the true order of dependence, the ego's dependence on consciousness, with what he takes to be the false order of dependence: consciousness's dependence on the ego. Sartre's account needs to be supplemented by an account of how this rather Buddhist status of the ego is possible.

According to Sartre a fundamental asymmetry obtains between consciousness and the ego. Consciousness is unaffected by anything outside itself, but the ego is affected by its own productions. This distinction requires careful formulation if it is to amount to a real distinction at all, perhaps more careful than the one Sartre presents:

> By virtue of this passivity the ego is capable of being affected. Nothing can act on consciousness, because it is cause of itself. But, on the contrary, the ego which produces undergoes the reverberation of what it produces. (82)[201]

Suppose 'A is the cause of itself' does not mean that A brings itself into existence but that if A is in some state 'S' then A has caused A to be in that state. This claim is then ambiguous between allowing and excluding a certain possibility. This possibility is that A be the cause of some second item 'B', or one of its states, and B, or some state of B caused by A, be the cause of A's state S. Then it would still remain true that A is the cause of A's state but only indirectly, or via B: A causes A to be in A's state by causing B to cause A to be in A's state.

I take that it is Sartre's view that precisely this possibility is excluded in the case of consciousness but admitted in the case of the ego. Consciousness causes its own states *tout court* but the ego causes its own productions and those productions of the ego cause the states of the ego.

I do not see that Sartre has good grounds for distinguishing productions of the ego from states of the ego, or, indeed, good grounds for introducing the concept of a production of the ego at all. If, as the following passage suggests, the productions of the ego are to be identified with its states and actions, then the productions of the ego are really constituents of the ego. But then the required contrast between the activity of consciousness and the passivity of the ego is not well drawn. If the ego is affected by a part of itself then arguably it is causing itself to be what it is and thereby possesses one of the essential characteristics of consciousness. This is a conclusion Sartre wishes to avoid but it is not excluded by:

> The ego is 'compromised' by what it produces. There a relation reverses itself: the action or the state returns upon the ego to qualify it. (82)[202]

Sartre requires an additional claim to mark the distinction successfully. For example the conjunction of:

1   Consciousness produces its states but those states have no effect on consciousness.

and

2   The ego produces its states but those states have an effect on the ego.

Sartre presents a version of (2) when he says:

> Each new state produced by the ego colours and tinges the ego slightly the moment the ego produces it. The ego is in some way spellbound by this action, it 'participates' with it. (82)[203]

But if what the ego produces is identical with what constitutes it, its parts, then it remains true that the ego, along with consciousness, falls under the description 'cause of itself'. The only real distinction made out by reference to causation is that expressed by (1) and (2) above, and Sartre has no explicit statement of (1).

Sartre ascribes the following properties to the ego:

1   'Everything the ego produces impresses it' (82)
2   'Only what it produces [affects it]' (82)
3   'The me can be transformed by external events' (82–3)
4   'The ego is an irrational synthesis of activity and passivity' (83)
5   'It is a synthesis of interiority and transcendence'. (83)[204]

I shall offer some definitions of the predicates used to ascribe properties (1)–(5) to the ego:

1   A produces B if and only if A causes B to exist.
2   A affects B if and only if A partly alters what B is.
3   A transforms B if and only if A wholly alters what B is.
4   A is active if and only if A is a cause but not an effect.
5   A is passive if and only if A is an effect but not a cause.
6   A is irrational if and only if A's description is contradictory.
7   A exhibits interiority if and only if A is both private and inalienable.
8   A is transcendent if and only if A is not exhausted by the present consciousness of it.

Using these definitions we may interpret the ascription of the five properties to the ego as follows:

1. Whatever the ego causes to exist partly alters what the ego is, so if the ego produces some states or actions then they were caused to exist by the ego but also contribute to making the ego what it is.

It is doubtful whether the doctrine of the causal efficacy of the ego (even if only apparent) may be shown to be consistent with the theory that the ego is the unity of its states. If A causes B then A is not B, but if A is the unity of (*inter alia*) B then A is ontologically nothing over and above (*inter alia*) B. This leads to the incoherent view that the ego both is and is not its states. In fairness to Sartre, he has claimed under (5) that the ego is an irrational synthesis.

2. Nothing alters what the ego is except what the ego has itself caused to be. Sartre claims the ego is only a pseudo-spontaneity, but there would seem to be a genuine spontaneity to an entity which is only affected by what it causes. If the ego is unaffected by whatever it does not cause but is itself a cause then it is active, and if the ego is active it is a spontaneity. If A causes B to be and thereby B alters what A is then A indirectly causes A to be what A is, and in that respect A is a cause of its own nature. Again, this entails a genuine spontaneity of the ego. The ego causes its states to be but its states alter what it is; so to that extent the ego is itself the cause of what it is. This barely suffices to distinguish the structure of the ego from the structure of consciousness.

3. Sartre considers as an objection to the immunity of the ego to any causal influences other than its own effects the claim that it may be transformed by events external to it. He gives the following examples of 'external events':

> catastrophe, mourning, trickery, change in social environment. (83)[205]

What Sartre has in mind is that I, as ego, may be caused to be in a different state by one of these sorts of events, even though none of them is the ego nor any part of it. That would violate the principle that only two sorts of causal relation are possible with regard to the ego: It either causes its states to be or its states alter what it is. An additional feature of the ego exists if what states the ego has or is in may be determined by events external to it.

Sartre's reply is that an external event may have this causal efficacy only in so far as it stands in a special relation to the ego:

> But this is so only in so far as external events are for the me the occasion of states or actions. (83)[206]

Sartre does not spell out exactly what it is for an event to be 'for the me', nor what it is for an event to be the 'occasion' of states or actions.

Suppose an event is for me if and only if that event is the intentional object of the me. We should rather say 'pseudo-intentional object' because only consciousness and not the ego exhibits intentionality.

Suppose further that an event is the occasion of states or actions of the ego if and only if the ego is in that state or exercises that action only if that event occurs.

We may now say that the ego is influenced by external events in just those two senses. The ego takes external events as pseudo-intentional objects, and there are no states that the ego is in when and only when certain external events occur. We could call this latter relation 'pseudo-causation' because there is no direct causal relation between an external event and a state of the ego: only a correlation. It is only *qua* pseudo-intentional objects of the ego that external events may be the occasion of state changes of the ego.

4. The ego is active if the ego is a cause but not an effect and the ego is passive if the ego is an effect but not a cause. Sartre claims that the ego is an irrational synthesis of activity and passivity. Now, *prima facie*, 'active' and 'passive' are mutually exclusive predicates because if A is active then, *qua* active, A is not an effect, but if A is passive then A is an effect, and if A is passive then, *qua* passive, A is not a cause but if A is active then A is a cause. Two mutually exclusive predicates cannot, logically, apply to the same entity at the same time and in the same respect, so it seems logically impossible that the ego in Sartre's sense should exist.

This irrationality, or appearance of contradiction, may be dispelled by drawing a distinction between how the ego appears to consciousness and how it is. It appears to consciousness that the ego constitutes consciousness, but in fact consciousness constitutes the ego. The ego is mistakenly taken by consciousness to be its own transcendental and subjective source, but the ego is an object of consciousness, constituted by acts of reflection. The ego is apparently active but really passive. The ego is passive because its existence and nature depend upon the operations of consciousness. It is apparently active because consciousness's operations seem to depend upon it. In this sense the ego is a synthesis of activity and passivity.

5. Finally, Sartre says the ego is a synthesis in another sense: a synthesis of interiority and transcendence. It is clear that the ego is transcendent in that it is an object for consciousness that is not wholly given to consciousness. (For example, dispositional states of the ego may not be immediately available to consciousness.) However, what is it for the ego to exhibit interiority? I have said (p. 127 above) that A exhibits interiority if and only if A is both private and inalienable.

I define 'private' as follows:

a   S is private if and only if awareness of S is only possible from a first-person singular point of view.

and 'inalienable' in this way:

b   S is inalienable if and only if S is a part of some person and logically could not be a part of any numerically distinct person.

So, if an ego is both private and inalienable then only the person whose ego it is may be directly aware of it, and that ego is a part of that person and could not be the ego of someone else.

Sartre says:

> It is, in a sense, more 'internal to' consciousness than one's states. (83)[207]

In the way I have defined 'interiority' it is not possible for interiority to admit of degrees, so what sense is Sartre allocating to the term here? He defines 'interiority' like this:

> Yet what do we mean by 'interiority'? Simply that to be and to be aware of itself are one and the same thing for consciousness. (83)[208]

So Sartre means by 'interiority' the Hegelian doctrine that there is no difference between consciousness being what it is and consciousness knowing what it is (that is, being conscious of what it is).[209]

Clearly, it is not inconsistent to speak of degrees of self-consciousness, but can sense be attached to 'more interior than' here? Again, an appearance/reality distinction is needed. The ego exhibits a two-fold interiority: one only apparent but the other real. The ego is an interiority because it exists only as an object of reflecting consciousness. It is private. But it has an illusory interiority of its own, as though it possessed a private awareness of its own states.

Sartre provides two characterisations of interiority, each intended as a partial explication of the Hegelian doctrine that consciousness's being is being conscious of itself:

1   'For consciousness appearance is the absolute to the extent that it is appearance' (84)
2   'Consciousness is a being whose essence involves its existence' (84).[210]

Appearance is an absolute because if there is awareness of appearance then *qua* appearance that appearance admits of no appearance/reality distinction. It is absolutely what it is. The contents of consciousness are given to consciousness *qua* contents of consciousness just as they are.

The essence of consciousness implies its existence for Sartre because it is wrong to say what consciousness is without acknowledging a commitment to the existence of consciousness. In describing what it is it is necessary to presuppose that it is.

Sartre says that a consequence of the interiority of consciousness and the stronger interiority of the ego is that

> one lives interiority (one 'exists inwardly'). (84)[211]

Living interiority is not the same as introspecting one's mental states. It consists in being in them, or partly being them. What I partly or even essentially am falls under the description 'private and inalienable' so what I partly am is accessible to me only through the first person singular perspective. What I partly am falls under true first person singular psychological descriptions.

For Sartre, living interiority is constitutive of what it is to be a person as opposed to observing a person. It is for this reason impossible for living interiority to be observed. I am partly co-extensive with my interiority and my being my interiority precludes the level of detachment or objectivity necessary for its observation. To put Sartre's point metaphorically, I am too close to my interiority to see it for what it is. This is only a metaphor, not only because of the spatial connotations of 'close to' but because I am my interiority and if A is close to B then A is not B. Nevertheless, the difficulty might well be compared with the incapacity of the seeing eye to see itself.

The fact that the ego may be an object for consciousness is a clue for Sartre to the falsity of its interiority. The ego is given to consciousness as a kind of interiority but this can only be illuminating because, as he puts it,

an absolute interiority never has an outside. (84)[212]

'Outside' is a spatial metaphor designed to capture a phenomenological fact about the ego, and, indeed, consciousness. Consciousness has no 'outside' because of its interiority, because there is something it consists in to be a consciousness. Consciousness may only be observed by the consciousness it is, and any interiority may only be apprehended by itself. The ego is an object for consciousness yet not part of consciousness. It follows that the notion of the ego is contradictory because if the ego is an interiority it cannot be observed by anything but itself. The ego is an interiority, but it is observed by something other than itself: consciousness. It follows that the ego both is and is not observed by something other than itself. This contradiction, according to Sartre, is a clue to the fact that the ego is only an appearance, an illusion, a postulated object for consciousness.

11 The structures of the interiority of the ego

Sartre claims that interiority has two structures: intimacy and indistinctness.

When Sartre says that the ego is given to consciousness as 'intimate' (85), I read this as follows: x is intimate if and only if x is a part of consciousness. Although the ego is given as intimate, this intimacy is illusory. The ego is not a part of consciousness but an object for consciousness, so the ego has a false intimacy.

Sartre says the ego is given as 'opaque' (85) to consciousness, and this opacity appears as indistinctness. To see more precisely what Sartre means by 'indistinctness' we need to inspect his examples.

In different philosophical contexts, God may be thought of as indistinct, as may pure being (what is, in abstraction from any of its properties). This suggests that if x is or appears indistinct then it is at least true that the concept of x is vague (or difficult to define) and it is perhaps true of x that x may not be (or may not be wholly) apprehended in its true nature. The ego as it features in Sartre's phenomenology falls under those two descriptions.

Sartre does provide us with an explicit characterisation of 'indistinctness':

> [This] is interiority seen from the outside. (85)[213]

'Seen' is a metaphor and is best unpacked as 'thought' or 'imagined', so if x is characterised by interiority but is imagined from a third-person point of view then x is thought as 'indistinct'; what x is is not clear in the imagining of x.

Both intimacy and indistinctness are relational structures of interiority. One is a relation to the consciousness whose ego exhibits interiority, the other is a relation to another, third-person, consciousness. They are not intrinsic properties of the ego.

12 Self-knowledge

Sartre's conception of self-knowledge is best understood as a systematic repudiation of Cartesian privacy. On a Cartesian epistemology of the self each person has a uniquely privileged access to their own mental states through introspection. Sartre maintains that the sorts of things I may know about myself are the sorts of things other people may know about me. Indeed, according to Sartre, others may understand me much better than I understand myself.

Nevertheless, Sartre begins his exposition of self-knowledge with an assertion *prima facie* inconsistent not only with Cartesianism, but with there being self-knowledge at all:

> The me, as such, remains unknown to us. (86)[214]

Sartre means the me as subject is unknowable because there is no such entity for our knowledge to be of. *Qua* object there are just four possible, but imperfect, modes of epistemological access to the me:

1 'observation' (86)
2 'approximation' (86)
3 'anticipation' (86)
4 'experience'. (86)[215]

Sartre does not explain what these procedures consist in, but he does say that each is only appropriate to apprehension of a non-intimate object, and the me is too intimate to be captured by any of them appropriately. We may understand them as follows:

1   There is *observation* of x if and only if there is either sense perception or introspection of x.

2   There is *approximation* to x if and only if there is some largely accurate estimation of the nature of x.

3   There is *anticipation* of x if and only if attention is paid to x.

4   There is *experience* of x if and only if x exists as an object for at least one consciousness.

If we unpack Sartre's four procedures in this way then room is left for knowledge of the ego by their means, but knowledge of an uncertain kind. Arguably there may only exist knowledge where there is room for error, and, in any case, part of Sartre's criticism of the Cartesian picture is that it makes it impossible to be in error as to one's (psychological) nature.

However, there is evidence that these procedures may be systematically misleading, or that it may in principle be impossible to acquire self-knowledge by their means. To understand why, we need to examine Sartre on the intimacy of the me. He says:

> It is too present for one to succeed in taking a truly external viewpoint on it. If we step back for vantage, the me accompanies us in this withdrawal. It is infinitely near, and I cannot circle around it. (86)[216]

Sartre's account is riddled with a spatial vocabulary: 'present', 'external', 'viewpoint', 'accompanies', 'withdrawal', 'circle around'. We could say we know intuitively what Sartre means by the intimacy of the me, but the difficult but worthwhile task would be to unpack the vocabulary non-metaphorically. The problem is that although the me is an object it behaves like a subject. If the me were a subject then it would, for example, be true that it 'accompanies us' in the sense that we are it, or perhaps as Kant's 'I think' must be capable of accompanying (*begleiten*) any of our perceptions. Suppose I try to think some thought about myself, or introspect myself, and try to thus introspect or think myself as something that exists independently of my thinking or introspecting. If not a paradox, there is a psychological difficulty in attempting this because the me is necessarily dependent on any thinking or introspecting I engage in. It is not dependent on my thinking as the subject of my thoughts but as an object of my thoughts, but no less dependent for that. We could formulate the difficulty in this way:

1   An 'external viewpoint' is possible on x if x exists independently of thought and perception.

2   An 'external viewpoint' is not possible on x if x depends on thought or perception.

Clearly, if the me *qua* the me depends upon thought or perception then an external viewpoint on it is not possible.

'Infinitely near' is also a spatial metaphor. Spatially, no matter how near x is to y it is always in principle possible for x to be nearer to y, but Sartre wishes us to entertain the idea of infinite nearness: x and y are near but it is in principle impossible for x and y to be nearer, or, there is no limit to how near they are. Unpacking the metaphor, Sartre is claiming that the me is as good a candidate as may be found for something that I am. Yet the me is not I myself as subject. It is not that psycho-physical human being that I am, but it is 'infinitely near' in the sense that there exists no better failed candidate for what I am. It is nearly what I am.

An epistemological problem is raised here which Sartre does not solve. Why should it be difficult to know the me? Spatially speaking, it is frequently difficult to see some object clearly which is close to one's eyes, and this difficulty is a result of certain empirical facts about focusing. It is hard to envisage a parallel difficulty about knowledge of the me, once the spatial metaphors are stripped away. Some argument would be needed to show that the Cartesian account of self-knowledge is radically mistaken. It cannot simply be taken for granted that if x depends on my consciousness then x is unknowable by me, nor that if x depends on my consciousness x's nature is self-evident to me.

Sartre provides a putative example of self-knowledge (86). If I ask myself whether I am lazy or hard-working then the best route to a correct answer to this question is to ask others, or perhaps, to collect information about oneself and to interpret it as dispassionately as if the information were about someone else. Either of these methods he regards as more reliable than direct introspection of the me.

It seems that Sartre has assimilated two pairs of distinctions which need to be distinguished. These are a subjective/objective distinction and a biased/unbiased distinction. Something counts as subjective if it pertains to consciousness. Something is objective if it does not pertain to consciousness. The subjective/objective distinction is thus an ontological distinction, a distinction between sorts of entity. The biased/unbiased distinction is, in contrast, an epistemological distinction. It makes sense to speak of beliefs, opinions, theories, ideologies and so on as biased or unbiased. Now, Sartre assumes that beliefs about a subjective entity, the me, are more likely to be biased than beliefs about objective entities. I see no reason to accept this. I should say an opinion is biased if and only if it is allocated a specific truth value because of a *desire* that it possess that truth value, and not because of evidence that it possesses that truth value. If we say I am more likely to favour myself than others and so self-knowledge is likely to be distorted, then even if this is true we may still ask Why?

It is understandable that a person's beliefs about themselves should make a difference to what they are and not merely tautologically. For example if someone believes they are confident then to that extent they are confident. If someone believes they are self-conscious then to that extent they are self-conscious. What is required is the construction of contrasting cases where a person generates false beliefs about themselves, or fails to acquire true beliefs about themselves, because it is himself that the beliefs are about.

Sartre considers the me an obstacle to self-knowledge. In the example of my deciding whether I am lazy or hard-working, it is possible to see how the me could bar such knowledge. If I think of my 'self' as a kind of introspectible psychological item, then this is a distraction from my coming to know what dispositions I have, and being lazy or hard-working is possessing a disposition.

Another person is better able to know my dispositions than I am because they are not acquainted with the me as an ontologically misleading inner entity in the way in which I am. So there does not exist for the other the same psychological obstacle to knowledge of me as exists in my knowledge of myself. In that respect at least another may know me better than I know myself.

To know oneself is for Sartre to know oneself as others know one, but to know oneself in that way is to ironically adopt a perspective which is necessarily false:

> Thus 'really to know oneself' is inevitably to take toward oneself the point of view of others, that is to say, a point of view which is necessarily false. (87)[217]

Sartre does not mean that the point of view others have on one is necessarily false. It is not necessary that of any set of sentences of third person grammatical form believed of a person some percentage will be false just because they are not autobiographical but third person. Sartre means that in self-knowledge I know myself as if I were another. The knowledge I have of myself is necessarily not third person knowledge and the knowledge another has of oneself is necessarily not self-knowlege. Clearly this is consistent with the fact that what I know about myself may be what another knows about me. The same propositional content may be truly expressed in first person singular and third person singular grammatical form. It follows that what one believes about oneself may be true even if it depends on the authority of others, or on adopting towards oneself the attitude of others, or both. Perhaps only to that extent is self-knowledge possible on Sartre's account.

13 The ego as ideal

There is a further obstacle to self-knowledge. The ego is taken as real but is in fact the ideal unity of its states and actions. It is ideal in that it only exists as an object for consciousness, and independently of that it has no reality so *a fortiori* no reality as the unity of states and actions. My states and actions are infinite according to Sartre (presumably because there are no non-stipulative criteria for their individuation and enumeration) but the ego is a finite entity. Nothing finite can be the real unity of something infinite so no ego can be the real unity of states and actions. This is what Sartre means by

> The intuition of the ego is a constantly gulling mirage, for it simultaneously yields everything and yields nothing. (87)[218]

The ego is putatively what the ontological unity of my states and actions consists in *qua* mine. Really it is incapable of fulfilling that role. It appears to have it, so it has it ideally only.

What does it mean to say that the ego is an *ideal* unity of states and actions? Sartre remarks

> Those who have some acquaintance with Phenomenology will understand without difficulty that the ego may be at the same time an ideal unity of states, the majority of which are absent, and a concrete totality giving itself to intuition. (88)[219]

Sartre has in mind the Husserlian distinction between fulfilled and unfulfilled intentions. Intentional acts are empty if their objects are absent, fulfilled if their objects are present. 'Fulfilment' is Husserl's term for the transition from absence to presence. The ego is the *ideal unity* of its states and actions in so far as these are possible objects of a series of unfulfilled intentional acts. The ego is a *concrete totality* in so far as it is the object of a fulfilled, present, act of consciousness. Clearly, that the ego has this status presents a further obstacle to self-knowledge. If I am directly acquainted with the ego only as an intentional object, and not with the states and actions which it unifies, then I am correspondingly ignorant of those states and actions.

Sartre also claims

> The ego is a noematic rather than a noetic unity. (88)[220]

As we have seen, the *noema*, in Husserlian phenomenology, is the intentional object, or object as meant or intended by an act of consciousness. The *noesis* is the act of consciousness itself. Sartre is thus reiterating his earlier claim that the ego is not a part of consciousness but an object for consciousness. It is not a property of or an inhabitant of consciousness but something consciousness is directed towards.

Within Sartre's phenomenological ontology the ego has much more the status of a physical object than an act of consciousness. As he puts it

> A tree or a chair exist no differently. (88)[221]

Sartre has in mind at least two salient phenomenological features common to the ego and a physical object. Both are given to consciousness as objects, as objects for consciousness, and both are constructions out of *Abschattungen* or perspectives. Indeed, a physical object, like the ego, is a unity of fulfilled and unfulfilled intentions. In establishing that there is much broadly in common between the phenomenology of the ego and the phenomenology of physical objects Sartre provides yet another reason for objecting to the Husserlian picture of the ego as subject, or transcendental condition for consciousness.

14 The ego and reflection

Sartre has consistently argued so far in *The Transcendence of the Ego* that the ego is an object of reflection. It exists in so far as it is given to reflexive consciousness. He now introduces two important reservations about that view. The ego only appears indirectly to reflection and, perhaps surprisingly, there is a sense in which the ego appears on the unreflected level. I shall treat each of these in turn.

i The indirect appearance of the ego

Sartre says

The ego never appears, in fact, except when one is not looking at it. (88)[222]

Clearly, 'looking at' is a metaphor here for 'reflecting on' (which is in turn metaphorical) or 'apprehending as object of reflexive consciousness'. If we read Sartre literally here then he is claiming that the ego only appears when there is no reflection on it, and that is clearly inconsistent with the thesis argued so far. The solution is that the ego does not appear as a direct object of reflection, only as an indirect one. It is not possible, to pursue Sartre's metaphor, to *focus* on the ego as a unique enduring particular clearly discriminable from other objects of reflection. On the contrary

It is, therefore, never seen except 'out of the corner of the eye'. (80)[223]

If an attempt is made to pay direct attention to the ego then the ego vanishes. This is because any such attempt takes the form of trying to apprehend the ego as an object for unreflected consciousness. The switch from reflexive to pre-reflexive consciouness loses the ego as object of consciousness because the ego only appears (if only indirectly) to reflexive consciousness.

This oscillation between reflexive and pre-reflexive consciousness accounts for the systematically elusive nature of the I according to Sartre. It is not that the I is perpetually subject but never object, and so may never be the object of any inner intuition. On the contrary, the I is an object, the indirect object of reflexive consciousness, but it is mistaken for an object of pre-reflexive consciousness. The attempt to make it a direct object of consciousness misconstrues it as an object of pre-reflexive consciousness and, in this way, the 'I' systematically evades direct apprehension by consciousness. The I is not *behind* consciousness.

ii The ego on the unreflected level

In a way that is *prima facie* inconsistent with a major thesis of his book Sartre asserts

It is certain, however, that the I does appear on the unreflected level. (89)[224]

and he provides this example:

> If someone asks me 'What are you doing?', and I reply, all preoccupied, 'I am trying to hang this picture' or 'I am repairing the rear tyre' these statements do not transport us to the level of reflection. (89)[225]

However, the I does not appear on the unreflected level in the same sense in which the I appears to reflection. What appears is the *thought* of the I. There is no intuition of the I as object, direct or indirect. Sartre equivocates between the view that the I is thought but not intuited in this example, and the view that the word I is used meaningfully but over and above that, there is no thought of I. The second view is suggested by

> But this 'I' which is here in question nevertheless is no mere syntactical form. It has a meaning: it is quite simply an empty concept which is destined to remain empty. (89)[226]

The I concept is thought but there is no intuition of the I to fulfil that thought.
   The second view is suggested by

> Just as I can think of a chair in the absence of any chair merely by a concept, I can in the same way think of the 'I' in the absence of the 'I'. (89)[227]

The two views are in fact mutually consistent if using the term 'I' (or a synonym) meaningfully and possessing the concept of I are mutually dependent capacities.
   On the unreflected level the I loses its intimacy. It is, as Sartre puts it, 'degraded' (91). In a sense the use of 'I' on the unreflected level is revealing of the nature of the I. This is because the term 'I', on that level, is used to refer to the psycho-physical whole who I am; an agent in the world.

4 Conclusions

Sartre claims that *La Transcendance de l' Ego* establishes three important conclusions. The correct understanding of the ego allows:

1 A correct transcendental phenomenology.
2 A refutation of solipsism.
3 A non-idealist phenomenology which provides a philosophical foundation for ethics and politics.

What all three conclusions have in common is the exhibiting of subject–object dualism as dependent upon a prior unity of subject and object. To make sense of this more needs to be said about what 'subject' and 'object' mean. I shall try to clarify both concepts in the course of examining Sartre's conclusions.

1 A correct transcendental phenomenology

Sartre's correction of Husserl's concept of the ego allows the following:

> The conception of the ego which we propose seems to us to effect the liberation of the transcendental field, and at the same time its purification. (93)[228]

The transcendental field is what appears to consciousness after the exercise of the transcendental reduction or *epoché*. It is what is given when ontological commitment to the objective reality of the external world is suspended. The transcendental field is 'liberated' by the abolition of the ego as subject because its disappearance leaves room for a phenomenological description of the contents of consciousness as they are given, without false commitments to a transcendental ego. The transcendental field is purified in the straightforward sense that we are no longer compelled to believe that an ego appears as a part of it. It recovers what Sartre calls its 'transparency' (93) 'limpidité' (TE 74).

In a sense the transcendental field is nothing but in a sense it is everything. This thought is reminiscent of Wittgenstein's claim in the *Tractatus* that realism and solipsism in a sense coincide:

In a sense it is nothing, since all physical, psycho-physical and psychic objects, all truths, all values are outside it, since my me has itself ceased to be any part of it. But this nothing is all since it is consciousness of all these objects. (93)[229]

At work in this passage is the subjective–objective distinction which Sartre is attempting to ground in a more primitive reality which is neither subjective nor objective.

The transcendental field is objectively nothing in the sense that no third person non-psychological ascription is made true by any feature of it. In other words, the transcendental field is nothing objective because it contains nothing which exists independently of consciousness. This is a predictable feature of the transcendental field because the phenomenological reduction is the suspension of ontological commitment to consciousness-independent particulars, and the transcendental field is what is disclosed by that reduction.

The transcendental field is however everything subjectively, that is, it makes true first person singular non-dispositional psychological ascriptions. The transcendental field is everything that is directly given, everything that constitutes the contents of consciousness.

In a sense, however, the subjective–objective distinction is undermined by the transcendental field as described by Sartre. This is because the I no longer features as its transcendental subject and, as for Husserl, consciousness-independent objects do not feature as its objects. The distinction between subject and object is thus dissipated, and the phenomenological content of the transcendental field is reduced to what was formerly thought of as the relation between subject and object. The relata are abolished so it no longer makes sense to talk of a relation.

Similarly, the abolition of the transcendental ego removes the grounds for an inner–outer distinction. 'Inner' and 'outer' are common metaphors in the philosophy of mind but they are rarely rendered literally so it is not clear what they amount to. I suggest the following:

x is inner if and only if x may be truly characterised *qua* x by some first person singular psychological ascription.
x is outer if and only if x may be truly characterised *qua* x by some third person non-psychological ascription.

Clearly this leaves room for the possibility that x may be both inner and outer because both sorts of description may in principle be true of one and the same item, or sort of item. At least, nothing in the definitions *prima facie* precludes that.

The contents of the transcendental field make possible the distinction between inner and outer in themselves. As they are given phenomenologically it does not make sense to think of them as intrinsically inner or outer. This is one direction from which Sartre undermines the subject–object distinction. He introduces a transcendental field which is neutral between subjective and objective descriptions which presuppose it. A second strategy is to deny the alleged privacy of the mental.

Here is the picture Sartre wishes to dissipate:

> To be precise: up to now a radical distinction has been made between the objectivity of a spatio-temporal thing or of an eternal truth, and the subjectivity of psychical states. (94)[230]

There are many ways in which such a putative subjective–objective distinction could be drawn. On any non-idealist ontology spatio-temporal things count as 'objective' in the sense of 'mind-independent'. They exist irrespective of whether they are thought about or perceived and irrespective of whether minds exist. Similarly, psychic states count as subjective because if some state is psychical it is a state of mind. This is necessarily true whatever account of minds we may wish to give. Spatio-temporal particulars are paradigmatically what make third person non-psychological ascriptions true, and count as 'objective' in just that sense. Psychic states are paradigmatically what make first person singular psychological ascriptions true, and count as 'subjective' in just that sense. Sartre, I think, is aware of these possible ways of drawing the subjective–objective distinction but he concentrates instead upon a particular epistemological criterion for it.

This criterion is itself a distinction, the private–public distinction. Here is the relevant notion of privacy:

> It seemed as if the subject had a privileged status with respect to his own states. (94)[231]

If some person A is in a state, S, then S counts as a privileged subjective state of A, just in case if A has a belief that A is in S then that belief is true, but that inference fails for persons other than A. Also, if S is a privileged subjective state of A then only A may have direct Russellian acquaintance with S.

This quasi-Cartesian conception of epistemological privacy contrasts with a relevant notion of objectivity. If some entity is an objective particular then it is both necessary and sufficient for its objectivity that it be intersubjectively accessible, both doxastically and perceptibly. If something is objective in this sense then (other things being equal) any two persons may perceive or hold beliefs about it but it does not follow that the resulting perceptions or beliefs are veridical. So, on the epistemological criterion, the subjective is characterised by epistemological privacy, the objective by epistemological publicity.

Sartre tries to draw this distinction in an additional way. He says that if two people talk about the same chair they are talking about the same thing, but if one person tries to understand another's mental state then only the other may directly intend that mental state. This distinction is not well drawn even though each claim when clarified comes out as analytic. The distinction fails because, as Sartre soon appreciates, if you talk and I talk about someone's mental state then we are talking about the same thing even though only the person whose state it is is in that state. The sound epistemological point may be extracted from this:

> Consequently, if Paul and Pierre both speak of Pierre's love, for example, it is no longer true that the one speaks blindly and by analogy of that which the other apprehends in full. They speak of the same thing. (95)[232]

Sartre thinks this is an undermining of the subjective–objective distinction which rests on the quasi-Cartesian epistemological criterion. If love is a disposition then a person may be as fully acquainted with another person's love as that person. The behavioural components are as essential to the state's being love as certain feelings so we are not dealing with two things here – inner love and its outer manifestation – but one state – love – which may be apprehended from a first or third person point of view. It may not be coherent to talk about observing someone's love, but it makes sense to talk of observing that someone is in love.

This 'correct' transcendental phenomenology is deployed by Sartre in his putative refutations of idealism and an attempt to ground the subject–object distinction itself.

2 The refutation of solipsism

The second consequence Sartre claims for his phenomenology of the ego is a refutation of solipsism. If solipsism is the doctrine that only my psyche exists then Sartre has refuted solipsism if he has proven a claim which is inconsistent with the thesis that only my psyche exists. He also says 'this conception of the ego seems to us the only possible refutation of solipsism' (103)[233] but he does not have a sound argument for this. It would in fact be extremely difficult to prove that one refutation of solipsism is the only possible one. This would require showing *a priori* that there is no other sound argument with a conclusion that is inconsistent with 'Only my psyche exists.'

Although he makes the point in a rather psychologistic and *ad hominem* way, Sartre does not think the putative refutations of solipsism presented by Husserl in *Formal and Transcendental Logic* and in *Cartesian Meditations* are sound and he does have the makings of an argument for this.

He characterises solipsism as follows:

> As long as the I remains a structure of consciousness, it will always remain possible to oppose consciousness, with its I, to all other existents. Finally, then, it is really the me who must produce the world. (103–4)[234]

Clearly this argument for solipsism is invalid. From the fact that a distinction may be drawn between consciousness and its I on the one hand and the rest of what is on the other it does not logically follow that the me produces the world. Nor, *a fortiori*, does it follow that the me must produce the world. However, it is possible to reconstruct a more useful observation on solipsism here.

So long as the I is maintained as a subject of consciousness and as a condition for the possibility of experience in a Kantian, Husserlian or, for that matter, Cartesian way room is left for scepticism about the existence of what the I is a condition for the possibility of. From the fact that the I is a necessary condition for experience it does not follow that it is sufficient for experience. The existence of the I, then, provides no guarantee of the existence of experience and its objects. It is this fact that leaves conceptual room for the kind of scepticism called 'solipsism'. The solipsist does not need a conclusion of the strength Sartre ascribes to him. He does not need to say that the me produces the world nor that the I necessarily produces the world. All the solipsist needs is the logical possibility that there is no world independent of his own psyche if *prima facie* there is only one's own psyche.

This provides materials for an argument that Husserl's putative refutations of solipsism fail. If Sartre can show that some thesis is vulnerable to solipsistic scepticism and that Husserl is logically committed to such a thesis then it follows that Husserl is vulnerable to solipsistic scepticism. Sartre thinks he has found precisely such a thesis in the Husserlian view that the transcendental ego is both subject of consciousness and transcendental ground of the possibility of experience.

This will always leave logical room for the reaffirmation of solipsism despite the manoeuvres of *Formal and Transcendental Logic* and *Cartesian Meditations*. Husserl's detailed phenomenology of the other is ultimately not logically inconsistent with solipsism despite Husserl's description of the differences between being presented with a human being as opposed to, say, a straightforward physical object. This is why Sartre says

> Small matter if certain layers of this world necessitate by their very nature a relation to others. This relation can be a mere quality of the world that I create and in no way obliges me to accept the real existence of other I's. (104)[235]

In this passage Sartre shifts modalities from 'it is' and 'must' to the more modest 'can be' and thereby moves from a version of solipsism on which what is depends or necessarily depends on the existence of my psyche to a version on which it is logically possible that what is depends on my psyche.

Sartre's argument against Husserl is sound because Husserl's phenomenological descriptions of the other have not removed this logical possibility. They are compatible with there being no such thing as what Sartre is calling 'the real existence of other I's' (104). *Pace* Husserl's descriptions the other might not have any psychological interiority, any subjectivity. The other might be wholly other.

The question now is whether Sartre's own phenomenology of the ego provides a genuine refutation of solipsism where Husserl's fails. Arguably it does.

Sartre's strategy is not to deny that the existence of other selves is dubitable. He accepts that it is dubitable. His strategy is to deny that the existence of other selves is any more or less dubitable than the existence of one's own self. He thus abdicates the rather Cartesian metaphysical assumption that Husserl's transcendental phenomenology rests on and so abdicates one part of the thinkability of solipsism.[236] Solipsism is partly the doctrine that other minds are doubtful but solipsism is also partly the doctrine that the existence of one's own mind is certain. It is this second tenet of solipsism that Sartre denies and it is just this tenet that Husserl is unable to escape.

Husserl cannot escape because he has made the self, *qua* transcendental ego, a necessary condition for experience and the 'ground' of the world. It follows that only extremely weak assumptions are sufficient to establish the ego's existence, viz. there is experience or there is a world. Sartre can accept the existence of experience and the world (in the sense of what experience is experience of) without thereby being logically committed to his own existence. This marks an important break with Cartesian philosophy; a break facilitated by Kant but continued by Sartre.

When Sartre says

> But if the I becomes a transcendent, it participates in all the vicissitudes of the world. (104)[237]

he means that the fact that the I is an object for consciousness rather than its subject entails that its existence is as dubitable as that of any other object of consciousness. What Cartesian philosophy, including Husserlian transcendental phenomenology, has mistakenly taken to be the 'owner' presupposed by consciousness is not in fact any kind of necessary condition for consciousness, therefore consciousness is not sufficient for its existence. If the existence of the I does not follow from the existence of consciousness then, to that extent, the existence of the I is dubitable. By 'dubitable' here I mean: *p* is dubitable if and only if there is no contradiction in denying the conjunction of *p* and 'consciousness exists'. (Even if, for example, 'consciousness exists' is true if doubt exists.) Clearly Sartre is right to suggest that Husserl's transcendental phenomenology is vulnerable to sceptical solipsism because it is committed to the view that the existence of the ego is indubitable but the existence of the external world is dubitable (even if not doubted).

If Sartre's arguments in *The Transcendence of the Ego* for the conclusion that 'there are moments of consciousness without the I' (32) are sound then he has adduced a ground for denying solipsism. By 'strong solipsism' I mean the conjunction of: 'Only I exist' and 'I necessarily exist'. (Or, more precisely, 'Only my mind exists' and 'My mind necessarily exists'.) If there are moments of consciousness without the I and moments of consciousness with the I then the I exists intermittently. If the I exists intermittently then it does not necessarily exist. If the I does not necessarily exist but it exists then it contingently exists. Although there are times when it exists there is no incoherence in the supposition that it does not exist because there are times when it does not exist. Any claim that it does not exist made at a time when it does exist is only false, not necessarily false. This implication of Sartre's thought relies on two assumptions which could be challenged. Nothing necessarily exists intermittently and everything is either necessary or contingent but not both. There seems no *a priori* objection to something's existing necessarily when it exists but sometimes not existing. Indeed, this seems to be Husserl's view of the transcdendental ego. Although it is logically impossible for something to be both necessary and contingent, there seems no incoherence in the idea that something should be neither.

Sartre says of the I reconstrued as object rather than subject 'It is not an absolute' (104). Something is an absolute if and only if it exists, it depends upon nothing else for its existence but the remainder of what exists does depend upon it for its existence. ('An absolute' in the sense of the first two conjuncts is roughly synonymous with 'substance' in Aristotelian metaphysics.) The I is not an absolute because although it exists it only exists intermittently and only *qua* object for consciousness. It depends upon consciousness for its existence and so is not an absolute.

Understood as object, not subject, the I is not any kind of precondition for experience. If experience does not depend on it then something does not depend on it so it is not an absolute. When Sartre says 'It has not created the universe' (104) he means the existence of the ego is not necessary for what is presented to consciousness (except, modally, itself).

It is an entailment of Sartre's view that the I 'falls like other existences at the stroke of the *epoché* (104), because whatever is an object for consciousness is open to that suspension of ontological commitment that is the phenomenological reduction. The ego is an object for consciousness so it falls by the *epoché*. If the ego is not any kind of precondition for consciousness it is coherent to suspend belief in its existence.

The phenomenological *epoché* is itself the implementation of a kind of solipsism. Although the *epoché* entails no disbelief in the external world it entails a kind of sceptical solipsism on which the existence of one's mental states is consistent with either the existence or non-existence of the external world.

Sartre summarises the consequences for solipsism of his reversal of the phenomenological role of the ego as follows:

> Instead of expressing itself in effect as 'I alone exist as absolute', it must assert that 'absolute consciousness alone exists as absolute', which is obviously a truism. (104)[238]

Sartre retains from solipsism the thesis that only consciousness depends upon nothing else for its own existence, but rejects the thesis that such a consciousness is necessarily one's own or 'mine'. He thinks it is a truism that consciousness alone exists as an absolute because the existence of consciousness logically and indubitably follows from the existence of consciousness.

Sartre has not refuted the various solipsist theses: only my consciousness exists, only one consciousness exists, nor the modal variants of these obtained by prefacing them by 'It is possible that' or 'It is necessary that'. He has succeeded in casting doubt on the ideas that a consciousness is necessarily owned, is someone's, that its being someone's is a necessary condition for its being, and that such ownership consists in the existence of a transcendental subject.

Sartre draws an important and possibly original distinction which damages a central tenet of Cartesian epistemology. It is the distinction between the *certainty* and the intimacy of the I:

> My I, in effect, is no more certain for consciousness than the I of other men. It is only more intimate. (104)[239]

This is not just a reiteration of the claim that my ego's existence is as dubitable as the ego of another, although it is partly that. It is the claim that there is a difference between the intimacy of the I, the privacy of access to it, and the certainty of the I, the incorrigibility of some first person singular claims about it. Sartre is saying that privacy is no guarantee of incorrigibility and in this he is right. From the fact (if it is a fact) that a consciousness has a kind of direct and perhaps introspective access to its own ego that no other consciousness shares and which it has to the ego of no other consciousness, it does not follow that such epistemological access yields incorrigible beliefs. There is no incoherence in the supposition that the deliverances of such access should be falsified.

Sartre's conclusion is

> Solipsism becomes unthinkable from the moment that the I no longer has a privileged status. (104)[240]

He is right in so far as solipsism has two essential entailments: the external world is dubitable and my own existence is indubitable. It is the second of these that Sartre undermines and, in doing so, damages not only Husserl's phenomenology but the profound Cartesianism it rests on.

3 A non-idealist phenomenology which provides a foundation for ethics and politics

Sartre is concerned to refute the view that phenomenology is a kind of idealism, both because that is a misunderstanding of phenomenology and because he thinks idealism politically and ethically undesirable. To evaluate Sartre's arguments we need a distinction between different kinds of idealism.

Idealism is paradigmatically the doctrine that only the mental exists and if anything putatively non-mental exists then it will turn out either to be mental or logically dependent on the mental for its existence. It follows that the thesis that only minds or only consciousnesses exist is an idealist thesis. Solipsism is an idealist thesis because 'Only my mind exists' entails 'only minds exist' and that is a kind of idealism.

All these kinds of idealism are to be sharply distinguished from so-called 'transcendental idealism' as advanced by Kant in the *Critique of Pure Reason*. Transcendental idealism is not a strong or ontological idealism of the kind advocated by Berkeley (although it is sometimes misunderstood as such). Transcendental idealism is the conjunction of two theses: there are non-empirical grounds for the possibility of experience ('transcendental' grounds) and it is not possible to know the world as it really is in itself but only as it presents itself to us within experience. Clearly neither doctrine, nor the conjunction of the two, entails that only minds exist, nor that everything that exists logically depends upon the mental for its existence. *Prima facie* transcendental idealism is consistent with idealism and this superficial appearance together with Kant's use of 'idealism' to refer to his own philosophy has understandably misled most commentators into identifying Kant as an ontological idealist. Kant himself tried to explicitly distance himself from idealism in the second 'B' edition of the *Critique of Pure Reason* by adding the chapter 'The Refutation of Idealism', but to little avail. (I cannot argue this here but I think that Kant's transcendental idealism is consistent with a kind of materialism that the philosophy of the *Critique of Pure Reason* in fact entails.)

Husserl characterised some phases of his philosophy as 'transcendental idealism' but it is an *aporia* within Husserl exegesis whether this should be interpreted as a kind of idealism. It is possible to read Husserl's transcendental idealism in two mutually consistent yet logically distinct ways: as a Kantian formal and *a priori* enquiry into the conditions of the possibility of experience, or as the claim that consciousness and its contents could exist even if nothing else existed. These readings are mutually consistent because the truth of one does not entail the falsity of the other. They are logically distinct because the truth of one of them does not entail the truth of the other.

Sartre says about phenomenology

> If it is a philosophy in which the effort of spiritual assimilation never meets external resistances, in which suffering, hunger, and war are diluted in a slow process of the unification of ideas, nothing is more unjust than to call phenomenologists 'idealists'. (104–5)[241]

Sartre is right to suggest that Husserlian transcendental phenomenology is consistent with any practical, including political, commitment. Also, it would be a crude and naive misunderstanding of Husserl to think that the phenomenological reduction or *epoché* entailed the non-existence of the external world. Manifestly and importantly the *epoché* entails no denial of a world existing outside consciousness. On the contrary, the existence of the world is neither affirmed nor denied in the *epoché*. It is neither believed nor disbelieved. Rather, both belief and disbelief are suspended. To this extent Sartre is right to deny that Husserlian phenomenology is a kind of idealism. If idealism is the doctrine that everything is mental then the phenomenological reduction does not entail idealism.

The kind of phenomenology that Sartre wishes to ultimately endorse is existential phenomenology, not Husserlian transcendental phenomenology. Crucial to the break with the phenomenology of *Ideas* and *Cartesian Meditations* is the repudiation of both the transcendental ego and the *epoché*. Sartre's existential phenomenology as developed in *Being and Nothingness* replaces the idea of a field of transcendental subjectivity with the quasi-Heideggerian existential category 'being-in-the-world' ('être-au-monde', 'in-der-Welt-sein'). This break with Husserl is continued in French existentialism in Maurice Merleau-Ponty's 1945 book *Phenomenology of Perception*, which also contains a critique of both the transcendental ego and the phenomenological *epoché*.

It is essential to the 'existential' phenomenology of Sartre and Merleau-Ponty that human being is inseparably in the world, as it is constitutive of Heidegger's fundamental ontology that the kind of being that pertains to *Dasein* is 'in-der-Welt-sein'. There is no doubt that in so far as Sartre is considering existential phenomenology he is right to say that

> The phenomenologists have plunged man back into the world; they have given full measure to man's agonies and sufferings, and also to his rebellions. (105)[242]

The 'existential' turn of the French phenomenologists would have appalled Husserl. Nevertheless, there are elements of his own later thought that are not inconsistent with existential phenomenology. I have in mind the notion of the *Lebenswelt* in *The Crisis of the European Sciences*. This lived reality of the human and the human environment entails an ontological inseparability of person and world which is equivalent to that entailed by human 'being-in-the-world'.

It is this later Husserl who Sartre approves and endorses and he regards it as an essential project of *The Transcendence of the Ego* to eliminate the features of Husserl's transcendental phenomenology which are inconsistent with being-in-the-world. It is those same features which are vulnerable to political criticism:

> Unfortunately, as long as the I remains a structure of absolute consciousness, one will still be able to reproach phenomenology for being an escapist doctrine, for again pulling a part of man out of the world and, in that way, turning our attention from the real problems. (105)[243]

Sartre means that in so far as the self is held not to be in the world it is thereby held not to be subject to suffering in the world, and that is the only kind of suffering there is. It is of immense ethical and political significance to Sartre that we are subject to such real suffering and philosophy should not conceal this.

There is a famous tenet of Husserl's thought which Sartre does not mention in the closing pages of *The Transcendence of the Ego* but which is conducive to his argument. One of the slogans of Husserl's philosophy is 'To the things themselves' (*Zu den Sachen selbst*). This slogan has been much misinterpreted but its meaning is as follows. Husserlian phenomenology deliberately eschews two ontological realms postulated by two competing kinds of philosophy. On the one hand phenomenology is anti-metaphysical and so does not postulate an ontology which transcends any possible experience, whether this be a realm of quasi-

Fregean mathematical objects, Platonic forms or spiritual substances. On the other hand, phenomenology is non-psychologistic because it does not postulate any sense-data, Humean impressions or other putatively self-subsistent sensory contents. Rather, phenomenology concerns itself with the objects of experience as they are presented: the things themselves.

Sartre could avail himself of this slogan at the end of *The Transcendence of the Ego* because phenomenology is, in a sense, neutral with regard to both metaphysics and psychologism. Sartre himself would regard both tendencies as distractions from ethical and political commitment.

If Sartre seeks to avoid idealism the same is true of its philosophical opposite, materialism. He emphasises that his political commitment to historical materialism does not entail metaphysical materialism:

> It has always seemed to me that a working hypothesis as fruitful as historical materialism never needed as a foundation the absurdity which is metaphysical materialism. (105)[244]

Metaphysical materialism is the thesis that everything is physical. On this view, putatively non-physical items will turn out to be either physical or logically dependent upon items that are physical. In its applications within the philosophy of mind, materialism is the thesis that a person is nothing but a highly complicated physical object, and a person's mental states, including their moods, emotions and sensations, are themselves either physical or logically dependent on the person *qua* physical object.

Historical materialism is the thesis that in order to change the way in which a society is politically, legally or religiously organised it is necessary to change the way in which it is economically organised. Economics are primitive because they are the means by which a society perpetuates itself. The way in which a society is organised economically is the set of ways in which it survives. It seems to follow that economic organisation is a necessary condition for ideological or epiphenomenal forms of organisation. If that is right, then arguably it is not possible to fundamentally change a society's ideology without changing its economics.

Now, clearly, although metaphysical materialism is consistent with historical materialism it is not entailed by it. Sartre is absolutely right therefore to say that historical materialism does not need metaphysical materialism as its 'foundation'. Here I take it that A is a foundation for B if and only if A is necessary for B and B is sufficient for A. Clearly, historical materialism is not sufficient for metaphysical materialism because other ontologies are consistent with the strong causal efficacy of economics. For example, on any kind of political epiphenomenalism where it is admitted that economic conditions may determine ideas but ideas may not, or may not essentially, determine economics historical materialism is not logically ruled out.

Perhaps ironically, metaphysical materialism might turn out to be the one ontology that is logically inconsistent with historical materialism. This is because a society must have some non-physical properties in order for its ideology to exist *qua* a mental effect of economics. The bare doctrine that the physical causes the mental is a dualist doctrine not a materialist doctrine.

Sartre conceives of phenomenology as a middle way that avoids individualistic psychologism, metaphysical ontology and ontological materialism. He is right. Phenomenology does provide such a middle way but it does not follow that the ontologies he eschews are inconsistent with the politics he wishes to endorse. It does not follow either that phenomenology is the best method for solving philosophical problems.

4 Subject–object dualism

The Transcendence of the Ego ends with the bold conclusion that subject–object dualism has been transcended. Unfortunately, as so often in philosophy, the intractability of the problem has been underestimated and the putative solution is too hasty.

Sartre says

> In fact, it is not necessary that the object precede the subject for spiritual pseudo-values to vanish and for ethics to finds its bases in reality. It is enough that the me be contemporaneous with the World, and that the subject–object duality, which is purely logical, definitely disappear from philosophical preoccupations. (105)[245]

Now, even if Sartre is right that the ontological priority of the subject over the object does not have to be reversed in order for the values which he regards as illusory to be criticised, it does not follow that subject–object dualism is 'purely logical'. Indeed, this seems wrong.

Subject–object dualism is the distinction between two seemingly mutually exclusive and collectively exhaustive portions of what is: the part that I am and the remainder that I am not. It is a profound metaphysical mystery why this distinction should obtain at all.

It is not clear how the subject–object distinction is to be drawn ontologically. In particular my body is on some views part of what I am, on other views part of the objective order, and on still other views part of both.

If the distinction were 'purely logical' as Sartre suggests then it would possess many properties which it lacks and lack many properties which it has. For example, the distinction would possess the property of obtaining *a priori*, on the minimal assumption that logic is *a priori*. However, not only may the distinction be established by experience, in a broad sense 'empirically', arguably it can only be established empirically. It follows that it is not *a priori* and so it is not purely logical.

The subject–object distinction is a pragmatic presupposition of our everyday dealings with the world. If it were purely logical it would be merely tautologous that it obtains. However, no analytic or tautological fact can be a pragmatic presupposition of everyday life. Only an ontological, transcendental or perhaps empirical fact can have that status.

If the distinction were purely logical it would obtain of necessity on the minimal assumption that logical facts are necessary facts. However, that there is a subject–object distinction is a contingent fact not a necessary one. Indeed, Sartre himself is logically committed to this view because he thinks that *everything* is contingent. That there is subjectivity is contingent. That there is objectivity is contingent. That out of all the people that there are I am one of them is contingent and that there is a portion of what is which is numerically and qualitatively distinct from myself is contingent. It is also contingent that the complex conjunction of all these facts obtain. But if the distinction obtains contingently it cannot be purely logical.

The fact that the distinction is contingent should not be confused with the fact (if it is a fact) that it follows with deductive necessity from the premise that there is experience. It may be that experience is a relation and it may be that, logically, there can be no relations without *relata*. In that case it follows that there is subject–object dualism because 'subject' means 'that which experiences' and 'object' means 'what experience is experience of'. However, the necessity of this inference should not be confused with the modality of the conclusion that subject–object dualism obtains. In general it is fallacious to infer the modal status of a conclusion from the modal status of the inference that yields it. In this case too, the fact that the subject–object distinction obtains even if its obtaining is a necessary condition for experience and even if there is experience, is insufficient to establish that its obtaining is a necessary truth. (This is a distinction which Kant systematically fails to grasp in the *Critique of Pure Reason*.)

It follows that Sartre is wrong to characterise subject–object dualism as 'purely logical'. It is also true that he has not shown that the distinction is not genuine or does not obtain.

Throughout *The Transcendence of the Ego* Sartre has sought to establish that the ego is an object not a subject: an item to be encountered in the course of experience, like the ego of another, and not an irreducibly subjective 'source' or precondition of consciousness. If his arguments are sound he has relocated the subject as another kind of object. The subject of intentionality has turned out to be one of the objects of intentionality. It is surprising then that he should misrepresent his own position as one which is neutral between subjectivist and objectivist ontologies, but there is no doubt that this is what he does:

> The World has not created the me: the me has not created the World. These are two objects for absolute, impersonal consciousness, and it is by virtue of this consciousness that they are connected. (105–6)[246]

If follows that subject–object dualism is a construction out of consciousness. Consciousness itself is intrinsically neither subjective nor objective but the distinction between ego and world is phenomenologically supervenient on it: a kind of phenomenological neutral monism.

Now, this topic neutrality of consciousness with regard to subjectivity and objectivity has simply not been established by the arguments of *The Transcendence of the Ego*. Even from the fact that there is a sound argument for the conclusion that the subject is an object it does not follow that both subject and object are constructions out of a consciousness that is intrinsically neither subjective nor objective. Of course, that ontology may be independently true; true on grounds that are logically independent of Sartre's arguments against Husserl's transcendental ego. It would however require separate argument to establish it.

Arguments for precisely that conclusion are advanced by Hegel in the final chapter of *Phenomenology of Spirit* called 'Absolute Knowing' but this is not the place to appraise their soundness.

5 Absolute interiority: towards a phenomenology of the soul

That something is me is not an empirical fact. Being me is not just the fact that a particular being exists. Nor is being me any modal fact, for example, that a particular being is numerically distinct from all other beings, or that some being is self-identical. Even if some of these facts are necessary for something's being me, none is sufficient. There is always more to something's being me than something's being.

If all the facts are empirical facts or modal facts or metaphysical facts and if being me is a fact but not an empirical fact nor a modal fact then being me is a metaphysical fact. Being me is a fact. It follows in a fairly precise sense that *I am out of this world*.

This metaphysical view is *prima facie* inconsistent with both the Husserlian doctrine that I am a transcendental ego and the doctrine of existential phenomenology that my being is essentially being-in-the-world. It is inconsistent with the view that I am a transcendental ego because Husserl, following Kant, denies that the transcendental I is *metaphysical*. It is inconsistent with my being being being-in-the-world because the terms of that putatively fundamental situation are existentially inseparable (even if separable in abstract thought) but my being being out of this world implies my separability from the world. How may phenomenology be reconciled with this metaphysics?

It is possible that I am a transcendental ego if *pace* Kant and Husserl the transcendental subject is metaphysical. It is possible for my being to be being-in-the-world if my being in the world but not my being is temporary.

The disagreement between Sartre and Husserl over the existence of the transcendental ego presupposes a common basis which they partly acknowledge. In Husserlian terminology it is the *transcendental field* or *field of transcendental subjectivity* after the *epoché*. In the existential phenomenological terminology of the Sartre of 1943 it is the *nothingness* of being-for-itself. In *The Transcendence of the Ego* Sartre calls it 'an inside without an outside' or 'absolute interiority'. We could call it 'subjective space' or 'inner space'. It is the space of one's own psychological interiority, the zone of awareness where my experiences happen. In the *non-*

psychologistic vocabulary of Heidegger's 1927 fundamental ontology which eschews 'subjective' and 'inner' it is the *Lichtung* or clearing in the forest where being is disclosed to being.

These spatial concepts differ sharply in sense but not in reference. That they differ sharply in sense establishes sharply different phenomenologies. That they do not differ in referent allows them to denote a common presupposition of the difference between Husserl and Sartre over the ego.

Subjective space has phenomenological properties. It is phenomenologically indistinguishable from physical space as perceptually presented to oneself at its centre: unbounded, in the sense that travel seems in principle possible for ever away from its centre.

Subjective space is Parmenidean: it is like the inside of a *sphere* with one's own being as its interior. Thoughts and experiences, including experiences of physical objects, arise and subside within it. It is the zone where being and phenomenological content coincide.

This space is primordial with regard to the dispute between Sartre and Husserl. It is hard to see how I could exist without it or it without me. It does not follow that I am it and we are left with the problem of exactly what I have said about subjective space if I do say I am it.

It is necessary and sufficient for my existence. It is not physical. I am or am directly acquainted with its interiority. It is hard to see how it could admit of natural generation or destruction. I conjecture that subjective space is the soul.

Notes

1 For a clear, argumentative introduction to Husserl's philosophy see Robert Sokolowski *Husserlian Meditations: How Words Present Things* (Northwestern University Press, Evanston, 1974). For a historical overview of phenomenology see H. Spiegelberg *The Phenomenological Movement: A Historical Introduction*, 2 vols. (Martinus Nijhoff, The Hague, 1976). Husserl's introduction to his own philosophy is *The Paris Lectures*, trans. Peter Koestenbaum (Martinus Nijhoff, The Hague, 1975). David Bell's *Husserl* (Routledge, London and New York, 1990) is clearly argued and informative.

2 For Brentano on intentionality see his *Psychology from an Empirical Standpoint* (Routledge, London, 1973). For an introduction to Brentano and Husserl on intentionality see Stephen Priest *Theories of the Mind* (Penguin, Harmondsworth, 1991), ch. 7, 'The Phenomeno-   logical View'.

3 On *noesis* and *noema* see *Ideen* I §§88–96.

4 *Erste Philosophie (1923–1924), Erster Teil: Kritische Ideengeschichte*, ed. R. Boehme (Martinus Nijhoff, The Hague, 1956); *Erste Philosophie (1923–1924), Zweiter Teil: Theorie der phänomenologischen Reduktion*, ed. R. Boehme (Martinus Nijhoff, The Hague, 1959); *Phänomenologische Psychologie: Vorlesungen Sommersemester 1925*, ed. Walter Biemel (Martinus Nijhoff, The Hague, 1962).

5 'Die ἐποχή ist, so kann auch gesagt werden, die radikale und universale Methode, wodurch ich mich als Ich rein fasse' (CM §8).

6 'Denken wir uns eine Selbstwahrnehmung vollzogen, aber jetzt in der Art, daß wir vom Leib abstrahieren' (*Ideen* II §22).

   Here I am identifying the transcendental ego with the pure ego or pure I. The translator has 'The pure ego' for 'Das reine Ich' and 'The pure ego as ego-pole' for 'Das reine Ich als Ichpol'.

7 'Wir finden uns dann als auf den Strom der Erlebnisse bezogene geistige Ich' (*Ideen* II §22).

8 In ordinary German *geistig* means *inter alia* 'spiritual', 'mental', 'intellectual'. It is an adjectival derivation from the noun *Geist*, which can mean 'spirit', 'mind', 'intelligence', 'wit', 'imagination', 'soul', 'morale', 'essence', 'ghost', 'spectre'. The adjective *seelisch* means 'mental', 'spiritual', 'emotional', 'psychical'. Its derivation from the noun *Seele* ('soul') is suggestive of a profound metaphysical commitment that Husserl seeks to eschew by the *epoché*.

9 'Das Ego erfaßt sich nicht bloß als strömendes Leben sondern als Ich, der ich dies und jenes erlebe, dies und jenes cogito als *derselbe* durchlebe' (CM §31).

10 'ich […] finde mich dabei als den einen und selben im Wechsel dieser Erlebnisse, als "Subjekt" der Akte und Zustände' (*Ideen* II §22).

11 It is an important claim of the present work that the problem Thomas Nagel identifies as that of *being someone* is genuine, important and difficult. Many philosophers who

I have spoken to about this do not see that Nagel has done this, so it is worth trying to state again just what the problem is.

Nagel himself says the problem really divides into two problems: 'What kind of a fact is it – if it is a fact – that I am Thomas Nagel? How can I be a particular person?' (*The View From Nowhere*, Oxford, Oxford University Press, 1986, p. 54) and, 'How can I be merely a particular person? The problem here is not how it can be the case that I am this one rather than that one, but how I can be anything as specific as a particular person in the world at all' (*The View From Nowhere* p. 55).

The essence of the problem is, if we try to answer the question What am I? no ontological answer seems adequate. Ontologically we might be whole human beings, minds, brains, living bodies, souls, or something else. The problem is saying what is claimed about one of these things when it is claimed I am it. What extra information is provided about something by claiming that you are it?

Now, the crux of the problem of getting people to see the Nagel problem is getting them to see that the straightforwardly ontological answers are inadequate. I think there are two reasons why people do not appreciate this inadequacy, one intellectual, the other existential. Intellectually, the objective view, or view from nowhere in particular, has not been abdicated even when a reader of Nagel thinks about himself. The oddness of being someone is thereby overlooked. The existential reason is this. It is probably necessary to experience, feel or appreciate being someone for it to strike one, so to speak 'in one's bones' that one is someone.

Possibly someone could be caused to experience being someone by paying attention to the peculiar asymmetries between one's experience of one's own body and one's observations of other people's bodies as described in existential phenomenology. This is not a theme of *The Transcendence of the Ego* but it is partly developed by Sartre in the chapter on the body in *Being and Nothingness* and more fully developed by Merleau-Ponty in the chapter on the body in *Phenomenology of Perception*. I discuss the asymmetries in my *Merleau-Ponty* (The Arguments of the Philosophers, Routledge, London, 1998).

Phenomenologically, other people are encountered as objectively discriminable beings in the external world. But, so far as I am concerned, one of these beings is not like that. I do not encounter it objectively 'over there'. I am it. Stating what this being one is, is what the problem consists in. To appreciate the problem you have to take seriously the fact that you exist.

12 'Ich, der ich jeweils "denke", den Ichstrahl auf das Gegenständliche des Aktes gerichtet haben' (*Ideen* II §22).

13 'in jedem Aktvollzuge liegt ein Strahl des Gerichtetseins, den ich nicht anders beschreiben kann als seinen Ausgangspunkt nehmend im "Ich" ' (*Ideen* II §22).

14 'Alles Weltliche, alles raum-zeitliche Sein ist für mich – das heißt gilt für mich, und zwar dadurch, daß ich es erfahre, wahrnehme, mich seiner erinnere, daran irgendwie denke, es beurteile, es werte, begehre usw. Das alles bezeichnet Descartes bekanntlich unter dem Titel *cogito*' (CM §8).

15 'Als absolut Gegebenes, bzw. zur Gegebenheit im a priori möglichen Blick fixierender Reflexion zu Bringendes, ist es ganz und gar nichts Geheimnisvolles oder gar Mystisches' (*Ideen* II §22).

16 '[Abstraktiv] es als etwas von diesen Erlebnissen, als etwas von seinem "Leben" Getrenntes nicht gedacht werden kann – ebenso wie umgekehrt diese Erlebnisse nicht denkbar sind, es sei denn als Medium des Ichlebens' (*Ideen* II §22).

17 'Mindestens, prinzipiell betrachtet, kann jede cogitatio wechseln, kommen und gehen, wenn Mann es auch bezweifeln mag, ob jede ein *notwendig* Vergängliches sei und nicht bloß, wie wir es vorfinden, ein *faktisch* Vergängliches. Demgegenüber scheint aber das reine Ich ein prinzipiell *Notwendiges* zu sein […]' (*Ideen* I §57).

18 'dann bietet sich mit ihm eine *eigenartige* – in gewissem Sinne nicht konstituierte – Transzendenz, eine *Transzendenz in der Immanenz* dar' (*Ideen* I §57).

19 For Sartre on Kant see *Being and Nothingness* translated by Hazel E. Barnes with an introduction by Mary Warnock (Methuen, London, 1969) pp. xlviii, l, lix, lxiv, 3, 6, 21, 62, 73, 81, 126, 130–5, 142–3, 148, 217, 225–30, 234–5, 247, 249, 253, 408, 431, 480, 582 and *Critique of Dialectical Reason, I: Theory of Practical Ensembles* trans. Alan Sheridan-Smith, ed. Jonathan Ree (NLB, London, 1976) pp. 22, 29, 35, 43, 65, 178.

In *L'Etre et le Néant* Sartre argues that Kant has no philosophy of the Other and so fails to solve the problem of solipsism. This pivotal criticism of Kant helps effect the transition from the existential phenomenology of *L'Etre et le Néant* to the Hegelian existential Marxism of the *Critique*: 'Nous trouverons pourtant peu de secours chez un Kant: préoccupé en effet, d'établir les lois universelles de la subjectivité, qui sont les mêmes pour tous, il n'a pas abordé la question des *personnes*' (*L'Etre et le Néant*, Gallimard, Paris, 1943, p. 269) 'We shall find little help in the Kantians. In fact they, preoccupied with establishing the universal laws of subjectivity which are the same for all, never dealt with the question of persons' (*Being and Nothingness* p. 225).

20 See Bernard Williams *Descartes: The Project of Pure Enquiry* (Penguin, Harmondsworth, 1978) Preface p. 9. Williams distinguishes the history of philosophy from the history of ideas by saying the history of ideas is history before it is philosophy and the history of philosophy is philosophy before it is history, where 'before' indicates the order of priorities. Williams says 'For the history of ideas, the question about a work *What does it mean?* is centrally the question *What did it mean?*'. See also John Dunn, 'The Identity of the History of Ideas', *Philosophy* 43 (1968), 85–104 (cited in Williams, op. cit.).

21 For Kant on the transcendental unity of apperception (*transzententalische Einheit der Apperzeption*) see Kant, *Kritik der reinen Vernunft*, herausgegeben von Ingeborg Heidemann (Phillipp Reclamm Jun., Stuttgart, 1980) 'Transzendentale Deduktion der reinen Verstandesbegriffe' pp. 173–206 esp. B131–2 and *Immanuel Kant's Critique of Pure Reason*, trans. Norman Kemp Smith (London, 1978) esp. pp. 135–61 esp. 152–3, 166, 168ff., 209ff., 329ff., 336ff., 375ff., 378n., 381ff., 408.

For interpretations see P.F. Strawson *The Bounds of Sense: An Essay on Kant's Critique of Pure Reason* (London, 1966) pp. 24, 26–7, 87, pt. II ch. 2 Sections 6 and 7, pp. 163ff.; Jonathan Bennett, *Kant's Analytic* (Cambridge, 1966) ch. 8 'Transcendental Deduction: The Main Thread' and ch. 9 'Transcendental Deduction: Further Aspects' (pp. 100–25 and 126–38); and Dieter Henrich *Identität und Objektivität: Eine Untersuchung über Kants transzendentale Deduktion* (Heidelberg, 1976).

22 Sartre's 'Le <Je> pense doit *pouvoir* accompagner toutes nos représentations' (TE 13) is a translation of Kant's 'Das: Ich denke, muß alle meine Vorstellungen begleiten *können*' (KRV B131). Note that the italicised emphasis of 'können' ('pouvoir') is not just Sartre's but Kant's. Kant is at pains to make clear that the transcendental unity of apperception is a doctrine about possibility, not necessarily about actuality.

For Hegel's Kant see G.W.F. Hegel *Sämtliche Werke*, Jubiläumsausgabe, ed. H. Glockner (Stuttgart, 1967) xix, and G.W.F. Hegel *Lectures on the History of Philosophy*, trans. E.H. Haldane and F.H. Simson (London, 1974) vol. 3. For Kant on Hegel on the transcendental unity of apperception see Stephen Priest 'Subjectivity and Objectivity in Kant and Hegel' in Stephen Priest (ed.) *Hegel's Critique of Kant* (Oxford, 1987) pp. 103–18.

23 See, for example, P.F. Strawson *Individuals: An Essay in Descriptive Metaphysics* (London, 1959), who mentions 'Kant's doctrine of the analytic unity of apperception of the "I think" which accompanies all "my" perceptions' (p. 82). Clearly, from the fact that *Ich denke* must be able to accompany all my presentations it does not logically follow that it does so. Nor is the analytic unity of apperception the same condition for the possibility of experience as the transcendental unity of apperception. The analytic unity of apperception is the modal point that 'I have my presentations' or 'all my presentations are mine' is a necessary truth. This is logically distinct from the dispositional claim that it must in principle be possible for any of my thoughts or perceptions to be a self-conscious thought or perception as a necessary condition for their being mine.

Interestingly, Kant makes the analytic unity of apperception (*analytische Einheit der Apperzeption*) rest on a synthetic condition: 'Die analytische Einheit der Apperzeption ist nur unter der Voraussetzung irgendeiner synthetischen möglich' (KRV B133). 'The analytic unity of apperception is possible only under the presupposition of a certain synthetic unity' (KRV B133).

Kant has made a logical mistake in thinking that the truth of some synthetic proposition is a necessary condition for the truth of an analytic proposition. This is never the case because the meaning of an analytic proposition is sufficient for its truth so nothing else is necessary. However, the exegetical point still holds against Strawson: Nothing is a necessary condition for the transcendental unity of apperception. Something is (putatively) a necessary condition for the analytic unity of apperception, therefore the transcendental unity of apperception is not the analytic unity of apperception.

24 'Das: Ich denke, muß alle meine Vorstellungen begleiten *können*; denn sonst würde etwas in mir vorgestellt werden, was gar nicht gedacht werden könnte, welches eben so viel heißt, als die Vorstellung würde entweder unmöglich, oder, wenigstens für mich nichts sein' (KRV B131–2).

A plausible explanation of Kant's italicisation of 'können' is his wish to distance himself from the 'occurrent' view of the relation between consciousness and self-consciousness. Notice too that 'Ich denke' should not be translated as 'the "I think"' (as Kemp Smith and several commentators have it) but as 'I think'. 'Das' in Kant's sentence is not the definite article. Kant means that any of my thoughts can in principle be prefaced by 'I think that … '. Notice that 'Ich denke' is a literal translation of Descartes' 'cogito' (even though Kant wishes to deny any Cartesian ontological implications). 'The *I think*' and 'The *cogito*' seem equally awkward.

25 C.D. Broad *Kant: An Introduction* (Cambridge, 1979). Although philosophically appropriate, the translation of 'Vorstellung' by 'presentation' in ordinary German would be normally correct when 'Vorstellung' denotes a presentation given: rather like a performance ('Darstellung'). I see nothing illegitimate in Broad's appropriation of 'presentation' even though the historical Kant's 'Vorstellung' is his rendering of Leibniz's 'representatio' via Wolff.

26 'Il s'agit en effet de déterminer les conditions de possibilité de l'expérience' (TE 14).

27 See Thomas Nagel *The View From Nowhere* ch. 4.1 'Being Someone'. As noted above Nagel thinks the problem of being someone divides into two questions. How many questions there are here depends partly on the criteria for individuating questions. It might be, for example, that if we were in a position to answer one of Nagel's two sub-questions we would be in a position to answer the other. Of course it would not follow from this that they were the same question because from the fact that knowing one answer enables one to know another it does not follow that they are answers to the same question. Even if the answers to the questions are the same (numerically and qualitatively identical) we would not wish to make that a conclusive ground for saying that they are the same question. This is because different questions could have the same answer. (For example, different questions could have the answer 'Yes'.)

I used to think the question 'What is it to be me?' could be answered, in principle, by mentioning:

1 Every empirical (including mental and physical) fact about a person.

2 Every uniquely specifying originating fact about that same person (the only person born at 11 St Andrew's Lane, Old Headington, Oxford, England at 1.00 a.m. on 22 August 1954, of such and such parents).

I now think that although these procedures provide individuating descriptions, descriptions which apply to me and to no one else, it is not logically or metaphysically impossible that they should have been false of me and true of someone else. Being me is some fact 'over and above' all empirical facts about me and all individuating descriptions of me. I have tried to show the seeming intractability of this problem of being oneself in my outline sketch of a possible solution to the mind–body problem at the end of Stephen Priest *Theories of the Mind* (London, Boston, New York, 1991) pp. 220–1.

28 See Christopher Peacocke 'No Resting Place: A Critical Notice of *The View From Nowhere*, by Thomas Nagel' *The Philosophical Review* 98/1 (January 1989).

29 Philosophy since Kant has been essentially Kantian. All the central movements of Anglo-American and European philosophy since Kant are species of anti-metaphysical transcendental philosophy. This is as true of so-called 'Modern continental philosophy': Dialectic, Phenomenology, Existentialism, Structuralism and Post-Structuralism, as it is of so-called 'Analytical' philosophy: Logical Positivism and Linguistic Analysis. Indeed, once their common Kantian presuppostions are made explicit the similarities between these movements are much more conspicuous than their stylistic differences. When these movements conceive of themselves as 'radical' or breaking with something called 'the tradition' they are repeating a Kantian conservatism.

The claim that all philosophy since Kant has been essentially Kantian is important to the present work because the difference between Husserl and Sartre is between two kinds of Kantianism: two different ways in which a Kantian consciousness may be unified. Solving the philosophical problem of how the unity of consciousness is possible may require our abdicating the Kantian framework. (This is true of many other problems.)

Although the Kantianism of post-Kantian philosophy is a premise of the present work it is the conclusion of a book I am presently working on: *The Critical View: Modern Philosophy's Kantian Assumptions* (forthcoming).

30 'Réaliser le Je transcendantal, en faire le compagnon inséparable de chacune de nos <consciences>, c'est juger sur le fait et non sur le droit, c'est se placer a un point de vue radicalement différent de celui de Kant' (TE 15).

Sartre may be supported by the Paralogisms chapter: KRV CPR (A341/B399–A405/B432) 'Von den Paralogismen der reinen Vernunft'. Any substantial reification of the subject is *prima facie* open to Kant's criticisms there.

31 'Si pourtant l'on prétend s'autoriser des considérations kantiennes sur sur l'unité nécessaire à l'expérience, on commet la même erreur que ceux qui font de la conscience transcendantale un inconscient préempirique' (TE 15).

32 'Si donc on accorde à Kant la question de *droit*, la question de fait n'est pas tranchée pour autant' (TE 15).

33 'Le Je que nous rencontrons dans notre conscience est-il rendu possible par l'unité synthétique de nos représentations, ou bien est-ce lui qui unifie en fait les représentations entre elles?' (TE 16).

34 See S.L. Hurley 'Kant on Spontaneity and the Myth of the Giving', *Proceedings of the Aristotelian Society* (1994).

35 For example, straight after claiming that Hume narrowly missed the opportunity to engage in genuine phenomenology Husserl says about Kant and phenomenology:

Und erst recht erschaut sie Kant, dessen größte Intuitionen uns erst ganz verständlich werden, wenn wir uns das Eigentümliche des phänomenologischen Gebietes zur vollbewußten Klarheit erarbeitet haben. Es wird uns dann evident, daß Kants Geistesblick auf diesem Felde ruhte, obschon er es sich noch nicht zuzueignen und es als Arbeitsfeld einer eigenen strengen Wesenwissenschaft nicht zu erkennen vermochte. So bewegt sich z.B. die transzendentale Deduktion der ersten Auflage der *Kritik der reinen Vernunft* eigentlich schon auf phänomenologischen Boden; aber Kant mißdeutet denselben als psychologischen und gibt ihn daher selbst wieder preis.

(*Ideen* I §62)

And then the first to correctly see it was Kant, whose greatest intuitions become wholly understandable to us only when we [had] (have) obtained by hard work a fully clear awareness of the peculiarity of the province belonging to phenomenology. It then becomes evident to us that Kant's mental regard was resting on that field, although he was still unable to appropriate it or recognize it as a field of work pertaining to a strict eidetic science proper. Thus, for example, the transcendental deduction in the first edition of the *Kritik der reinen Vernunft* was actually operating inside the realm of phenomenology, but Kant misinterpreted that realm as psychological and therefore he himself abandoned it.

(Ideas I §62)

Even in this admission Husserl underestimates Kant's anticipation of phenomenological method. For example, Kant does not misinterpret the findings of the A version of the transcendental deduction as psychological. This is something that Husserl has done. Kant is engaged in transcendental logic *(transzendentale Logik)*: a method that contains the essence of Husserl's eidetic phenomenology. See Stephen Priest *The Critical View* (forthcoming).

36 Despite Husserl's repeated search for a phenomenology that will be a 'science' *(Wissenschaft)* or 'strict science' *(strenge Wissenschaft)* it would be a naive mistake to assimilate his phenomenology to empirical or natural science. Husserl draws the distinction as follows:

Ist nun alle eidetische Wissenschaft prinzipiell von aller Tatsachenwissenschaft unabhängig, so gilt andererseits das Umgekehrte hinsichtlich der *Tatsachenwissenschaft*. Es gibt *keine*, die *als Wissenschaft voll entwickelt*, rein sein könnte von eidetischen Erkenntnissen und somit *unabhängig sein könnte* von den, sei es formalen oder materialien eidetischen Wissenschaften.

(Ideen I §8)

But although every eidetic science is necessarily independent of every science of matters of fact, the reverse holds, on the other hand, for the latter sciences. There is no science of matters of fact which, were it fully developed as a science, could be pure of eidetic cognitions and therefore could be independent of the formal or the material eidetic sciences.

(Ideas I §8)

37 'La conscience transcendentale de Kant, Husserl la retrouve et la saisit par l'ἐποχή' (TE 18).

38 It is worth raising the question of why the transcendental ego does not feature in the Husserl of *Logische Untersuchungen* (1900–1901) and *Vorlesungen zur Phänomenologie des innern Zeitbewußtseins* (in *Jahrbuch für Philosophie und phänomenologische Forschung* 9 (1928) pp. 367–498, but delivered from 1905) but is introduced only in *Ideen* I (and even then under the name 'pure ego' not 'transcendental ego') because we may legitimately read Sartre in *La Transcendance de l'Ego* as endorsing the Husserl of 1900 against the Husserl of 1913 and later. (As noted above, note 4, 'transcendental ego' is first used in the lectures in the early 1920s on *Erste Philosophie* and *Phänomenologische Psychologie*.)

This transition from the early to the middle Husserl on the ego is effected by the *epoché*. The transcendental ego is putatively revealed or discovered through the *epoché* and there is no *epoché* in the work of 1900–1 or 1905 (even though there is a suspension of attitude towards objective time in the 1905 lectures which interestingly anticipates the *epoché*). For example, in *Cartesianische Meditationen* Husserl claims:

Jeder von uns, als cartesianisch Meditierender, wurde durch die Methode der phänomenologischen Reduktion auf sein transzendentales Ego zurückgeführt und natürlich mit seinem jeweiligen konkret-monadischen Gehalt als dieses faktische, als das eine und einzige absolute Ego.

(CM §34)

By the method of transcendental reduction each of us, as Cartesian meditator, was led back to his transcendental ego – naturally with its concrete-monadic content as this de facto ego, the one and only absolute ego.

(CM §34)

Once ontological commitment to the external world is suspended it is not the case that there is nothing at all. The field of transcendental subjectivity is revealed.

We may still ask, as Sartre will ask, whether this transcendental field is necessarily personal, necessarily someone's, even though it does not belong to any empirical self because the empirical self has fallen by the *epoché*.

Arguably, although the empirical self falls by the *epoché*, *being someone* does not. If we ask what the external world is external to, part of the answer is 'me'. Husserl thinks it is intuitive that I am given to myself as myself even after the transcendental reduction:

Ich bin für mich selbst und mir immerfort durch Erfahrungs-evidenz als Ich Selbst gegeben.

(CM §33)

I exist for myself and am continually given to myself, by experiential evidence, as 'I myself'.

(CMT §33)

39 'cette conscience n'est plus un ensemble de conditions logiques, c'est un fait absolu' (TE 18).
40 Here I assume that what a philosopher (or anyone else) thinks, says or writes is not necessarily identical with what that philosopher either intends to think, say or write or believes he thinks, says or writes. This is because the propositions expressed by a set of token indicative sentences may not coincide with the propositions the producer of the sentences might allocate to them. To argue otherwise would be a *non sequitur*.
41 A proposition is synthetic if and only if it is not true by definition but provides non-tautological information. A proposition is *a priori* if and only if its truth value is decidable purely intellectually. A proposition is necessary if and only if, if it is true it could not have been false and if it is false it could not have been true.
42 'c'est bien elle qui constitue notre conscience empirique, cette conscience <dans le monde>, cette conscience avec un <moi> psychique et psychophysique. Nous croyons volontiers pour notre part à l'existence d'une conscience constituante' (TE 18).
    On Husserl's *noesis/noema* distinction see *Ideen* I paras 87–96 inclusive.
43 See CM §11 where Husserl draws a clear contrast between the the existence of the pre-phenomenological empirical self of the natural attitude: 'Ich, dieser Mensch, bin' ('I, this man, exist') and the 'reduced' ego of the transcendental field: 'Ich bin, ego cogito' ('I exist, ego cogito').
    Dorion Cairns has mistranslated Husserl's German here. 'Exist' and 'man' have no warrant in the original and 'Ich, dieser Mensch, bin' would be better translated as 'I, this human being am' and 'Ich bin, ego cogito' would be better rendered as 'I am, ego cogito'.

Note too that in Husserl's Latin 'cogito' is prefaced by 'ego' for emphasis. In Latin the inflexion of 'cogito' is grammatically sufficient to indicate the first person singular form and the present tense and active mood. 'Ego' is grammatically redundant. However, Husserl exploits the fact that 'ego' may be used for emphasis in Latin to express more forcibly his phenomenological claim that being me survives the suspension of belief in my empirical self.

44 'ce moi psychique et psycho-physique n'est-il pas suffisant? Faut-il le doubler d'un Je transcendantal, structure de la conscience absolue?' (TE 18–19).

45 'Le champ transcendantal devient impersonnel, ou, si l'on préfère, <prépersonnel>, il est sans Je' (TE 19).

46 'Un Je transcendantal qui serait comme en arrière de chaque conscience, qui serait une structure nécessaire des consciences, dont les rayons tomberaient sur chaque phénomène qui se présenterait dans le champ de l'attention' (TE 20).

47 On the problem of what the unity of consciousness consists in see Thomas Nagel 'Brain Bisection and the Unity of Consciousness', *Synthèse* 22 (1971) pp. 396–413 reprinted in Jonathan Glover (ed.) *The Philosophy of Mind* (Oxford, 1976) pp. 111–25 and in Thomas Nagel *Mortal Questions* (Cambridge, 1979) as ch. 11; Michael S. Gazzaniga *The Bisected Brain* (New York, 1970); R.W. Sperry 'The Great Cerebral Commissure' *Scientific American* 210 (1964), 'Brain Bisection and the Mechanisms of Consciousness' in J.C. Eccles (ed.) *Brain and Conscious Experience* (Berlin, 1966); Erwin Schrodinger *Mind and Matter* (Cambridge, 1958) ch. 4; Sydney Shoemaker *Self-Knowledge and Self-Identity* (New York, 1963) ch. 3; J.C. Eccles *The Brain and the Unity of Conscious Experience* (Cambridge, 1965). Kant tries to dissolve the problem *qua* metaphysical or ontological at KRV/CPR (A341/B399–A405/B432) and substitutes his 'formal' and 'transcendental' account at KRV/CPR (A84/B130–A130/B169).

48 On the putative intentionality of all and only mental events see Stephen Priest *Theories of the Mind* (London, Boston, New York, 1991) pp. 116, 186, 193–7, 198, 199, 202–7; Franz Brentano *Psychologie vom empirischen Standpunkt* (Leipzig, 1874), *Psychology From an Empirical Standpoint* trans. A.C. Rancurello, D.B. Terrell and L.L. McAlister (London, 1973); Edmund Husserl *Logische Untersuchungen* (1900–2), *Logical Investigations* trans. J.N. Findlay (New York, 1970); John Searle *Intentionality* (Cambridge, 1983).

49 'L'unité des mille consciences actives par lesquelles j'ai ajouté, j'ajoute et j'ajouterai deux à deux pour faire quatre, c'est l'objet transcendant <deux et deux font quatre>' (TE 21).

50 If p is an *eternal truth* then p is true at all times and so never false. If p is an *eternal falsehood* then p is false at all times and so never true. May p nevertheless be contingent? 'Necessarily not' contains modal information lacking in 'never' so there is logical room for the possibility of p's truth even if, as a matter of fact, choose any time you like, p is false at that time. p could have been true even if p is never true. p could have been false even if p is never false.

51 'Qui dit <une conscience> dit toute la conscience' (TE 22).

52 I have in mind here the putative transition from 'Die Wahrheit der Gewissheit seiner Selbst', 'The Truth of Self-Certainty' to 'Das absolute Wissen', 'Absolute Knowing'. See G.W.F. Hegel *Phänomenologie des Geistes*, herausgegeben von Hans-Friedrich Wessel und Heinrich Clairmont mit einer Einleitung von Wolfgang Bonsiepen (Hamburg, 1988), translated as *Hegel's Phenomenology of Spirit* by Arnold Miller (Oxford, 1977). Whether numerically and qualitatively distinct and mutually antagonistic forms of consciousness may be ultimately *aufgehoben* ('absorbed', 'preserved', 'taken up', 'abolished', 'relieved') by *Geist* is an unsolved philosophical problem. Hegel's conclusion should certainly not be endorsed glibly.

53 'Il faut un principe d'unité *dans la durée* pour que le flux continuel des consciences soit susceptible de poser des objets transcendants hors de lui. Il faut que les consciences soient des synthèses perpétuelles des consciences passées et de la conscience présente. C'est exact.' (TE 22)

54 This distinction is introduced by Husserl in the *Lectures on the Phenomenology of Inner Time Consciousness*. See *Vorlesungen zur Phänomenologie des inneren Zeitbewußtseins* herausgegeben von Martin Heidegger, *Jahrbuch fur Philosophie und phänomenologische Forschung* 9 (1928).

55 'Aufgehoben' is the past participle of the verb 'aufheben', a crucial technical term in Hegel's dialectical reasoning. The infinitive means not only 'to relieve' (as in to relieve a tension) but 'to preserve' and 'to abolish', a paradoxical ambivalence which Hegel exploits to denote the relationship between a pair of antithetical categories and their speculative synthesis. The antitheses are allegedly abolished in their disunity or independence but preserved as the new synthetic whole.

   Applying this to Sartre, although there are no intentional objects without the unity of consciousness and there is no unity of consciousness without intentional objects both the unity of consciousness and intentional objects exist. Logically, the relation is: if not A then not B and if not B then not A, but both A and B exist. Sartre has no new term for the putative dialectical synthesis. It is typical of him to only partly endorse Hegelian thinking in this manner. (See, for example, the impossibility of a synthesis of *l'être pour-soi* and *l'être en-soi* in *L'Etre et le Néant, passim*.)

56 In *L'Etre et le Néant*, although Sartre concedes that 'la temporalité est évidemment une structure organisée', 'temporality is obviously an organised structure', he suggests that 'ces trois prétendus <éléments> du temps: passé, présent, avenir, ne doivent pas être envisagés comme une collection de <data> dont il faut faire la somme' (p. 145), 'these three putative "elements" of time: past, present, future, should not be envisaged as a "collection" out of which it is necessary to make a sum'.

   His motivation is to avoid creating a philosophical problem by making an unnecessary assumption. If we think of past, present and future atomistically (as not mutually dependent) it will be impossible to understand them *qua* whole. If we think of their mutual dependence as prior to the distinctions between them then they are available for phenomenological description *qua* dialectical moments or 'ekstasies' of time. It is typical of Sartre's 'phenomenological ontology' to make synthesis prior to analysis and wholes prior to parts.

   One of the central conclusions of the discussion of presence in *L'Etre et le Néant* is conspicuously consistent with the dependence of the unity of consciousness on the world of objects in *La Transcendance de L'Ego*. Sartre says 'Mon présent c'est d'être présent', 'My present is to be present' (p. 159) but then, assuming that all presence is presence to, asks 'Présent a quoi?', 'Present to what?'. He provides various empirical examples and says 'bref à l'être en-soi', 'in brief, to being in-itself'. The critique of Husserl on the transcendental ego thus removes a phenomenological obstacle to the depiction of consciousness *qua l'être pour-soi* as dependent on *l'être en-soi* in his existential phenomenology.

57 In so far as he recognises the existence of a subject prior to the sophisticated articulation of *l'être pour-soi* in *L'Etre et le Néant*, Sartre equivocates between its being consciousness and its being the human being *qua* psycho-physical whole. Although it is open to Sartre *qua* phenomenologist to hold that both of these are presented *qua* subject at different times this ambivalence is open to a Husserlian interpretation which he has to repudiate. Before the *epoché*, for Husserl, the subject is the empirical human being of the natural attitude. After the *epoché* the subject is revealed as transcendental consciousness essentially structured by the pure ego. Sartre cannot accept this, not just because he rejects the transcendental ego, but because he rejects the *epoché*. In *La Transcendance de L'Ego* the *epoché* is still partly endorsed, indeed, it is used as an ironic weapon against Husserl. In *L'Etre et le Néant* however it is abandoned and the the Heideggerian notion of being-in-the-world substituted. Heidegger, Merleau-Ponty and Sartre in differing degrees abandoning the *epoché* is partly criterial of their practising 'existential phenomenology' (a label Merleau-Ponty and Sartre but not Heidegger would be happy with but which applies to all three). On the alleged

impossibility of the *epoché* see Stephen Priest, *Merleau-Ponty* (Routledge, London, 1998) pp. 2, 7, 9, 18–23, 28, 29, 35, 208.

58 One can sympathise with a reader who despairs of Sartre at this point. *Prima facie* he has fallen into that common intellectual naivety of thinking contradictions insights rather than confusions. Construed sympathetically, however, Sartre is distinguishing awareness from content and saying the structure of content is the best guide to the structure of consciousness. Awareness of content is not another content (at least for pre-reflexive consciousness).

59 'L'individualité de la conscience provient évidemment de la nature de la conscience. La conscience ne peut être bornée (comme la substance de Spinoza) que par elle-même' (TE 23).

60 See Benedictus de Spinoza *Ethics*, trans. A. Boyle (London, 1977) *passim*. Spinoza's concept of substance is essentially Aristotelian:

> I understand 'substance' [*substantia*] to be that which is in itself and is conceived through itself; I mean that the conception of which does not depend on the conception of another thing from which it must be formed.
>
> (*Ethics* p. 1)

Spinoza offers both an ontological and an epistemological criterion for being a substance. Ontologically, x is a substance if and only if if x exists then x's existence depends upon nothing but x. Epistemologically, if x is known then knowledge of x does not depend upon knowing anything but x. *Prima facie* it is only the ontological criterion which Sartre appropriates in his discussion of consciousness. Nevertheless, the epistemological criterion is implicitly at work. For example, consciousness is given phenomenologically to itself as if it is (or could be) all there is.

61 'Elle constitue donc une totalité synthétique et individuelle entièrement isolée des autres totalités de même type' (TE 23).

62 'La conception phénoménologique de la conscience rend le rôle unifiant et individu-alisant du Je totalement inutile. C'est la conscience au contraire qui rend possible l'unité et la personnalité de mon Je' (TE 23).

  Here the translator has 'the I' but Sartre has 'mon Je', 'my I'.

63 The Cartesian and Freudian conceptions are mutually inconsistent because their conjunction implies a contradiction. Cartesianism is:

  (C) If a subject, S, is in any mental state, M, then S knows that S is in M.

and Freudianism (here) is:

  (F) For some S and for some M, if S is in M, then S does not know that S is in M.

which jointly imply that S both knows and does not know that S is in M. We have to understand Cartesianism as thoroughgoing: as entailing that if S knows of M under some description then that is sufficient for 'S knows that S is in M' and if S is in M then S does know M under such a description. Without this qualification Cartesianism and Freudianism could in principle be reconciled, for example if S could know M under some (Cartesian) description but not under any (Freudian) description.

64 'Elle prend conscience de soi *en tant qu'elle est conscience d'un objet transcendant*' (TE 24).

65 'Tout est donc clair et lucide dans la conscience: l'objet est en face d'elle, avec son opacité caractéristique, mais elle, elle est purement et simplement conscience d'être conscience de cet objet, c'est la loi de son existence' (TE 24).

66 A criterion for the self-evidence of propositions is this:

(SE) P is self-evident if and only if knowledge of P's truth value is a necessary condition for understanding P.

We could call Sartre's pre-reflexive consciousness 'self-intimating' with regard to its states:

(SI) Some consciousness is self-intimating if and only if its knowledge of its states is a necessary condition for being in its states.

Clearly 'knowledge of its states' must not be taken to imply knowledge of the truth values of its propositional attitudes or knowledge of which experiences are veridical and which non-veridical. Consciousness, putatively, only knows which states it is in if it is in them, not their veracity (although, equally clearly, their veracity and consciousness's knowledge of it are not precluded either).

67 I discuss this problem in Stephen Priest *Theories of the Mind* pp. 216–18. It is metaphysically unclear whether awareness of objects is nothing at all or something non-physical, but appearances arguably presuppose a *phenomenological space* in which to appear. There are good metaphysical grounds for the ultimate identification of such phenomenological space with the interiority of the soul. See Stephen Priest *Merleau-Ponty* (London, Routledge, 1998) ch. 15 'Parousia: Existential Phenomenology and the Return of Metaphysics'; and Stephen Priest 'On Aquinas' Claim "Anima mea non est ego"' *The Heythrop Journal* 42 (1999).

68 It is hard to answer the question What is consciousness? from phenomenological resources alone, *pace* Husserl's claim that intentionality is the essence of consciousness. Phenomenologically, consciousness could be nothing at all or all that there is. Philosophically, consciousness is *prima facie* open to elimination through extreme reductivism (as in eliminative materialism) or to inflation to all there is (as in Hegel). If *pace* Husserl we construe transcendental subjectivity metaphysically, room is opened up for the description of the interiority of the soul. In a sense this would involve the 'elimination' of consciousness, but in a way that would appal the eliminative materialist. Consciousness is redescribed as phenomenological space. Phenomenological space is redescribed as the inside of the soul.

The problem of consciousness is potentially fatal to phenomenology. Phenomenology is the description of what appears to consciousness. Does consciousness appear to consciousness? If so, what does it appear to? If no consciousness appears there is nothing for phenomenology to describe. If, strictly speaking, there are only phenomena then consciousness must fall by the *epoché*: a consequence neither Husserl nor Sartre envisages.

69 'Nous demandons: y a-t-il place pour un Je dans une pareille conscience? La réponse est claire: évidemment non. En effet ce Je n'est ni l'objet (puisqu'il est intérieur par hypothèse) ni non plus *de la conscience*, puisqu'il est quelquechose *pour* la conscience' (TE 24–5).

70 See Immanuel Kant's *Critique of Pure Reason* trans. Norman Kemp Smith (London, 1978) pp. 92, 93, 105, 130, 151, 153, 165, 169, 382, 411, 465. Kant contrasts 'spontaneity' (*Spontaneität*) with 'receptivity' (*Rezeptivität*) like this:

Wollen wir die Rezeptivität unseres Gemüts, Vorstellungen zu empfangen, so fern es auf irgend eine Weise affiziert wird, Sinnlichkeit nennen; so ist dagegen das Vermögen, Vorstellungen selbst hervorzubringen, oder die Spontaneität des Erkenntnisses, der Verstand. (A51/B75)

If the receptivity of our mind, its power of receiving (re)presentations in so far as it is in any wise affected, is to be entitled sensibility, then the mind's power of producing (re)presentations from itself, the spontaneity of knowledge, should be called the understanding.

It follows that 'receptivity' and 'sensibility' do not differ in reference, and 'spontaneity' and 'understanding' do not differ in reference. Part of the sense of 'sensibility' is the sense of 'receptivity' and part of the sense of 'understanding' is the sense of 'spontaneity'. By 'sense' I mean: a word has a sense if and only if it has a verbal definition. Plausible senses of 'receptivity' and 'spontaneity' are:

(R) A mind exhibits receptivity if and only if has a disposition to be caused to acquire knowledge.

(S) A mind exhibits spontaneity if and only if it has a disposition to cause itself to acquire knowledge.

The obtaining of the receptivity/spontaneity distinction is necessary but not sufficient for the obtaining of the sensibility/understanding distinction.

71 'ce n'est plus une spontanéité, elle porte même en elle comme un germe d'opacité' (TE 25).

72 In *L'Etre et le Néant*, although consciousness is not straightforwardly identified with the *nothingness* of the title, nothingness, or non-being, is introduced into the universe by consciousness (or that kind of being called '*l'être en-soi*'). It is common in discussion of Sartre and Heidegger to accuse them of the reification of nothing. Far from their falling into this naivety it is essential to the existential ontology of both thinkers that nothingness (*Nichts, néant*) does not exist. However, according to Sartre there is, for example, the *phenomenon* of Pierre's absence from the café or the possibility of 'negating' political institutions: thinking that they could cease to exist or could be otherwise. It is in these sorts of case that it makes sense to talk of consciousness producing nothingness. I take it they are psychologically uncontroversial whatever the merits and demerits of Sartre's phenomenological descriptions.

73 'On est contraint d'abandonner ce point de vue original et profond qui fait de la conscience un absolu non substantiel' (TE 25).

74 The thought is that if consciousness *per impossibile* were one item amongst others discriminable in its contents, then it could not exist *qua* awareness of those contents. Consciousness is, so to speak, too subjective to be objective.

75 'Une conscience pure est un absolu tout simplement parce qu'elle est conscience d'elle-même. Elle reste donc un <phénomène> au sens très particulier où <être> et <apparaître> ne font qu'un. Elle est toute légèreté, toute translucidité. C'est en cela que le Cogito de Husserl est si différent du Cogito cartésien' (TE 25).

76 See George Berkeley *The Principles of Human Knowledge with Other Writings* edited and introduced by G.J. Warnock (London, 1977). On the *esse est percipi* principle, see esp. pp. 30, 66–8, 109, 133, 154, 219–20, 264, 271. See also Stephen Priest *The British Empiricists* (London, 1990) pp. 104–31.

77 See G.W.F. Hegel *Phänomenologie des Geistes* neu herausgegeben von Hans-Friedrich Wessels und Heinrich Clairmont mit einer Einleitung von Wolfgang Bonsiepen (Hamburg, 1988) ch. 8 'Das absolute Wissen' pp. 516–31 and *Hegel's Phenomenology of Spirit* trans. A.V. Miller with a foreword by J.N. Findlay (Oxford, 1979) ch. 8 'Absolute Knowing' pp. 479–93.

Absolute knowing is the dialectical synthesis and speculative culmination of the forms of consciousness described in *Phänomenologie des Geistes*:

Das Ziel, das absolute Wissen, oder der sich als Geist wissende Geist hat zu seinem Wege die Erinnerung der Geister, wie sie an ihnen selbst sind und die Organisation ihres Reiches vollbringen. (pp. 530–1)

The goal, Absolute Knowing, or Spirit that knows itself as Spirit, has for its path the recollection of the Spirits as they are in themselves and as they accomplish the organisation of their realm.

(*Phenomenology of Spirit* p. 493)

Because it is self-consciousness its being (or becoming) what it is is not independent of its knowing what it is. If it fully knows what it is then it has fully become what it is.

78 It is Hegel's view that ultimately there is no ontologically self-sufficient individual subject and *a fortiori* no individual transcendental subject. By 'individual' here I mean 'corresponding to each individual human being'. In this sense Hegel and Husserl offer mutually inconsistent accounts of subjectivity. Nevertheless, there is a subject according to Hegel and the subject is substance and in a sense transcendental. The true subject of experience is *Geist*, or what is *qua* spiritual whole. *Geist* is substance because *Geist* depends upon nothing except itself for its existence. *Geist* is subject because *Geist* has my experiences and *Geist* is transcendental because *Geist* is a condition for the possibility of experience.

Qua *Geist* consciousness is conscious of itself and there is no ultimate subject of experience other than *Geist*. It is this picture of consciousness as *self-sufficient* which results from Sartre's subtraction of the transcendental ego from Husserl's field of transcendental subjectivity, or consciousness after the *epoché*.

79 Descartes thinks of the mind as a quasi-Aristotelian substance: It could exist even if nothing else existed (with the exception of God). Husserl is not committed to this despite his construal of the full concretion of the ego as a *monad* (CM §33). Nevertheless, neither the Cartesian soul nor the Husserlian transcendental ego is nothing over and above its psychic operations. It is that which exercises them.

For Descartes the mind is never directly acquainted with itself *qua* soul, only with its own *pensées*. For Husserl the transcendental ego is never available to the ordinary consciousness of the natural attitude but is revealed by the *epoché* as the condition for the possibility of experience within the transcendental field. On Sartre's rather Humean view, consciousness is aware of its own operations, implicitly through pre-reflexive consciousness and explicitly through reflective consciousness, but there is no ego *qua* subjective source of consciousness. Sartre thus endorses Descartes' epistemology of the mind but rejects his ontology.

80 'Tous les résultats de la phénoménologie menacent ruine si le Je n'est pas au même titre que le monde un existant relatif, c'est à dire un objet pour la conscience' (TE 26).

81 'Le <Je pense> kantien est une condition de possibilité. Le Cogito de Descartes et de Husserl est une constatation de fait' (TE 26).

82 'On a parlé de la <nécessité de fait> du Cogito et cette expression me paraît très juste. Or il est indéniable que le Cogito est personnel' (TE 26–7).

83 A *prima facie* construal of the logical status of 'I think' is:

(IT) 'I think' is true if and only if the token sentence 'I think' exists (or is produced).

Unfortunately this will not do because 'I think' could be produced by a tape recorder or similar non-conscious or unthinking object. Clearly, too, the existence of the token sentence 'I think' could survive the death of the thinker who produced it (for example, if it were written down). Its production is not then sufficient for its truth. That its production is necessary for its truth does not distinguish it from other sentences.

Another *prima facie* candidate for the logical status of 'I think' is

(IT') 'I think' is true if and only if the token sentence 'I think' is thought.

This provides us with a sufficient condition for the truth of 'I think': if I think 'I think' then it logically follows that 'I think' is true. It is not however necessary because it could be true that I think, and hence 'I think' could be true, even if I do not think 'I think'. If I think any thought that will do. On any of these 'I think' is contingent, even if *a priori*. Descartes' 'cogito' is usually translated as 'I think'. A more natural and philosophically plausible translation would be 'I am thinking'.

Cartesian self-knowledge, the Kantian doctrine of the unity of consciousness, and Husserl's transcendental phenomenology all logically depend for their formulation on the possibility of deploying the operator 'I think that' in a way that prefaces and embeds any thought by one thinker. This deployment must be by the thinker himself as a putative condition for the unity of that thinker's thought (and experience).

84 'Dans le <*Je* pense> il y a un *Je* qui pense' (TE 27).

85 To make this intuitively clearer: 'I think' is one thought amongst others for Sartre.

86 'Le fait qui peut servir de départ est donc celui-ci: chaque fois que nous saisissons notre pensée, soit par une intuition immédiate, soit par une intuition appuyée sur la mémoire, nous saisissons un *Je*' (TE 27).

87 'Si, par exemple, je veux me rappeler tel paysage aperçu dans le train, hier, il m'est possible de faire revenir le souvenir de ce paysage en tant que tel, mais je peux aussi me rappeler que *je* voyais ce paysage' (TE 27).

88 See Derek Parfit *Reasons and Persons* (Oxford, 1984).

89 (1) 'Je peux toujours opérer une remémoration quelconque sur le mode personnel et le *Je* apparaît aussitôt' (TE 27).
(2) 'Ainsi apparaît-il qu'il n'est pas une de mes consciences que je ne saisisse comme pourvue d'un Je' (TE 27).

90 That a being has to be self-conscious in order to be consciousness always needs special argument. *Prima facie*, from the fact that x is conscious it does not logically follow that x is conscious of x (still less that x is conscious that x is both what is conscious and what its consciousness is consciousness of). However, the move from 'I am conscious' to 'I am self-conscious' requires less argument because of the indexical role of 'I'. One plausible explanation for x's being a successful 'I' user is that x is conscious of x *qua* x and knowingly uses 'I' to refer only to himself. However, it cannot be ruled out *a priori* that non-conscious beings, for example robots, could be I users yet neither conscious nor self-conscious.

91 'Telle est la garantie *de fait* de l'affirmation *de droit* kantienne' (TE 27).

92 'Tous les auteurs qui ont décrit le Cogito l'ont donné comme une opération réflexive, c'est-à-dire comme une opération du second degré' (TE 27–8).

93 'Ce Cogito est opéré par une conscience *dirigée sur la conscience*, qui prend la conscience comme objet' (TE 28).

94 'Or, ma conscience réfléchissante ne se prend pas elle-même pour objet lorsque je réalise le *Cogito*. Ce qu'elle affirme concerne la conscience réfléchie' (TE 28).

95 'Entendons-nous: la certitude du Cogito est absolue' (TE 28).

96 'Comme le dit Husserl, il y a une unité indissoluble de la conscience réfléchissante et de la conscience réfléchie (au point que la conscience réfléchissante ne saurait exister sans la conscience réfléchie)' (TE 28).

97 On this quasi-Hegelian construal, consciousness *qua* reflecting depends upon reflected consciousness because arguably there could be no reflecting consciousness without consciousness being reflected on. Consciousness *qua* reflected depends upon reflecting consciousness because there could be no reflected consciousness without consciousness reflecting on it. Although contrasting forms of consciousness they are thus mutually dependent.

98 'Il n'en demeure pas moins que nous sommes en présence d'une synthèse de deux consciences dont l'une est conscience *de* l'autre' (TE 28).

Hegel's 'synthesis' is the name of two antithetical concepts united in their 'identity-in-difference'. The relation between A and B is identity-in-difference, if and only if; if not A then not B but A and B are numerically distinct. A is not B and B is not A but A and B are mutually dependent. The synthesis of A and B is A and B *qua* new whole.

99   The phenomenological claim to advance only descriptions so no explanations is probably unrealisable. In the description of essences, questions of the form 'What is *x*?' are being answered. However, any vocabulary used in such an answer will be theory-laden and open to possible argumentative refutation. A pure phenomenological vocabulary is as unlikely as a pure sense data language. On this point as on many others phenomenology and Logical Positivism are essentially similar philosophies; a fact surprising and abhorrent to practicioners of both but nonetheless true for that. See Stephen Priest *The Critical View: Modern Philosophy's Kantian Assumptions* (forthcoming).

100   I have in mind here the chapter of Hegel's *Phänomenologie des Geistes* VI, A, 'Selbständigkeit und Unselbständigkeit des Selbstbewußtseins; Herrschaft und Knechtschaft', Hegel's *Phenomenology of Spirit* VI, A, 'Independence and Dependence of Self-Consciousness: Lordship and Bondage'.

The thought Sartre needs is that my self-conception is built from my perception of others. I think of myself as like them but not as them. Sartre may resist this suggestion because it is not obviously consistent with his view that I fashion my own essence through my spontaneous freedom.

101   For intentionality as a putative criterion of being mental see Stephen Priest *Theories of the Mind* (London, New York, Boston, 1991) ch. 7 'The Phenomenological View' pp. 182–209. Arguably, the intentional is neither necessary nor sufficient for the mental because some non-mental things are intentional and some mental things are non-intentional. Missiles, rockets, pilotless bombs and even bullets exhibit a directedness towards an object but are not mental. It follows that the intentional is not sufficient for the mental. Pains, objectless depressions, aches and feelings of 'angst' do not exhibit intentionality, they are not 'about' anything, yet they are mental (or at least felt or undergone). It follows that the intentional is not necessary for the mental.

102   'Le principe essentiel de la phénoménologie "toute conscience est conscience *de* quelquechose", est sauvegardé' (TE 28).

103   The token thought 'I think' is thought by reflecting consciousness. The token thought 'I think' is not thought by reflected consciousness. Sartre thinks it is the thinking done by reflected consciousness that makes 'I think' true. He sees that this is sufficient but misses the point that it is not necessary. Any thought thought by the thinker of 'I think' is necessary and sufficient for the truth of 'I think' thought by him, including just that thought itself. So the thinking of one thought rather than another in reflected consciousness is not necessary.

104   'En tant que ma conscience réfléchissante est conscience d'elle-même, elle est conscience *non-positionelle*. Elle ne devient positionelle qu'en visant la conscience réfléchie qui, elle-même, n'était pas conscience positionelle de soi avant d'être réfléchie' (TE 28).

105   Locke thinks that if a being is conscious then it is self-conscious 'it being impossible for anyone to perceive without perceiving that he does perceive' *An Essay Concerning Human Understanding* ed. A.S. Pringle-Pattison (Oxford, 1950) II.27.9. Locke is involved in a *non sequitur* here. From '*x* perceives' we cannot validly derive '*x* perceives that *x* perceives', unless in giving '*x*' the value 'anyone' we assume it is a necessary truth that persons are self-conscious and include only persons in the scope of 'anyone'. This is not a route open to Locke however, because he needs the transparency of consciousness as a premise for his view that persons are self-conscious.

106   'Ainsi la conscience qui dit <Je pense> n'est précisément pas celle qui pense. Ou plutôt ce n'est pas *sa* pensée qu'elle pose par cet acte thétique' (TE 28).

107 'Nous sommes donc fondés à nous demander si le *Je* qui pense est commun aux deux consciences superposées ou s'il n'est pas plutôt celui de la conscience réfléchie' (TE 28–9).

108 'Toute conscience réfléchissante est, en effet, en elle-même irréfléchie et il faut un acte nouveau et du troisième degré pour la poser' (TE 29).

109 'Il n'y a d'ailleurs pas ici de renvoi à l'infini puisqu'une conscience n'a nullement besoin d'une conscience réfléchissante pour être consciente d'elle-même. Simplement elle ne se pose pas à elle-même comme son objet' (TE 29).

110 Plausibly, a necessary condition of '*x* believes that *p*' is '*x* has a disposition to allocate the truth value "true" to *p*'. This cannot possibly be sufficient because the allocation of truth values could be quite arbitrary. Indeed, *x* could allocate the truth value true to *p* without understanding *p*; for example by ticking a token sentence 'S' on a blackboard where (unknown to *x*) S means that *p*. If we introduce an evidential requirement: '*x* has evidence that *p*' we have to guard against circularity. For example, '*x* has evidence that *p*' had better not mean '*x* believes E is evidence that *p*' and we have to allow for the apparent fact that people believe things on no or very little evidence.

111 Iteration imposes a limit on phenomenology. Although any consciousness may in principle be described by a meta-consciousness this means that phenomenology is in practice incompletable.

112 'Mais ne serait-ce précisément l'acte réflexif qui ferait naître le Moi dans la conscience réfléchie? Ainsi expliquerait-on que toute pensée saisie par l'intuition possède un Je, sans tomber dans les difficultés qui signalait notre précédent chapitre' (TE 29).

113 'Le résultat n'est pas douteux: tandis que je lisais, il y avait conscience *du* livre, *des* héros du roman, mais le *Je* n'habitait pas cette conscience, elle était seulement conscience de l'objet et conscience non-positionnelle d'elle-même' (TE 30).

114 'Il suffit […] de chercher à reconstituer le moment complet où parut cette conscience irréfléchie' (TE 30).

115 'Cette saisie non-réflexive d'une conscience par une autre conscience ne peut évidemment s'opérer que par le souvenir et […] elle ne bénéficie donc pas de la certitude absolue inhérente à l'acte réflexif' (TE 31).

116 1 'Un acte certain qui me permet d'affirmer la présence du Je dans la conscience réfléchie' (TE 31).

    2 'un souvenir douteux qui tendrait à faire croire que le Je est absent de la conscience irréfléchie' (TE 31).

117 'Tous les souvenirs non-réflexifs de conscience irréfléchie me montrent une conscience *sans moi*' (TE 32).

118 'Il n'y a pas de *Je* sur le plan irréfléchi' (TE 32).

119 'Quand je cours après un tramway, quand je regard l'heure, quand je m'absorbe dans la contemplation d'un portrait, il n'y a pas de Je. Il y a conscience *du tramway-devant-être-rejoint*, etc., et conscience non-positionelle de la conscience. En fait, je suis alors plongé dans le monde des objets, ce sont eux qui constituent l'unité de mes consciences, qui se présentent avec des valeurs, des qualités attractives et répulsives, mais *moi*, j'ai disparu, je me suis anéanti. Il n'y a pas de place pour *moi* à ce niveau, et ceci ne provient pas d'un hasard, d'un défaut momentané d'attention, mais de la structure même de la conscience' (TE 32).

120 'je suis […] plongé dans le monde des objets' (TE 32).

121 See Martin Heidegger *Sein und Zeit* (Tubingen, 1986) esp. pt I, ch. 3 'Die Weltlichkeit der Welt' pp. 63 ff.

122 'Quant aux significations, aux vérités éternelles, elles affirment leur transcendance par ceci qu'elles se donnent dès qu'elles apparaissent comme indépendantes du temps, alors que la conscience qui les saisit est, au contraire, individualisée rigoureusement dans la durée' (TE 33).

123 'La réponse est claire: le Je ne se donne pas comme un moment concret, une structure périssable de ma conscience actuelle: il affirme au contraire sa permanence par
delà cette conscience et toutes les consciences et – bien que, certes il ne ressemble
guère à une vérité mathématique – son type d'existence se rapproche bien plus de
celui des vérités éternelles que de celui de la conscience' (TE 33–4).

124 'Il est même évident que c'est pour avoir cru que *Je* et *pense* sont sur le même plan
que Descartes est passé du Cogito à l'idée de substance pensante. Nous avons vu
tout à l'heure que Husserl, quoique plus subtilement, tombe au fond sous le même
reproche' (TE 34).

125 Plausibly: p is self-evident if and only if perceiving the truth of p is a necessary
condition for understanding p (or, conversely, understanding p is sufficient for
perceiving p's truth). Within the Cartesian–Husserlian framework it is self-evident
that I think, if and only if, if I think then I know that I think.

126 Sartre does not spell out what he means by these terms so I suggest:
    1 'Metaphysical': (MM) M is a metaphysical method if and only if M putatively
      yields knowledge of what is as it is (as opposed to how it appears to be) or what is
      qua whole, or both.
    2 'Critical': (CM) M is a critical method if and only if M demonstrates that some
      enquirer or enquiry is so constituted as to be able to formulate philosophical
      questions but as to be unable to answer those questions.
    3 'Phenomenological': (PM) M is a phenomenological method if and only if M
      yields descriptions only of phenomena, or what is as it appears to consciousness.

127 'Puisque le Je s'affirme lui-même comme transcendant dans le <Je pense> c'est qu'il
n'est pas de la même nature que la conscience transcendantale' (TE 35).

128 'Remarquons d'ailleurs qu'il n'apparaît pas à la réflexion comme la conscience
réfléchie: il se donne *à travers* la conscience réfléchie' (TE 35).

129 'Certes, il se manifeste comme la source de la conscience' (TE 35).

130 See for example Ludwig Wittgenstein *Philosophical Investigations* (Oxford, 1958) §573
where it is claimed that the ascription of mental states is their public ascription to a
person, say 'Mr. N.N.'.

131 See Gilbert Ryle *The Concept of Mind* (London, 1949). 'Stephen Priest *Theories of the
Mind* (London, Boston, New York, 1991) ch. 3.

132 (1) 'Rien sauf la conscience ne peut être la source de la conscience' (TE 35–6).
    (2) 'Si le Je fait partie de la conscience, il y aura donc *deux* Je' (TE 36).

133 'Le Je est un *existant*. Il a un type d'existence concrète, différent sans doute de celui
des vérités mathématiques, des significations ou des êtres spatio-temporels, mais
aussi réel. Il se donne lui-même comme transcendant' (TE 36).

134 'Il se livre à une intuition d'un genre spécial qui le saisit derrière la conscience
réfléchie, d'une façon toujours inadéquate' (TE 36).

135 'Il n'apparaît jamais qu'à l'occasion d'un acte réflexif […]. Il y a un acte irréfléchi
de réflexion sans Je qui se dirige sur une conscience réfléchie […]. En même temps
un objet nouveau apparaît qui est l'occasion d'une affirmation de la conscience
réflexive' (TE 36–7).

136 'Le Je transcendant doit tomber sous le coup de la réduction phénoménologique. Le
Cogito affirme trop. Le contenu certain du pseudo <Cogito> n'est pas *"J'ai conscience
de cette chaise"*, mais *"il y a* conscience de cette chaise"' (TE 37).

137 'La Rochefoucauld est un des premiers à avoir fait usage, sans le nommer, de l'inconscient; pour lui l'amour propre se *dissimule* sous les formes les plus diverses. Il faut
le dépister avant de le saisir. D'une façon plus générale on a admis par la suite que le
Moi, s'il n'est pas présent à la conscience, est caché derrière elle et qu'il est le pôle
d'attraction de toutes nos représentations et de tous nos désirs. Le Moi cherche donc
à se procurer l'objet pour satisfaire son désir' (TE 38–9).

138 The anti-Cartesian epistemology of the self common to the thinkers Sartre attacks
here is:

(AC) It is possible that (*x* is in a mental state but *x* does not know that *x* is in that mental state).

which is inconsistent with Cartesianism:

(C) If *x* is in a mental state then *x* knows *x* is in that mental state.

Freud in particular must not endorse anything stronger than (AC) for example:

(AC1) If *x* is in a mental state then *x* does not know *x* is in that mental state.

or

(AC2) It is necessary that if *x* is in a mental state then *x* does not know that *x* is in that mental state.

because that would be inconsistent with his view that someone might come to have knowledge of otherwise repressed states through analysis.

139 'Il n'y a pas de Moi: je suis en face de la douleur de Pierre comme en face de la couleur de cet encrier. Il y a un monde objectif des choses et d'actions, faites ou à faire, et les actions viennent s'appliquer comme des qualités sur les choses qui les réclament' (TE 39–40).

140 'Même si l'inconscient existe, à qui fera-t-on croire qu'il recèle des spontanéités de forme réfléchie? La définition du réfléchi n'est il pas d'être posé par une conscience? Mais, en outre, comment admettre que le réfléchi est premier par rapport à l'ir-réfléchi?' (TE 41).

141 'Nous arrivons donc à la conclusion suivante: la conscience irréfléchie doit être considérée comme autonome' (TE 41).

142 'Tout se passe comme si nous vivions dans un monde où les objets, outre leurs qualités de chaleur, d'odeur, de forme, etc., avaient celles de repoussant, d'attirant, de charmant, d'utile, etc., etc., et comme si ces qualités étaient des forces qui exerçaient sur nous certaines actions' (TE 41–2).

143 'Le Moi ne doit être cherché *dans* les états de conscience irréfléchis ni *derrière* eux. Le Moi n'apparaît qu'avec l'acte réflexif' (TE 43).

144 'Nous commençons à entrevoir que le Je et le Moi ne font qu'un. Nous allons essayer de montrer que cet Ego, dont Je et Moi ne sont que deux faces, constitue l'unité idéale (noématique) et indirecte de la série infinie de nos consciences réfléchies' (TE 43).

145 'Le Je c'est l'Ego comme unité des actions' (TE 44).

146 'Le Moi c'est l'Ego comme unité des états et des qualités' (TE 44).

147 'La distinction qu'on établit entre ces deux aspects d'une même réalité nous paraît simplement fonctionnelle, pour ne pas dire grammaticale' (TE 44).

148 Sartre's vocabulary is again Kantian:

x is transcendental if and only if *x* is a necessary condition for experience.

is a use of 'transcendental' common to Kant, Husserl and Sartre.

x is transcendent if and only if *x* is not a possible object of experience.

is the use of 'transcendent' by Kant.

x is transcendent if and only if *x* is not exhausted by experience.

is the use of 'transcendent' by Sartre and Husserl. It is consistent with Kant's use if we allow that '*x* is not exhausted by experience' is consistent with 'there is no experience of *x*'. We see in the deployment of this vocabulary that Husserl and Sartre have not escaped the fundamentally Kantian way of posing problems about the self.

149 'C'est le flux de la Conscience se constituant lui-même comme unité de lui-même' (TE 44).

150 'les états et les actions' (TE 44).

151 'L'Ego est unité des états et des actions' (TE 44).

152 'Il est l'unité d'unités transcendantes et transcendant lui-même' (TE 44).

153 'C'est un pôle transcendant d'unité synthétique, comme le pôle-objet de l'attitude irréfléchie. Seulement ce pôle n'apparaît que dans le monde de la réflexion' (TE 44).

154 'L'*état* apparaît à la conscience réflexive' (TE 45).

155 'Il se donne à elle et fait l'objet d'une intuition concrète. Si je hais Pierre, ma haine de Pierre est un état que je peux saisir par la réflexion' (TE 45).

156 'Faut-il conclure de là qu'il soit immanent et certain? Certes non. Nous ne devons pas faire de la réflexion un pouvoir mystérieux et infaillible, ni croire que tout ce que la réflexion atteint est indubitable *parce qu'il* est atteint par la réflexion' (TE 45).

157 'Je vois Pierre, je sens comme un bouleversement profond de répulsion et de colère à sa vue (je suis déjà sur le plan réflexif): le bouleversement est conscience' (TE 45).

158 'Mais cette expérience de répulsion est-elle haine? évidemment non. Elle ne se donne d'ailleurs pas comme telle. En effet, je hais Pierre depuis longtemps et je pense que je le haïrai toujours. Une conscience instantanée de répulsion ne saurait donc être ma haine' (TE 45–6).

159 'Ma haine m'apparaît en même temps que mon expérience de répulsion' (TE 46).

160 'La haine n'est pas *de la* conscience' (TE 46).

161 'Elle déborde l'instantanéité de la conscience et elle ne se plie pas à la loi absolue de la conscience pour laquelle il n'y a pas de distinction possible entre l'apparence et l'être' (TE 46).

162 'Il est certain que Pierre me répugne, mais il est et restera toujours douteux que je le haïsse' (TE 47).

163 1 'conscience *active*' (TE 51)
    2 'conscience simplement spontanée' (TE 51)
    1 'actions [...] dans le monde des choses' (TE 51)
    2 'actions purement psychiques' (TE 51–2)

164 'Nous voudrions simplement faire remarquer que l'action concertée est avant tout [...] un transcendant. Cela est évident pour les actions comme <jouer du piano>, <conduire une automobile>, <écrire>, parce que ces actions sont <prises> dans le monde des choses' (TE 51).

165 'Mais les actions purement psychiques comme douter, raisonner, méditer, faire une hypothèse, doivent, elles aussi, être conçues comme des transcendances' (TE 51–2).

166 'Ce qui trompe ici c'est que l'action n'est pas seulement l'unité noématique d'un courant de conscience: c'est aussi une réalisation concrète' (TE 52).

167 1 'unité noématique' (TE 52)
    2 'réalisation concrète' (TE 52)
    3 'temps' (TE 52)
    4 'articulations' (TE 52)
    5 'moments' (TE 52).

168 'A ces moments correspondent des consciences concrètes actives et la réflexion qui se dirige sur les consciences appréhende l'action totale dans une intuition qui la livre comme l'unité transcendante des consciences actives' (TE 52).

169 'L'Ego est directement [...] l'unité transcendante des états et des actions. Cependant il peut exister un intermédiaire entre ceux-ci et celui-la: c'est la qualité' (TE 52–3).

170 1 'un intermédiaire' (TE 52)
2 'une disposition' (TE 53)
3 'un objet transcendant' (TE 53)
4 '[...] substrat' (TE 53)
5 'un rapport d'actualisation' (TE 53)
6 'une potentialité' (TE 53)
7 'une virtualité' (TE 53)
8 '[...] unité de passivités objectives' (TE 53).

171 'De ce type sont naturellement les défauts, les vertus, les goûts, les talents, les tendances, les instincts, etc.' (TE 54).

172 'Le psychique est l'objet transcendant de la conscience réflexive' (TE 54).

173 'Die Prädikate sind aber Prädikate von "*etwas*", und dieses "etwas" gehört auch mit, und offenbar unabtrennbar, zu dem fraglichen Kern: es ist der zentrale Einheitspunkt, von dem wir oben gesprochen haben. Es ist der Verknüpfungspunkt oder "Träger" der Prädikate, aber keineswegs Einheit derselben in dem Sinne, in dem irgendein Komplex, irgendwelche Verbindung der Prädikate Einheit zu nennen wäre. Es ist von ihnen notwendig zu unterscheiden, obschon nicht neben sie zu stellen und von ihnen zu trennen, so wie umgekehrt sie selbst seine Prädikate sind: ohne ihn undenkbar und doch von ihm unterscheidbar' (*Ideen* I §131).

174 'Une totalité synthétique indissoluble et qui se supporterait elle-même n'aurait nul besoin d'un x support' (TE 56).

175 'Pour ces raisons mêmes nous nous refuserons à voir dans l'Ego une sorte de pôle X qui serait le support des phénomènes psychiques' (TE 57).

176 'L'Ego n'est rien en dehors de la totalité concrète des états et des actions qu'il supporte' (TE 57).

177 'Si nous cherchions un analogue pour la conscience irréfléchie de ce qu'est l'Ego pour la conscience du second degré, nous pensons plutôt qu'il faudrait songer au *Monde*, conçu comme la totalité synthétique infinie de toutes les choses' (TE 57–8).

178 'L'Ego est aux objets psychiques ce que le *Monde* est aux choses' (TE 58).

179 'Seulement l'apparition du *Monde* à l'arrière plan des choses est assez rare; il faut des circonstances spéciales, fort bien décrites par Heidegger en *Sein und Zeit*, pour qu'il se <dévoile>. L'Ego, au contraire, apparaît toujours à l'horizon des états' (TE 58).

180 'Chaque état, chaque action se donne comme ne pouvant être sans abstraction séparée de l'Ego' (TE 58).

181 *Being and Nothingness*, p. xxix.

182 'Cette totalité transcendante participe au caractère douteux de toute transcendance: c'est à dire que tout ce que nous livrent nos intuitions de l'Ego peut toujours être contredit par des intuitions ultérieures et se donne comme elle' (TE 58–9).

183 'Par exemple, je puis voir avec évidence que je suis coléreux, jaloux etc., et cependant je puis me tromper' (TE 59).

184 'Ce caractère douteux de mon Ego – ou même l'erreur intuitive que je commets – ne signifie pas que j'ai un *vrai* Moi que j'ignore, mais seulement que l'Ego intentionné porte en lui-même le caractère de la dubitabilité (dans certains cas celui de la fausseté)' (TE 59).

185 'Ce pouvoir du <Malin Génie> s'étend jusque-là' (TE 59).

186 'En effet l'Ego est l'unification transcendante spontanée de nos états et de nos actions. A ce titre il n'est pas une hypothèse. Je ne me dis pas <Peut-être que j'ai un Ego> comme je peux me dire <Peut-être que je hais Pierre>' (TE 59).

187 'Je ne cherche pas ici un *sens* unificateur de mes états. Lorsque j'unifie mes consciences sous la rubrique <Haine> je leur ajoute un certain sens, je les qualifie. Mais lorsque j'incorpore mes états à la totalité concrète *Moi*, je ne leur ajoute rien' (TE 59).

188 1 'émanation' (TE 59)
2 'actualisation' (TE 60)

3 'production poétique' (TE 60).

189 'Ce mode de création est bien une création ex nihilo, en ce sens que l'état n'est pas donné comme ayant été auparavant dans le Moi' (TE 60).

190 'Même si la haine se donne comme actualisation d'une certaine puissance de rancune ou de haine, elle reste quelquechose de neuf par rapport à la puissance qu'elle actualise' (TE 60).

191 1 'l'acte unificateur de la réflexion' (TE 60)
    2 'un rapport qui traverse le temps à l'envers' (TE 60)
    3 'le Moi comme la source de l'état' (TE 60).

192 'L'acte unificateur de la réflexion rattache chaque état nouveau d'une façon très spéciale à la totalité concrète *Moi*' (TE 60).

193 'Elle ne se borne pas à le saisir comme rejoignant cette totalité, comme se fondant à elle: elle intentionne un rapport qui traverse le temps à l'envers' (TE 60).

194 '[…] rapport […] donne le Moi comme la source de l'état' (TE 60).

195 'L'Ego maintient ses qualités par une véritable création continuée. Cependant, nous ne saisissons pas l'Ego comme étant finalement une source créatrice pure en deçà des qualités' (TE 60–1).

196 'Il ne nous paraît pas que nous pourrions trouver une pôle squelettique si nous ôtions l'une après l'autre toutes les qualités' (TE 61).

197 'Au terme de ce dépouillement, il ne resterait plus rien, l'Ego se serait évanoui' (TE 61).

198 'Mais cette spontanéité ne doit pas être confondue avec celle de la conscience. En effet, l'Ego, étant objet, est *passif*. Il s'agit donc d'une pseudo-spontanéité qui trouverait des symboles convenables dans le jaillissement d'une source, d'un geyser, etc. C'est à dire qu'il ne s'agit que d'une apparence' (TE 62).

199 'L'Ego est un objet […] *constitué* par la conscience réflexive' (TE 63).

200 'L'ordre est renversé par une conscience qui s'imprisonne dans le Monde pour se fuir, les consciences sont données comme émanant des états et les états comme produits par l'Ego' (TE 63).

201 'En vertu de cette passivité l'Ego est susceptible d'être *affecté*. Rien ne peut agir sur la conscience, parce qu'elle est cause de soi. Mais, au contraire, l'Ego qui produit subit le choc en retour de ce qu'il produit' (TE 64).

202 'Il est <compromis> par ce qu'il produit. Il y a ici inversion de rapport: l'action ou l'état se retourne sur l'Ego pour le qualifier' (TE 64).

203 'Tout nouvel état produit par l'Ego teinte et nuance l'Ego dans le moment où l'Ego se produit. L'Ego est en quelque sorte envoûté par cette action, il en participe' (TE 65).

204 1 'Tout ce que produit l'Ego l'impressionne' (TE 65)
    2 '*Seulement* ce qu'il produit [l'impressionne]' (TE 65)
    3 'Le Moi peut être transformé par des événements extérieurs' (TE 65)
    4 'L'Ego est une synthèse irrationnelle d'activité et de passivité' (TE 65)
    5 'Il est synthèse d'intériorité et de transcendance' (TE 65).

205 'ruine, deuil, déceptions, changement de milieu social' (TE 83).

206 'Mais c'est seulement en tant qu'ils sont pour lui l'occasion d'états ou d'actions' (TE 65).

207 'Il est, en un sens, plus <intérieur> à la conscience que les états' (TE 65).

208 'Qu'entendons-nous en effet par intériorité? Simplement, ceci que pour la conscience être et se connaître sont une seule et même chose' (TE 66).

209 'Une seule et même chose' (TE 66), 'one and the same thing' (TET 83) is used in a loose and exaggerated way by Sartre (a tendency he inherits from Hegel). However close the mutual dependency between 'être', 'being', and 'se connaître', 'to be aware of itself', in 'la conscience', 'consciousness', it falls short of numerical identity. It is incoherent to claim that self-knowledge is being or being self-knowledge. This would even be incoherent if self-knowledge were all that there is. Nevertheless, something

close to what Sartre wants is coherent: That which has self-knowledge is numerically identical with something that is (has being), viz. consciousness.

210 1 'Pour la conscience, l'apparence est l'absolu en tant qu'elle est apparence' (TE 66).

2 'La conscience est un être dont l'essence implique l'existence' (TE 66).

211 'on *vit* l'intériorité (qu'on <existe intérieur>)' (TE 66).

212 'une intériorité absolue n'a jamais de dehors' (TE 66–7).

213 'C'est l'intériorité vue du dehors' (TE 67).

214 'Tel que, le Moi nous reste inconnu' (TE 68).

215 1 'l'observation' (TE 68)

2 'l'approximation' (TE 68)

3 'l'attente' (TE 68)

4 'l'expérience' (TE 68).

216 'Il est trop présent pour qu'on puisse prendre sur lui un point de vue vraiment extérieur. Si l'on se retire pour prendre du champ, il vous accompagne dans ce recul. Il est infiniment proche et je ne puis en faire le tour' (TE 68).

217 'Ainsi, <bien se connaître>, c'est fatalement prendre sur soi le point de vue d'autrui, c'est à dire un point de vue forcément faux' (TE 69).

218 'L'intuition de l'Ego est-elle un mirage perpétuellement décevant, car, à la fois, elle livre tout et elle ne livre rien' (TE 69).

219 'Ceux qui ont quelque connaissance de la Phénoménologie comprendront sans peine que l'Ego soit à la fois une unité idéale d'états dont la majorité sont absents et une totalité concrète se donnant tout entière a l'intuition' (TE 69–70).

220 'L'Ego est une unité noématique et non noétique' (TE 70).

221 'Un arbre ou une chaise n'existent pas autrement' (TE 70).

222 'En effet, l'Ego n'apparaît jamais que lorsqu'on ne le regarde pas' (TE 70).

223 'Il n'est donc jamais vu que <du coin de l'œil>' (TE 70).

224 'Il est certain cependant que le Je paraît sur le plan irréfléchie' (TE 70).

225 'Si l'on me demande <Que faites-vous?> et je réponde, tout occupé <J'essaie d'accrocher ce tableau> ou <Je répare le pneu arrière>, ces phrases ne nous transportent pas sur le plan de réflexion' (TE 70–1).

226 'Mais ce <Je> dont il est ici question n'est pourtant pas une simple forme syntaxique. Il a un sens; c'est tout simplement un concept vide et destiné à rester vide' (TE 71).

227 'De même que je puis penser une chaise en l'absence de toute chaise et par simple concept, de même je peux penser le Je en l'absence du Je' (TE 71).

228 'La conception de l'Ego que nous proposons nous paraît réaliser la libération du Champs transcendantal en même temps que sa purification' (TE 74).

229 'En un sens c'est un *rien* puisque tous les objets physiques, psycho-physiques et psychiques, toutes les vérités, toutes les valeurs sont hors de lui, puisque mon Moi a cessé, lui-même, d'en faire partie. Mais ce rien est *tout* puisqu'il est *conscience de* tous ces objets' (TE 74).

230 'Précisons: jusqu'ici on faisait une distinction radicale entre l'objectivité d'une chose spatio-temporelle ou d'une vérité éternelle et la subjectivité des <états> psychiques' (TE 75).

(The translation has 'external' but the French has 'éternelle'. The translation should be 'eternal'.)

231 'Il semblait que le sujet eût une position privilégiée par rapport à ses propres états' (TE 75).

232 'Par suite, si Pierre et Paul parlent tout deux de l'amour de Pierre, par exemple, il n'est plus vrai que l'un parle en aveugle et par analogie de ce que l'autre saisit en plein. Ils parlent de la même chose' (TE 76).

233 'Cette conception de l'Ego nous paraît la seule réfutation possible du solipsisme' (TE 84).

234 'Tant que le Je demeure une structure de la conscience, il restera toujours possible
     d'opposer la conscience avec son Je à tous les autres existants. Et finalement c'est
     bien *Moi* qui produit le monde' (TE 85).
235 'Peu importe si certaines couches de ce monde nécessitent par leur nature même
     une relation à autrui. Cette relation peut être une simple qualité du monde que je
     crée et ne m'oblige nullement à accepter l'existence réelle d'autres Je' (TE 85).
236 Husserl emphasises the essentially Cartesian nature of his phenomenology in the
     opening remarks of *Die Pariser Vorträger* delivered at the Sorbonne in 1929. See *The
     Paris Lectures*, trans. P. Koestenbaum (The Hague, 1975) esp. §1. When Husserl
     expanded the lectures into *Cartesianischen Meditationen* the title alluded to his incorpo-
     ration of Descartes' methodological doubt into phenomenology. See *Cartesianischen
     Meditationen: Eine Einleitung in die Phänomenologie* (Hamburg, 1987), *Cartesian Meditations:
     An Introduction to Phenomenology*, trans. Dorian Cairns (The Hague, 1982).
237 'Mais si le Je devient un transcendant, il participe à toutes les vicissitudes du monde'
     (TE 85).
238 'Au lieu de se formuler, en effet: <J'existe seul comme absolu>, il devrait s'énoncer:
     <La conscience absolue existe seule comme absolue>, ce qui est évidemment un
     truisme' (TE 85).
239 'Mon *Je*, en effet, *n'est pas plus certain pour la conscience que le Je des autres hommes*. Il est
     seulement plus intime' (TE 85).
240 'le solipsisme devient impensable dès lors que le Je n'a plus de position privilégiée'
     (TE 85).
241 'Si c'est une philosophie où l'effort d'assimilation spirituelle ne rencontre jamais de
     résistances extérieures, où la souffrance, la faim, la guerre se diluent dans un lent
     processus d'unification des idées, rien n'est plus injuste que d'appeler les
     phénoménologues des idéalistes' (TE 85–6).
242 'Ils ont replongé l'homme dans le monde, ils ont rendu tout leurs poids à ses
     angoisses et à ses souffrances, à ces révoltes aussi' (TE 86).
243 'Malheureusement, tant que le Je restera une structure de sa conscience absolue, on
     pourra encore reprocher à la phénoménologie d'être une <doctrine-refuge>, de
     tirer encore une parcelle de l'homme hors du monde et de détourner par là l'atten-
     tion des véritables problèmes' (TE 86).
244 'Il m'a toujours semblé qu'une hypothèse de travail aussi féconde que le matérial-
     isme historique n'exigeait nullement pour fondement l'absurdité qu'est le
     matérialisme métaphysique' (TE 86).
245 'Il n'est pas nécessaire, en effet, que *l'objet* précède *le sujet* pour que les pseudo-valeurs
     spirituelles s'évanouissent et pour que la morale retrouve ses bases dans la réalité. Il
     suffit que le *Moi* soit contemporain du Monde et que la dualité sujet–objet, qui est
     purement logique, disparaisse définitivement des préoccupations philosophiques'
     (86–7).
246 'Le Monde n'a pas créé le Moi, le Moi n'a pas créé le Monde, ce sont deux objets
     pour la conscience absolue, impersonnelle, et c'est par elle qu'ils se trouvent reliés'
     (TE 87).

Select bibliography

Bell, David, *Husserl* (London and New York, 1990)

Bennett, Jonathan, *Kant's Analytic* (Cambridge, 1966)

Berkeley, George, *The Principles of Human Knowledge with Other Writings*, ed. G.J. Warnock (London, 1977)

Boer, Steven E. and Lycan, William G., *Knowing Who* (Cambridge, Mass., 1986)

Brentano, Franz, *Psychologie vom empirischen Standpunkt* (Leipzig, 1874)

Brentano, Franz, *Psychology from an Empirical Standpoint*, trans. A.C. Rancurello, D.B. Terrell and L.L. McAlister (London, 1973)

Broad, C.D., *Kant: An Introduction* (Cambridge, 1979)

Dunn, John, 'The Identity of the History of Ideas', *Philosophy* 43 (1968)

Eccles, J.C. (ed.), *Brain and Conscious Experience*, see 'Brain Bisection and the Mechanisms of Consciousness' (Berlin, 1966)

Eccles, J.C., *The Brain and Unity of Conscious Experience* (Cambridge, 1965)

Gazzaniga, Michael S., *The Bisected Brain* (New York, 1970)

Hegel, G.W.F., *Hegel's Lectures on the History of Philosophy*, trans. E.H. Haldane and H.H. Simson (London, 1974)

Hegel, G.W.F., *Phänomenologie des Geistes*, herausgegeben von Hans-Friedrich Wessels und Heinrich Clairmont mit einer Einleitung von Wolfgang Bonsiepen (Hamburg, 1988)

Hegel, G.W.F., *Phenomenology of Spirit*, trans. Arnold Miller, foreword by J.N. Findlay (Oxford, 1977)

Hegel, G.W.F., *Sämtliche Werke*, Jubiläumsausgabe, ed. H. Glockner (Stuttgart, 1967)

Heidegger, Martin, *Sein und Zeit* (Tubingen, 1986)

Henrich, Dieter, *Identität und Objektivität: Eine Untersuchung über Kants transzendentale Deduktion* (Heidelberg, 1976)

Hurley, S.L., 'Kant on Spontaneity and the Myth of the Giving', *Proceedings of the Aristotelian Society* (1994)

Husserl, Edmund, *Cartesian Meditations: An Introduction to Phenomenology*, trans. Dorion Cairns (The Hague, 1982)

Husserl, Edmund, *Cartesianische Meditationen: Eine Einleitung in die Phänomenologie*, ed. S. Strasser (The Hague, 1950)

Husserl, Edmund, *Erste Philosophie (1923–1924), Erster Teil: Kritische Ideengeschichte*, ed. R. Boehme (The Hague, 1956)

Husserl, Edmund, *Erste Philosophie (1923–1924), Zweiter Teil: Theorie der phänomenologischen Reduktion*, ed. R. Boehme (The Hague, 1959)

Husserl, Edmund, *Ideas Pertaining to a Pure Phenomenology and to a Phenomenological Philosophy, First Book: General Introduction to a Pure Phenomenology*, trans. F. Kersten (The Hague, 1983)

Husserl, Edmund, *Ideas Pertaining to a Pure Phenomenology and to a Phenomenological Philosophy, Second Book: Studies in the Phenomenology of Constitution*, trans. Richard Rojcewicz and Andre Schuwer (Dordrecht, Boston, London, 1989)

Husserl, Edmund, *Ideen zu einer reinen Phänomenologie und phänomenologischen Philosophie, I. Buch: Allgemeine Einführung in die reine Phänomenologie*, neu herausgegeben von Karl Schuhmann (The Hague, 1976)

Husserl, Edmund, *Ideen zu einer reinen Phänomenologie und phänomenologischen Philosophie, Zweites Buch: Phänomenologische Untersuchungen zur Konstitution*, ed. Marly Biemel (The Hague, 1952)

Husserl, Edmund, *Logical Investigations*, trans J.N. Findlay (New York, 1970)

Husserl, Edmund, *Logische Untersuchungen* (1900–1901)

Husserl, Edmund, *The Paris Lectures*, trans. Peter Koestenbaum (The Hague, 1975)

Husserl, Edmund, *Phänomenologische Psychologie: Vorlesungen Sommersemester 1925*, ed. Walter Biemel (The Hague, 1962)

Husserl, Edmund, *Vorlesungen zur Phänomenologie des innern Zeitbewußtseins*, in *Jahrbuch für Philosophie und Phänomenologische Forschung* 9 (1928)

Kant, Immamuel, *Critique of Pure Reason*, trans. Norman Kemp Smith (London, 1978)

Kant, Immanuel, *Kritik der reinen Vernunft*, herausgegeben von Ingeborg Heidemann (Stuttgart, 1980)

Locke, John, *An Essay concerning Human Understanding*, ed. A.S. Pringle-Pattison (Oxford, 1950)

Lowe, E.J., *Kinds of Being: A Study of Individuation, Identity and the Logic of Sortal Terms*, Aristotelian Society Series, 10 (Oxford, 1989)

Lowe, E.J., *Subjects of Experience* (Cambridge, 1996)

Mackie, J.L., 'The Transcendental "I"', in Zak van Straaten (ed.), *Philosophical Subjects: Essays presented to P.F. Strawson* (Oxford, 1980)

Moore, A.W., *Points of View* (Oxford, 1997)

Nagel, Thomas, 'Brain Bisection and the Unity of Consciousness', *Synthèse* 22 (1971) 396–413, reprinted in his *Mortal Questions*

Nagel, Thomas, *Mortal Questions* (Cambridge, 1979)

Nagel, Thomas, *The View from Nowhere* (Oxford, 1986)

Parfit, Derek, *Reasons and Persons* (Oxford, 1984)

Peacocke, Christopher, *Being Known* (Oxford, 1999)

Peacocke, Christopher, 'No Resting Place: A Critical Notice of *The View From Nowhere*, by Thomas Nagel', *The Philosophical Review* 98/1 (January 1989)

Priest, Stephen, *The British Empiricists* (London, 1990)

Priest, Stephen (ed.), *Hegel's Critique of Kant* (Oxford, 1987)

Priest, Stephen, *Merleau-Ponty* (London, 1998)

Priest, Stephen, 'On Aquinas' Claim "Anima mea non est ego"', *The Heythrop Journal* 42 (1999)

Priest, Stephen, *Theories of the Mind* (London, 1973; London, Boston, New York, 1991)

Ryle, Gilbert, *The Concept of Mind* (London, 1949)

Sartre, Jean-Paul, *Being and Nothingness*, trans. Hazel E. Barnes, introduction by Mary Warnock (London, 1969)

Sartre, Jean-Paul, *Critique of Dialectical Reason, I: Theory of Practical Ensembles*, trans. Alan Sheridan-Smith, ed. Jonathan Ree (London, 1976)

Sartre, Jean-Paul, *L'Etre et le Néant* (Paris, 1943)

Sartre, Jean-Paul, *La Transcendance de l'Ego: Esquisse d'une description phénoménologique*, Introduction, notes et appendices par Sylvie Le Bon (Paris, 1985)

Sartre, Jean-Paul, *The Transcendence of the Ego: An Existentialist Theory of Consciousness,* translated and annotated with an introduction by Forrest Williams and Robert Kirkpatrick (New York, 1957)

Schrodinger, Erwin, *Mind and Matter* (Cambridge, 1958)

Searle, John, *Intentionality* (Cambridge, 1983)

Shoemaker, Sydney, *Self-knowledge and Self-identity* (New York, 1963)

Sokolowski, Robert, *Husserlian Meditations: How Words Present Things* (Evanston, 1974)

Sperry, W.R., 'The Great Cerebral Commissure', *Scientific American* 210 (1964)

Spiegelberg, H., *The Phenomenological Movement: A Historical Introduction*, 2 vols. (The Hague, 1976)

Spinoza, Benedictus de, *Ethics,* trans. A. Boyle (London, 1977)

Strawson, P.F., *An Essay on Kant's Critique of Pure Reason* (London, 1966)

Strawson, P.F., *Individuals: An Essay in Descriptive Metaphysics* (London, 1959)

Williams, Bernard, *Descartes: The Project of Pure Enquiry* (Harmondsworth, 1978)

Wittgenstein, Ludwig, *Philosophical Investigations* (Oxford, 1958)

Index